Bio

As I Live and Breathe

AS I LIVE

AND BREATHE
Stages of
an Autobiography

MALCOLM BOYD

Random House   New York

1643

First Printing

10 9 8 7 6 5 4 3 2

Library of Congress Catalog Card Number: 76–85608

Grateful acknowledgment is extended to the following periodicals, in which passages from this book initially appeared in a different form: *Ave Maria, The Christian Century* (November 11, 1964 and September 15, 1965 issues), *Commonweal, Motive, National Catholic Reporter, The New Journal of Yale University,* and *Television Quarterly: The Journal of the National Academy of Television Arts and Sciences.*
An excerpt from a press release of the Greater Lansing branch of the American Civil Liberties Union of Michigan is reprinted by permission. Hymn 437 in The Hymnal of the Protestant Episcopal Church in the United States of America is reprinted by permission of LeRoy Percy; Hymn 172 is reprinted by permission of J. Curwen & Sons Ltd., London. Portions of "A Study in Color," in THE FANTASY WORLDS OF PETER STONE are reprinted by permission of Harper & Row, Publishers. Excerpts from FREE TO LIVE, FREE TO DIE, by Malcolm Boyd, are reprinted by permission of Holt, Rinehart and Winston, Inc. Copyright © 1967 by Malcolm Boyd. A portion of the article, "A Cry from the Underground Church" is reprinted by courtesy of the editors from the December 24, 1968 issue of *Look* Magazine. Copyright © 1968 by Cowles Communications, Inc.
A short excerpt from THE HUNGER, THE THIRST, by Malcolm Boyd, is reprinted by permission of Morehouse-Barlow Co., Inc. Copyright © 1964 by Morehouse-Barlow Co.

Manufactured in the United States of America
by Kingsport Press, Inc., Kingsport, Tennessee

Book designed by Vincent Torre

T O

William Sloane Coffin, Jr.
Chaplain, Yale University

Paul Moore, Jr.
Suffragan Bishop of the
Episcopal Diocese of Washington

R. W. B. Lewis
Professor of English and American Studies
at Yale University
and Master of Calhoun College,
whose hospitality and friendship
have made
my stay at Yale
a most creative experience

James H. Silberman
my friend
long before he became my editor,
who asked me to write
this book

Richard Allyn English
on the faculty of
the University of Michigan School
of Social Work

AUTHOR'S NOTE

This book is simply a look at, and into, a man's life—my own. I am forty-five; it seems unlikely that I shall be writing a sequel to this book at ninety. In any event I have found it a cathartic task to write it at my present age. It has made me introspective, and therefore outgoing. I am grateful that I could do it for the purpose of better understanding my life; perspective leaps out of new paragraphs.

It brings me, in a curiously freeing way, face to face with my own mortality. I am constantly turning corners and observing my own death, as I have done in given moments of the past forty-five years. This brings a salutary objectivity to any enterprise—a book *or* a life.

This is not a treatise explaining my theology or position on a number of contemporary subjects. It is only between the lines that a reader may experience a sense of what I might, on another occasion, place in the context of a "sermon." Instead, here are some of the men and women I have known; places I have lived; laughter I have laughed, and pain I have suffered; fears that have engulfed me and visions that have lifted me up; motivation that has impelled me to go on, and the sense of life itself which I have used to make sense *of* life.

In the stages of my forty-five years I have known love and hate, anger and peace, the spirit of God and the spirits of man; I have worn many faces and masks in sad and happy dramas. Yes—in certain strangely natural and wonderful moments I have glimpsed the fragments coming together as a whole.

Malcolm Boyd

Yale University/March 5, 1969

CONTENTS

FOREWORD

Malcolm Boyd showed up on the Yale campus in the summer of 1968. He had no particular plan or program in mind;
he had simply heard from his friend William Sloane Coffin,
chaplain of Yale, that there were a good many concerned
and interesting students there, and he wanted to meet some
of them. It happened that one of the resident Fellows (associated faculty) in Calhoun College had just then decided
to go on leave, so as Master of Calhoun I invited Malcolm to
take over the absent professor's suite. This was quite irregular, as it turned out. Malcolm had been given the courtesy title of "visiting chaplain," but he had in fact no formal
connection with the university whatever, and was not eli-
gible to occupy rooms. But the Yale authorities thoughtfully
averted their eyes, and Malcolm moved in.

When the students came back in September, they instantly flocked around the new guest Fellow, and from that
moment Malcolm could always be seen in the courtyard or
the dining hall, in his rooms or at tea in the Master's House
—engaged in conversation on every variety of subject. In
November, when Yale instituted its "coed week" (a preview
of the way things would be when women students actually
enrolled in September, 1969), the ceremonies began with
Malcolm engaging about four hundred young men and women—his stocky figure perched on a kitchen stool to ease
his painful back—on the basic and engrossing topic of men,
women, and Yale. The general effect of his presence has
been both stimulating and unsettling. Malcolm, in talk, goes
to the human core of the matter, and touches people where
they ought to be living, but aren't.

His position vis-à-vis Yale was typical, and not entirely

unlike his position in the Episcopal Church, into which he was ordained priest in 1955. He is the irregular man, the informal man, but (anything but an alienated man) he always prefers to do his work and have his say *within* the peripheries of whatever establishment he is inhabiting. He retains some connection with the diocese of Washington, D.C., but he is not there very often. He reminds me of a clerical person of my youth who was away from his diocese so much that he was known as the Bishop from Colorado.

My father was an Episcopalian clergyman of high Anglican persuasion; in politics, a registered Socialist. (My maternal grandfather was a clergyman, too, but according to family lore he was something of a rogue.) I can imagine nothing my father would have approved more than Malcolm Boyd's unstinting effort to make fresh connections, and remake forgotten ones, between the contemporary church and American society—that is, the actual lives and personalities, the ambitions, daily needs and life-styles of the individuals who are that society. My father would have greatly enjoyed holding long converse with Malcolm over cigars, of an evening, teasing him gently by pointing out that if Malcolm were better grounded in Church history he would be aware of countless precedents for his own particular mission.

What Malcolm also seems to know mainly by instinct is that his mission is altogether in the American grain. It harks back to the days of Emerson and Theodore Parker and Orestes Brownson, to those restive ministers who found that their church had gone dry, that it was rationalistic and comfortable and far removed from human urgencies; and who, in their attempt to restore vitality to the religious life, expanded their ministerial activities into the whole range of human experience.

Emerson, more of a radical than Malcolm Boyd, eventually "signed off" from his church. But his definition of the role of the minister is close to Malcolm's. It is a question of bringing the church much more closely to bear upon immediate life, of mediating between the religious vision with which one has been entrusted and the common aspirations of common people. And this involves new forms and idioms of prayer, new rituals of worship, new assumptions of priestly responsibility, new areas—sometimes, literally, new *places*—in which to exercise the religious energy. A new form of the sacramental life. Malcolm, to be sure, can on occasion be a good deal more antic than Emerson allowed himself to be; and though Emerson faced audiences all across the country, it is not easy to think of him performing, as Malcolm has done, in a California nightclub. But I dare say Emerson would have understood the impulse. He understood Whitman and *Leaves of Grass* at once:

Unscrew the locks from the doors!
Unscrew the doors themselves from their jambs!
                    .   .   .
Whoever degrades another degrades me . . .
                    .   .   .
Through me many long dumb voices . . .
Voices of the diseas'd and despairing, and of thieves and
    dwarfs . . . by me clarified and transfigured.

How Malcolm arrived at his so-to-say regularized irregularity is the subject of this book, and an utterly absorbing account it is. His first mature experience was in the most secular field that even this secular culture has to offer: Hollywood and the television industry. Then, after divinity school and postordination study, came the peace marches, the parochial work among the poor and the victimized ("the diseas'd and despairing"); the startling success of his books of prayers, and the evolution of a new style of religious expression; the campus attachments. Somehow the order of things in this educational process was exactly right. Out of it came one kind—certainly not the only kind, but one important and invaluable kind—of contemporary churchman. The best churchman, I remember my father saying (per-

haps quoting) is the man who is most at home in the universe. I don't know about the universe; but it is hard to think
of any churchman more at home than Malcolm Boyd in the
depths and heights, on the fringes and at the center of the
world of America today.

R. W. B. Lewis

As I Live and Breathe

I

Mal Boyd, radio-television partner of Mary
Pickford and Charles (Buddy) Rogers,
yesterday announced plans to abandon the
entertainment fields and to commence studies
for the Protestant Episcopal priesthood. The
27-year-old producer, whose paternal grandfather was a priest in the Episcopal Church,
said he had been admitted as a postulant for
holy orders in the Diocese of Los Angeles
and has made application to enter a seminary
this fall. "This has not been a simple decision," said Boyd. "I am leaving behind an
industry which contains many friends, has
treated me with happiness and good fortune
and has called for all my energy and devotion.
I have found out, however, that the road
to peace and happiness in my personal life
lies in my ability to serve whomever it may
be within my power to serve."

Los Angeles Times,
May 8, 1951

Mal Boyd, first president of the Television
Producers Association of Hollywood, will
leave for Berkeley tomorrow to enter the
Church Divinity School of the Pacific and
begin studies for the Episcopal priesthood.
Boyd gave up a TV-radio partnership with
Mary Pickford and Buddy Rogers when he
felt the call to enter church service. Last week
200 TV, radio and motion picture friends
gave a luncheon in honor of Boyd. He will
register for his three years of study on
Thursday.

Los Angeles Examiner,
September 4, 1951

HOLLYWOOD

I packed my suitcase with a very few things—wouldn't life be a simple matter now?—and on an early September morning in 1951, got into my car and started the drive from Hollywood to the theological seminary in Berkeley, California, where I would spend the next three years of my life.

What did I feel? The elation of expectation, and enough hope to cover my fear. I was actively setting out, on that September morning, upon a pilgrimage inside as well as outside myself. To heal or to die; to treat life as a charade or as reality . . . On the morning I began driving toward the seminary, "God" was as hidden from me as my "brother." Although I felt quite alone, I knew for certain that I was commencing a complex journey, a journey on which I would meet strangers.

When it was announced in the press that I was leaving Hollywood to enter a seminary, the story shared space with reports of a leading film idol's tragic, unexpected death, and a suicide attempt by a prominent actress. All three stories were headlined in identical shocking boldface type.

At the going-away party for me (it was at the old Ciro's on Sunset Strip) even the bartenders stood and bowed their heads when the Lord's Prayer was said.

Many people wept openly. They seemed to see the whole thing almost as a funeral—certainly not a joyful new beginning in life.

I sat on a dais, flanked by several Hollywood stars and a priest. After we ate, people stood up one by one to eulogize me. The mood was terribly sad. To them, religion obviously meant an area closed off from real life. Here I sat, a lively, enthusiastic young man with whom everybody in the room had enjoyed some kind of human relationship—and I was about to walk inside the forbidding ghetto of religion and close the door behind me. Some songs were offered. The priest prayed. Finally, I got up to say a few words. I nearly broke down. If the truth were faced—and everybody present was facing it —I was throwing out an irrevocable good-bye to life *here* and *now*. Inside the religious stockade, would my head be shaved? Could I receive mail in the cell where I would be engaged in meditation all day? "Can I write to you?"

Henceforth I would be as dead.

Candles flicker on a high altar.
> I am a young boy kneeling inside a great cathedral
>> during the Holy Eucharist.
> I hear a priest's voice saying the words.
> Then a shuffling of feet as people go up to the altar.

I am praying
> For my mother
> For my father
> For my grandmother
> For my dead grandfather
> For my schoolwork

God is listening
> God is inside this holy place
> Be quiet in his presence
> Think holy thoughts

Forget the discomfort of the old wooden pew and kneeler.

The pain of kneeling on the hard wood is a sacrifice.

The organ music adds to the holiness and mystery.

The priests' embroidered robes moving against the shining gold of the high altar transport me to the glory and majesty of heaven.

It would all be over when I stepped outside the church into the sunlight.

Looking back on my childhood, I remember a particular morning in 1935. I was seated in a junior high school auditorium in Colorado. The room was packed with students, teachers and a few invited parents. Prizes for achievement were being handed out. I sat there, not expecting to be touched in any way by such a happening.

Suddenly my name was called. People around me were clapping. I couldn't think clearly, get my breath, or move. Friends were pushing me out of my seat and up the aisle toward the big stage. People were friendly, reaching out to me. I wanted to cry but instead managed a set smile on my face. I was a child withdrawn from other boys and girls, living most of my days in fantasies about adulthood or somewhere deep inside myself, so this experience was both thrilling and very, very threatening. The ovation was exuberant. It was irrational and unexpected—someone else should have been up there in that high place of honor. I felt a happy circus feeling: I *could* do something; I had *done* something. The prize was for writing an essay about why I liked history and considered it important. I did love history. I loved the teacher who spent many hours with me after class, making it come alive in an exciting way.

Winning this prize gave me a sense of confidence I had not known before. I started to write for the newspaper at North Junior High School in Colorado Springs. My forte, it was discovered, lay in interviewing artists and writers who visited our town. I had learned the hard way. My first subject for an interview was the violinist Mischa Elman. I asked him to give me the names of his father and mother, his birthplace, and date of birth. He told me to refer to an encyclopedia, abruptly terminating the interview. He had kindly given me lesson number one, to do research on my subjects before encountering them in the flesh.

As a very young boy, I was rich and lived in New York city.
  Accompanied by my governess, I rode my tricycle in Central Park.
  I played outside a weather station which resembled a castle, and fantasized about life in a medieval royal court.
  From there I looked down upon shantytown, where poor people resided in makeshift huts with tin roofs.
  A chauffeur taught me how to tie my shoelaces and read a clock face.
I spent one summer on a farm in Pennsylvania.
  Everybody got up early.
  The men ate a big breakfast of soup, meat, potatoes, bread, vegetables, and dessert.
  Then they set out to work all day in the fields.
I went rowing on the lake.
  I sat in a hammock on the porch, reading books.
  I visited with an elderly great-uncle who showed me around his ramshackle, immense house with its empty rooms, antiques, and a family Bible.

As a boy, I also lived for a year on a small farm in Texas.

This was after my mother and father were divorced.

I raised vegetables, had a pet dog, and daydreamed in dry rocky gorges.

I loved the Indian blankets and bluebonnets—great fields of flowers.

I climbed up immense tanks and smelled the oil inside them.

At nights I was frightened when the wind blew.

On Saturdays I bathed in a tin tub filled with hot water which was placed on papers in the kitchen.

I played with a little girl named Kathleen from the next farm.

I kept a diary (Kathleen was in it).

One day I saw some men killing a pig.

They hit it, again and again, with an axe.

They were having a good time and laughing. They were drinking from a bottle which they passed around.

The pig was bleeding and running, terrified, but boxed in by the men.

A schoolteacher hated my New York handwriting (my *r*'s were different) and flunked me in all my composition work. I was stubborn and would not change for her.

One day a flash flood almost caught our car as we drove over a country wooden bridge while returning in a rainstorm from a visit to a chiropractor.

We moved to Colorado when I was twelve.

We were seated in the baroque lobby of the Brown Palace Hotel in Denver. Carl Van Doren had given me four full hours on a Saturday afternoon for an interview. I had researched him so carefully that I had read four of his books preceding the interview. Finally his wife had him paged, and the press conference with the animated junior high school journalist came to an end. I interviewed John Gunther, Harold Laski and H. V. Kaltenborn; Lotte Lehmann, Kirsten Flagstad. Wanda Landowska received me in her hotel suite for a full afternoon's conversation over tea. I chatted with Josephine Antoine, a Metropolitan Opera soprano, backstage at the Ute Theatre in Colorado Springs, where she had given a concert. Learning from our conversation that I sang, too, she asked me to render "O Sole Mio" for her onstage. My mother, arriving to drive me home, was startled to hear my voice thundering through the empty hall.

As a young New Yorker isolated in the Western town of Colorado Springs, I impatiently awaited the Sunday *New York Times*. Stiff blizzards could delay its arrival for several agonizing days. On Saturdays I listened with religious zeal to the radio broadcasts of the Metropolitan Opera. Once a week my mother drove across town to an ancient European baker for a loaf of homemade pumpernickel. It was a sensual experience for me to eat a slice of this bread, simultaneously reading the *Times* and listening to the opera. Yet none of these things could make me happy. I was always conscious of myself as a young prince who had gone into exile as a pauper. My father, separated from my life, sometimes wrote letters, but I felt rejected and unloved by him, despite his protestations and occasional gifts which seldom met my own moods or needs.

My mother worked hard to support me during these years. (Remarkably, she continued working, until she turned seventy, as an extremely able legal secretary in Beverly Hills. Now, past seventy, she studies French, does oil painting, and works as a volunteer with children in a hospital. She embodies an extraordinary combination of vitality and serenity. It has been one of the very good things in my life to see our relationship move from the formal pattern of mother-son to the more mutually freeing one of close friends.)

My mother's mother, a gallant woman in her sixties, tried to help out financially by opening a boarding house. She rented rooms to overnight guests and cooked meals for them. Her hot breads, I remember, were a wonder. I had a collie dog, Laddie, and I felt genuine grief when he was run over by a speeding car. On the radio I listened to *Major Bowes' Amateur Hour, Fibber McGee and Molly, Amos 'n' Andy,* and the gruesome account of Bruno Hauptmann's execution; considered Will Rogers' death in a plane crash a personal loss; followed Dick Tracy in the comics; felt Franklin D. Roosevelt was the closest equivalent to God; read great stacks of books which I procured from the library on Saturday mornings; and wrote poems, pieces of literary criticism and essays at a furious pace.

She was a devoutly religious old lady.
(I knew her when I was in junior high school.)
Every Sunday morning she went to church, and to prayer meetings during the week.
Seated beside her radio, she would listen to broadcasts of the Mass.
At the moment of consecration in the Mass, she would shake with angry laughter.
She was Protestant. She hated Catholics.
As the Rosary was being said she would shout insults at all Catholics.
She would scream obscenities at the radio.
Then, looking kindly in her old frame glasses, she would resume her knitting.

Every Sunday morning she faithfully went to
church.

When I attended East High School in Denver, I encountered "the Establishment" for the first time in my
life—monied, privileged students who moved in a
clique, passing the ball of honors and leadership from
one to the other, running the school, shutting out, unintentionally perhaps, more than nine-tenths of "the
Others." I was in the latter group. In my next-to-last year
in the school I had been writing most of the unsigned
editorials in the student newspaper, the *Spotlight,* and
in some issues was responsible for more stories than any
other reporter. But when editorial positions were assigned for the senior year I was not included in any
capacity. I felt a gnawing hurt. I didn't have an important father or a socialite mother (mine worked in a
downtown office as a secretary so that we could pay rent
in an old apartment and eat three meals a day) or country club connections or a car to drive to school: so I
couldn't have an editorial position on the *Spotlight.* It
was my first encounter with "it isn't what you know, but
who you know"; I raged against it, but was helpless to do
anything. I continued to write my interviews but my
heart wasn't in it; I felt no pride in the paper. However I
earnestly poured out poems and book reviews for the
little-noticed school literary magazine.

Later, in college, I did little creative writing, content-
ing myself instead with fairly surface reporting for a
student newspaper and, when I became bored, editing a
gossip sheet called the *Bar Nuthin'.* One typical "item"
read as follows: " 'It's so quiet in here,' commented
[insert name of coed] seated in [insert name of popular
campus beer joint], 'you can almost hear the zippers in
the men's room.' "

Ironically, in college I moved in a crowd similar to the one which had excluded me in high school. It was a set that drank a lot of beer every night, considered itself pretty damned sophisticated, and more or less established what it meant to be "in." My initiation into the acrobatics of social power grew out of a curious experience when as a high-school senior, I was appointed (God knows why) publicity chairman for a school dance that was to take place on St. Patrick's Day. I promptly named it the Shamrock Shag. Quite innocently, I selected the thirty or forty "most popular" girls in school to be "wearers of the green," as part of a promotional stunt for the event. The effect was staggering. Indignant mothers phoned the school principal ("Why wasn't my daughter on that list?"), desperately frightened that such an affront might keep a college-bound daughter from pledging Theta or being accepted by Sarah Lawrence. Pressure was brought to bear on me, suddenly the high school's "Cholly Knickerbocker" and "Suzy" rolled into one. Out of nowhere, I had become a terrible, shaking, godlike force to be reckoned with. I don't remember whether I decided to be flexible enough to add a dozen or so forlorn outcasts to the now-golden list. This first smell of success was positively overpowering.

At the University of Arizona I became a veritable wheeler-dealer in campus power. I was president of my fraternity, chairman of some dozen committees, editor of the "in" gossip sheet, and even managed to get caught in a cheating scandal. Obviously, I *needed* to cheat, for I simply did not study. In high school I had been chosen by the National Honor Society in my junior year, but now campus glamour had replaced serious pursuits. Finally, I became aware of the fact that I was going nowhere at jet speed, and also was not enjoying it. Out of sheer boredom I had published a particularly dirty issue

of the *Bar Nuthin'*. A member of the board of trustees
felt I should be expelled. A kind and wise college official
asked me to come by his house for a talk; the gist of it
was that I would have to leave school. Just at that moment his wife walked through the room, carrying a copy
of *Forever Amber,* a notorious bedroom novel of the
period. After a moment of silence the official stood up.
He told me to go back to the fraternity and forget the
problem; I would not be expelled. However, the *Bar
Nuthin'* was henceforth banned from the campus. Naturally, I had to put out just one more under-wraps issue in
order to prove my manhood. But soon afterward the
superficiality and sameness of the campus social scene
began to wear on me. Also, I began to spend more time
working my way through college, which took me out of
the "in" crowd; by the time I graduated I had become
something of a social recluse.

I took a night job at the local radio station (an N.B.C.
affiliate) where I read commercials, played records and
even swept the floors and locked up the place around
midnight. I also waited on tables and washed dishes in a
sorority house. We had no union; I was up before dawn
—every morning seemed like the middle of the night—
to work the breakfast shift; then, immediately following
my last morning class, I raced to do the luncheon duties;
and in late afternoon I hurried back to the sorority house
to work the dinner shift. Vegetable soup; the respectable
house mother seated at the head of her table; avocado
salad (if there were three slices on each plate, we often
removed one, thereby creating a gigantic salad for ourselves); bowls of chili; the sorority girls singing in the
dining room when one of their number had just received
a fraternity pin; glasses of milk (one day, we placed a
dead fly in the milk glass of a particularly snobbish girl

who looked down on us); great vats of chocolate ice
cream; mopping the kitchen floor after dinner: it all
blurs into a single "Greek" montage. One summer I got a
job running a power mower in a park system. I was
assigned a lawn area adjoining an expressway and overlooking a creek. I remember the morning when the
mower—just as I was executing an elegant turn with it
at the very edge of the steep creek-bank—leaped out of
my calloused hands, pirouetted gaily in midair, and dis-
appeared beneath the water below. I wasn't fired, but I
was hastily reassigned to a park without a creek. Night
after night, as I soaked my perpetually blistered feet in
salts and hot water in order to work the next day, I read
my way through *War and Peace,* then the myriad works
of Chekhov and Dostoyevsky.

Of all my odd jobs the one that interested me most
was my stint in broadcasting. It combined a variety of
tasks and the bustle of people with the glamour of local
showmanship. And there was a sense of power when
one thought of broadcasting into a vast number of
homes. After college days, I wanted to continue communications work in Hollywood. I moved there, looking for
a job.

My grandmother, in her will, had left a thousand
dollars to be given me when I became twenty-one years
old. This legacy enabled me to enroll in a radio workshop conducted by the National Broadcasting Company
in Hollywood. The students' spirit was highly competitive, for the workshop was seen as a possible spring-
board to a job in Hollywood. Writing a script was the big
assignment. Mine was a panorama of American history;
I told the story with dozens of voices, massed choruses,
innumerable sound effects and considerable moralizing.
I crowded everything—including, literally, the Statue of

Liberty—into my mammoth, uncoordinated writing effort. It was never produced. However, out of the workshop experience came my first job in the industry.

After receiving my diploma I was down and out, with literally only a few dollars left. I lived in a five-dollar-a-week butler's pantry in an immense rundown rooming house. The smell of escaping gas mingled with that of frying fish in the adjoining kitchen. When I left my room to look for a job, I had to lock the windows which faced an alley. Later, upon returning, it was necessary to air out the room before I could stay in it because of the constantly escaping gas. On such occasions, while awaiting relief from my personal air-pollution problem, I would sit in the kitchen (which operated night and day at a consistently heavy level of traffic) and chat with other roomers.

My tiny, claustrophobic room in that old house sometimes terrified me. For it reminded me of the day, as a child, when my family was away and an elderly maid, angry with me, had locked me inside a dark closet. "A white rat is inside! He will eat you!" she shouted. I wept. For an hour I threw my body against the locked door in desperate anguish. The darkness. The stifling, small space in which there could be no escape from attack, torture and certain death. The awful loneliness. And I can remember, also as a child, my darkened bedroom. I lay alone. There was a light in the hall outside. Don't put out the light! For if you do there can be no escape from attack and death. Now, outside my room in the boarding house kitchen I could sense the presence and movement of people. There was a sense of mutual belonging and security; I was not alone.

One of the half-dozen largest advertising agencies in the country hired me for its Hollywood office as a junior executive. I was to learn the business from the inside. I was soon producing my own radio show, a fifteen-minute, five-times-a-week, "live" network program, featuring a philosopher, a home economist and the late Buddy Cole who played a combination organ-celeste-piano. In addition I was agency contact man for both a Sunday evening high-rated newscast and a daily network soap opera.

I smelled clean. I had the antiseptic, remote look of success. My suit was a paragon among suits. My shoes carried the aroma of fresh leather. My ties had an avant-garde relationship with my shirts. My barber had a celebrity clientele on an appointment basis. I dined on an expense account, and the martini before lunch became a sacrament. I dated very beautiful young starlets. My deodorant, after-shave and cologne made me a walking collection of tasteful smells. I was chatting with stars, writers, producers and others who were then making the Hollywood scene. I was seething inside with macabre visions of success, while outwardly learning how to cultivate cool, and was in the process of becoming a bright, shiny, pushing, well-groomed snot. I wanted more success. The people with whom I worked had already achieved it. The men were established at the top of their profession; the women had either made it or slept with men who had.

My real interest was in writing scripts. And I wrote them. Most of my writing was abjectly unsuccessful. Yet night after night I returned to my office to spend hours at the typewriter. I had a friend who, like me, was an ambitious young man working in communications. We sat up together many nights, fashioning a script idea that nobody wanted. We considered ourselves sorry failures. (I was delighted to find, several years later, that Bob Merrill had hit his stride in song writing. He is probably best known as the writer of the lyrics for *Funny Girl.*)

I wrote a script about an alchemist for a series called *The Count of Monte Cristo.* The setting was medieval; the plot laden with action and mystery. Time ran out at the end of the program so my writing credit had to be eliminated in the rush to get off the air—I was heartbroken. I did a lot of research for a program about trains called *Mainline,* for which the train sounds had to be accurately described in the script. The sound man was far more important than the actors. To my horror, just before the show I noticed that he had had a lot of drinks. I stood petrified inside the control booth, watching him do work that seemed as precise as that of a wood carver. He mixed train whistles and choo-choos with voices, faded locomotives in and passing trains out, raised a majestic train sound while increasing yet another train's speed to heighten the drama; it was thrilling to hear. All this without missing a cue or seeming to stop for breath, although he was sweating hard. When the show was over, we bought him black coffee.

I was "the kid" in the advertising agency. At the end of a long day, I joined the oldtimers for drinks at their favorite bars. I learned agency politics and found out what gave ad men their ulcers. Along with the ribbing I got came a welcome to almost any events going on inside or outside the agency.

My first Hollywood office party was a complex affair. I was asked to mix the drinks and to see that a particular guest—the mistress of a tycoon—received very, very stiff ones. This was ostensibly to test the legend of her wooden leg. Naturally she drank everybody else under the table, showing none of the ravages of liquor or power politics. The latter she knew well: She had come to her present eminent position from lowly beginnings on the tycoon's switchboard, later moving into his public relations department. I learned afterward that she ultimately married him. When he died, she inherited his empire.

> My heart is turning to aluminum, my balls steel, my liver silver, my soul gold.
> To be totally functional would mean not to waste man-hours.
> Laughter could be filed on old tapes. I might eliminate pain, depression and fear.
> Credo: Do; don't be.
> *How* not to turn into a machine?

The agency had a radio show starring a top musical personality who hit the bottle whenever his program was being taped for a network. Every week the ritual was repeated. The director and production crew gathered, waiting for the star, who was hosting a party next door at a prestigious restaurant. Finally—only after the musicians had gone on "golden hours" (overtime) and the budget had once again snapped—the star arrived to start taping. Even then the atmosphere was charged with temperament, missed cues, and infighting. I always attended these taping sessions, somewhat in awe of the combined glamour, power, and madness. One night the agency producer, after concluding the taping, evidently returned to his office and kicked a gaping hole in the door. We found it the next morning along with a cryptic note of resignation. The door was famous for a day; other agency people arrived to look at it, muttering suitably lugubrious remarks, casting heavenward glances, and gnashing their teeth (this life was rough for them, too). He never returned. I missed him.

As "the kid" I was not threatening to anybody. From my place in the circle I could see all but was seldom asked to speak. I spent some time in the downtown Los Angeles office of the agency. It was a block from Pershing Square, which used to be a palm-tree-lined square block where speakers harangued anyone who would listen, debates springing up at a moment's notice. It was like Hyde Park Corner in London.

I knew little about Pershing Square at that time. One afternoon, after an agency luncheon downtown, I decided to take my first walk through it. A sharp debate was going on. I stopped to listen for a few minutes. My blood pressure was stirred a bit, but not too seriously because I was thoroughly the junior executive in a major ad agency: my role was to be quiet, earnest, and dignified in a youthful way, as befitted someone being groomed for advancement in the club.

Moving on from that sharp debate, I came to yet another one. This time I became angered by what I heard, but kept my temper in check. However, just ahead a third man was delivering a raucously leftist message with which I found myself in violent disagreement. He was addressing a growing and spirited crowd. Shouting "Now, wait a minute!" I fought my way through to the speaker. Delighted to have an opponent, especially a junior executive type, he gave me a soapbox to stand on. We went at it furiously. The crowd seemed vastly entertained. After a while, looking out over the crowd, I was discomfited to see two of the top agency men standing on the sidelines, looking quizzically and with cool disdain on the scene. I was acting distinctly out of character—that is, out of my correct image. Without a word or a hint of recognition, they went executively on their way.

The show I had been producing was to move to San Francisco. It was a dead town for radio and, at that time, a place best suited for persons in the industry who were retired or independently wealthy. I was neither. I went job-hunting in Hollywood again. The large motion picture studios employed men to act in a liaison capacity with the then supremely important radio industry, representing both literary properties and film personalities to be utilized on radio programs. The purpose was nation-wide publicity for new movie releases. I was hired as such a liaison man, as well as publicity unit-man on some movies. My salary leaped.

Here was the celebrity system, not as an abstraction or occasion for rhetoric, but in the flesh. Here was the motion picture, not as art but as pure commercial. This was exploitation straight-across-the-board. (My title was actually "director of radio exploitation.") Here was the curious tribal world: studio chiefs, mistresses receiving homage from those at my level, forgotten wives who came out of retirement once a year to pour at stockholders' meetings, alcoholic old directors (some clutching their Oscars) and bright new ones on the make, writers who frankly considered themselves whores alongside others who felt they were Faulkners, friendly switchboard operators, and hard starlets lugging their mothers around with them.

Mildred Thornton, business associate of a top movie producer, who had company stock literally pasted on the soles of her shoes, sided up to me. It was about eleven and the party was going full swing. An Old-Fashioned in hand, I was standing expectantly on the sidelines. I'd never had a good chance to become acquainted with Mildred Thornton and had just about decided to wipe out my error. She seemed to have had the same idea.

I wondered what made her one of the most stunning women in the room and I decided it was her bearing. Her slightly graying hair was piled on top of her head, and she was wearing a regal-looking white satin gown. The fact that she was weighted down with enough diamonds to sink the *Queen Elizabeth* was one of the few indications she was pushing fifty. I knew she'd been married once, a long time ago, and wondered who in hell she belonged to now.

"Who do you think is the most attractive woman here?" she asked me.

"I don't think you take second place," I told her, looking straight at her and meaning what I said—if she could lose ten years.

"Come now," Mildred laughed in her tired, bored way which wasn't really either tired or bored. "Let's not stand on formality."

Two friends of mine were writers. They spent their days grinding out portions of scripts in the writers' building. What a factory it was. During shooting, a writer could never set foot on the set of a movie he had written. After a script had supposedly been completed, a second writer would invariably work on it, restructuring it and providing new dialogue. My writer friends went to studio sneak previews of their films. They were not invited, but got word via a grapevine as complex and foolproof as that of a medieval court. Sometimes I tagged along. Often the writers couldn't make sense of a film for which they had been given screen credit. They might not even be able to recognize several of the characters—added later by another hand. The bewildered writers generally ended up getting loaded. It was all very funny and very destructive.

I was working in my Hollywood office on a Saturday morning, trying to catch up on paper work on a day when the switchboard would be closed and interruptions minimal. Loud voices outside my window distracted me. They continued, growing in intensity. I leaped from my desk and ran to the window. Two men stood, talking, on the pavement below. I would outshout them, ordering them to be more quiet and considerate. Just in time I noticed that one of the men was Samuel Goldwyn. The other was Howard Hughes. I retreated in silence from the window.

A production assignment once kept me working at a film studio for three nights in a row. I was tired and angry when the third night rolled around. A union regulation stipulated that personnel directly related to my project must be given a time break and fed at midnight. I decided management needed to be taught to respect workers' feelings. I contacted the most expensive catering service in Beverly Hills. Could they cater a sit-down dinner party at midnight? Yes?

At twelve o'clock, on an empty, dimly lighted, ghost-ridden movie stage in the studio, a curious, perhaps unprecedented affair began. I invited the night guards to join us; I compelled the cleaning women. Dinner was preceded by cocktails. Shrimp came before the steak entrees. There was wine. The desserts were lavish pastries. The cost was outrageous.

The next morning, I was called in by a studio executive. I was fired, he said. No, I replied, I quit. He looked disconcerted. Would I reconsider and stay, he asked. No,

I definitely would not, I said. He begged me to stay. All right, I said, if I were given a raise. He consented. I departed his office with an anomalous new dignity within the studio.

I went to San Francisco on a vacation where I spent all my money. Returning to Hollywood, I found that I had been fired.

It had all seemed so important, and I had felt important because I was part of it. At least I had worked hard at it. I had quite sincerely *tried* (whatever that meant) but suddenly what I had accomplished on the job didn't mean very much. When I knew I was leaving I wasn't sure of anything any more—what I'd be taking with me, or what I'd be leaving behind.

Remembering how quickly others had been forgotten, on the very last day I took a penknife and carved my initials—very small—on the bottom part of the wooden desk in my office. It was absurd, of course, but I had left a mark. Even then, part of me realized that the only real way to leave a mark was to do something with my life, to use it in a way that would have meaning, but at the time I didn't think I could.

The next day I was gone, the hidden mark remained, and the telephone rang in my empty office.

Now, instead of job-hunting, I decided I wanted to write a novel. A friend provided an office for me to work in. I checked in every night at 7 o'clock and wrote until dawn, interrupted only by the cheerful greeting of cleaning women. I started to make my novel a mystery but unfortunately ended up by trying to render a serious social commentary. I was represented by an excellent Beverly Hills literary agent who sent the completed manuscript to a New York colleague. She replied: "I have now read the manuscript and agree with you that

Mr. Boyd has not written another 'Hucksters.' In fact, the whole novel, which has considerable merit, suffers from attempting to do a more serious job than it accomplished. As a matter of fact, when I first started it I thought it was going to be an extremely superior 'whodunit' and when I discovered it was not, it became pretty pretentious in my opinion. I still think it should be a murder story and in this category it would be outstanding. I don't suppose though that the author will agree to this. Thank you for the opportunity of letting me see this novel. I really do think there is a property here if the author is willing to revise."

The author was not. Instead, I gambled with my career. Because of my previous contact with liaison work for the major movie studios, I decided that the independent movie producers, who were mushrooming all over Hollywood, needed their own liaison with radio. One fine New Year's Day in southern California I opened up Mal Boyd & Associates, to represent a group of independent motion picture producers.

As one of its first assignments, my office handled the radio exploitation for an insignificant film called *It Happened on Fifth Avenue*. The presence of Victor Moore in the cast was the only good thing about the picture. I was given a Fifth Avenue bus, which had been driven to the West Coast from New York by order of the producer. It was to be used to promote the movie. I worked out an arrangement with a women's daytime radio program on one of the major networks. I would take a busload of ladies from the studio audience for a sightseeing ride to the homes of various motion picture stars. A report of the trip would be made on a subsequent program. A motion-picture magazine would photograph the event.

One morning, after the show, network ushers in uniform escorted a group of selected ladies onto the bus waiting at the curb outside the studio. Our strange pilgrimage got under way. Most of the ladies were excited about the idea but a few were actually tearful. They said good-byes to husbands and children. The ladies were to return in late afternoon. Lunch on the bus was catered by Hugo, the Hot Dog King.

The first stop was the Beverly Hills mansion of Maria Montez and her husband, Jean Pierre Aumont. Miss Montez was at home in bed that day because the astrologer, whose advice she scrupulously followed, had warned of mishap if she left home. Outside, the ladies from the bus stomped in their high heels through the wet soil of a freshly planted garden. Then they walked into the mansion with its white wall-to-wall carpeting. Mr. Aumont graciously entertained the ladies. A sister of Miss Montez served sandwiches and coffee to the members of my staff in an attractive den. As we enjoyed our repast a cat vomited on a carpeted stair off the den. It was a bad omen.

The next stop was Pickfair, the fabled estate of Mary Pickford and Buddy Rogers, located up a hill from the mansion of Miss Montez and Mr. Aumont. When the ladies, the members of my staff, and a half-dozen film stars who were accompanying us boarded the bus for this next excursion, we discovered that the bus could not manage the sharp incline. We asked several of the ladies to get off and await a second trip. But still the bus could not make it. It would start grinding up the hill, then come crashing back dangerously near the Montez-Aumont driveway. A couple of the ladies were crying again. I decided that a fleet of cars should be summoned to take the ladies, in relays, up the hill to Pickfair. Meanwhile, our schedule was wrecked. The ladies who were left behind, awaiting cars to drive them to Pickfair, reentered the Montez-Aumont mansion, several of them demanding ice water.

At Pickfair, the ladies from the tour were ushered onto the grounds of the estate. They walked across the great sweep of lawn to the swimming pool, which overlooked Beverly Hills, commanding a view of many illustrious homes including Falcon's Lair where Rudolph Valentino had lived and which was now occupied by Doris Duke. Miss Pickford was away but Mr. Rogers came down from the main house, which was once a hunting lodge, to greet the ladies.

Next on our agenda was the home of Jeanette MacDonald and her husband, Gene Raymond. The middle-aged women, crowding around the well-known couple in the garden, seemed momentarily almost overcome by this proximity to Hollywood holiness. Ladies reached out with timid aggressiveness to touch Miss MacDonald's gown. Once again that afternoon, tears came to the eyes of a few.

The Paul Henried home at Malibu was on our list but had to be scratched. We were running very, very late. However, we could try to visit the home of Peter Lawford and his parents. It was near Pacific Palisades. When we got there, young Peter was out playing cricket or football somewhere, but Lady Lawford invited my staff to come inside for a quick libation which she sensed we badly needed. Due to the limitation of time, the ladies remained on the bus observing the facade of the Lawford residence.

When we emerged from the house a few minutes later, the bus had vanished.

It was a bad moment. Perhaps the ladies were lying in a ditch somewhere beneath an overturned bus which they had commandeered from the driver following a decision to mutiny. We soon learned that, fortunately, they had merely decided to use—immediately—the closest public restroom facilities they could find. Lady Lawford, who had driven with her maid to a nearby bus stop, came back to tell us that the ladies were queuing up outside the ladies' room of a gasoline station several blocks away. As soon as they returned, by unspoken common assent we headed quickly back down Sunset Boulevard toward the heart of Hollywood. Light was rapidly diminishing. Husbands were no doubt worrying.

To bolster sagging morale, I led the ladies on the Fifth Avenue bus in song. We were in the middle of "Three Blind Mice" when the bus passed the Cock 'n' Bull bar and restaurant on the Sunset Strip. At that moment the indefatigably sophisticated Monty Woolley emerged from the doorway. He caught one glimpse of the Fifth Avenue bus speeding by, heard the briefest strain of "Three Blind Mice," then urbanely turned back into the bar. Soon the ladies were delivered to their spouses; the day's adventure was gratefully over.

On another occasion my radio promotion featured a cow. The lady chosen for that day's "Queen for a Day," on the now-defunct network radio program of that name, had received the cow as one of her gifts. It came from a leading dairy products firm. It was arranged that the queen, accompanied by her cow, would visit cowboy star Roy Rogers' famous horse Trigger at his farm. Photographers would be present to record the classic meeting. Roy Rogers' new movie would receive publicity on *Queen for a Day*.

A fleet of black limousines bore the queen, a group of somber advertising men, the cow and me out to the farm. The cow rode in the rear, in a trailer attached to the last car of the entourage. Liveried chauffeurs drove each of the five or six cars. The cow was extremely irritable; it needed to be milked, but nobody seemed to know how to do it. As we drove along residential streets to reach the farm, little children ran alongside the elegant open trailer bearing the discomfited cow.

At the farm the creature was led forth, along with the queen, to stand next to Trigger for photographs. Kids had by now gathered in a circle around us, gripped by a proper awe. I will never be sure what happened next. It seems that the queen, quite innocently, had tweaked the cow's ear. The beast was gone in a cloud of dust. The dead-serious ad men, in their shiny black shoes and expensive black suits, were soon lost in the cloud in hot pursuit. During the confusion one huckster, who had decided not to take part in the hunt, sidled up to me. Would I, he asked, take special care with the photo captions. I said I would. They should stress, he continued, that the cow had been provided by the firm's canned milk division, not its fresh milk division . . .

Soon the creature was captured and the tableau regrouped itself. Trigger, the queen and the subdued cow were photographed for posterity. The queen good-naturedly wore a combination of her own clothes and gifts that had been showered upon her. Over her housedress she gallantly sported a double silver-fox fur. On her head was a modish new hat; on her feet, her old flat shoes. Her fingers and arms fairly glittered with pieces of gift jewelry. I admired her good grace and sense of humor about it all. However, trouble lay ahead with the cow. That afternoon, the beast was manicured, feet and tail, by a leading cosmetics house. All went smoothly. But in the evening, while accompanying the queen to dinner, the cow had an unfortunate accident on the carpet of Ciro's nightclub.

.   .   .

At this stage in my life, I decided to give The Party. It is the only Hollywood party I ever gave. It was in honor of a visiting Canadian newspaper columnist who had turned Hollywood momentarily on its ear. The film colony was always impressed by a foreign accent, preferably British, and by journalistic credentials from London, Paris, Rome—or even Toronto. I resolved to give the party in my extremely modest bungalow in the hills of Hollywood. To my great surprise, suddenly a Canadian picture magazine decided to "cover" the party and all the film studios in town were calling to tell me which of their stars, accompanied by which press agents and photographers, were planning to attend.

The matter showed signs of getting out of hand. There would undoubtedly be too many people and probably not enough liquor, let alone space. For once at least in my life, I remained completely relaxed and attempted to do nothing at all. I left my office at the usual time, showered, shaved and dressed for the party. Liquor was ordered, food catered, and one well-known actor volunteered to be bartender, another to greet people at the door. But while I was still alone in the house an hour before party time, shaving, the first four guests arrived. They had not been invited. Extremely well-dressed, they rang the doorbell and casually walked in. They said they had read about the fete in the daily newspapers and thought it sounded like fun. Then, largely because of the incongruity of their presence alone with me, as the silence seemed to close in around us, they departed and I never saw them again.

The guests didn't trickle in—they arrived like a tidal wave. It seemed that, as if on cue, the entire immense crowd of them converged on the house and poured in. Almost immediately, people were queuing up for use of

Let's stay there all afternoon
And plot some baroque scheme that will be fun, not
    power
Tomorrow the sun will shine again.
    Today we'll let the king feed us cake
    But oh the longing
    For a good plain resolve
    For a sturdy heart
    And a loaf of hot bread.

Undoubtedly, I was looking for a playwright, priest, or prophet who might present me with the accouterments of my identity. I knew there had always been a form to my life, although I could not have defined it. The self: Malcolm. Who was he? At first, words had constituted my reality. Love. Success. Happiness. But I had never known what the words meant. Surely many sounds and images flowed into and through these words: I knew what it was to dream. My heart was still closed in upon itself. I could not comprehend either myself as a real person or the world as a real world.

It is hard for me now to feel a relationship with myself then. A great deal of what is called glamour touched my life, but only very lightly on the surface. I moved in the company of Stars and Other Successful People in a strange setting called Hollywood. I might rub elbows with Ava Gardner or Gary Cooper, Ingrid Bergman or Clark Gable. Dancing late at Mocambo's on a week night, I might find Lana Turner on the uncrowded dance floor. At a party or screening, Louella Parsons or Hedda Hopper, the royal chroniclers of the magic scene, might enter, transforming the so-so event into an *important* one.

Miss Parsons had a Sunday night national radio program which was of supreme importance in the Hollywood world. I tried to place a stuntman as a guest on the show, which had its choice of top stars, and was amazed when he was accepted and scheduled for an early broadcast. He would be a "different" guest.

I went to work interviewing the stuntman about the times when, impersonating a star at a distance when the script called for his being caught in a burning building, on a wild horse, or in the raging rapids of a swollen river, he gave an effective portrayal—and saved his own life. I prepared a detailed biography for the writer of the program. After the writer had conducted a long, involved personal interview with the stuntman, she wrote the script. Things were going well; there seemed to be no problems.

Then, to my horror, I discovered that the stuntman could not read English. This meant, of course, that he could not read his portion of the script on the program, which was scheduled to be broadcast live, coast-to-coast, on the next Sunday night. He obligingly agreed to work with me, for however long it might take, to memorize the script.

We spent twelve hours a day working on our task. He succeeded brilliantly in committing the script to memory. Everything was going to be all right. Then the head of the studio (the stuntman was employed on a John Wayne movie which I was promoting) managed to get hold of a copy of the script. He had changes to make, i.e., more plugs for his picture. All was lost. The program producer very rightly would not accept the changes. There were hurried conferences at levels far above my lowly estate. A compromise was reached: certain changes would quickly be incorporated into the script. This was done, a new script typewritten, and a copy sent to me by messenger. The stuntman and I—on the day before the broadcast—went to work again. But our task was a hopeless one: on the air the next night, as the nation listened attentively, there was nearly a full minute of dead time as the stuntman gallantly tried to think of the answer to a question which Miss Parsons had gracefully posed. After that interview, Louella taped all of her programs.

I had another brush with fate linked to the Louella Parsons' program. The David Selznick studio had promised me Gregory Peck as a guest on the show, in conjunction with promotion for the Motion Picture Relief Fund, of which I was radio chairman. A few days before the broadcast, a Selznick studio representative informed me that Mr. Peck would be working on a film away from Hollywood and therefore be unavailable to do the radio interview.

I had to come up with a substitute guest star whose magnitude equaled that of Mr. Peck. What could I do? The writer, a good friend of mine, suggested a solution. A major male star was away honeymooning with his new wife. However, the writer had the private telephone number of the star's cabana in a luxury hotel. I could telephone him. The situation would be saved if he consented to cut short his honeymoon and come back to Hollywood to do the interview.

The writer took me to Louella's home to make the call from Miss Parsons' office on the second floor. As we entered, I saw Miss Parsons and Louis B. Mayer, then head of M-G-M, sitting in the living room, looking at a print of the new technicolor movie *Son of Lassie*. We passed them and walked upstairs. I sat down at a desk, picked up the phone, and dialed the number.

One of the most famous voices in the world answered. I plunged ahead. "I am calling for Louella Parsons," I said. "Miss Parsons would like you to be a guest on her radio program next Sunday night. What shall I tell Miss Parsons?"

There was a long silence. My heart was pounding. Then the famous voice spoke; I was saved.

During this period of my life I was steadily drinking too much. Always there was the cocktail party. It provided lots of good, free liquor in glamorous settings with highly interesting, well-known people. Afterward I would retreat, with just a few others to an appropriate bar or someone's place to continue imbibing and savor the sex that was offered. It seemed fun.

On a New Year's Eve I was driving, in a new black Cadillac his father had just given him, with Charles Chaplin, Jr., from one popular nightclub to another. We had both been drinking. The accident occurred on Sunset Strip in front of the old Mocambo club. Charlie ran his car into another brand new Cadillac—driven by my boss at Samuel Goldwyn Studios, where I was working on an assignment. The *cause célèbre* that ensued monopolized newspaper headlines for days. It was, very sadly, all because a driver involved in a minor traffic accident happened to bear the name Charles Chaplin, Jr., at a time when the great comedian was being pilloried by segments of the American press.

Television was just getting under way, and I became one of the first West Coast producers. I also appeared in an early Hollywood TV series. My function was to interview celebrity guests. I was terrified. Foolishly, I attempted to memorize a script rather than ad-lib. On my first show I was to walk through a door, make a few opening remarks, and introduce a guest. The door stuck. I had to kick it open. Then, with sweat pouring down my face, which was stiff with pancake make-up, I confronted the camera with a glazed smile, and parroted the lines I had learned by rote. The reviews were decidedly mixed.

We had no money to pay guest stars in those days. Kirk Douglas, Ruth Roman, Charles Brackett, the producer, and James Wong Howe, the cinematographer, all appeared on one of my programs—without fee; Edgar Bergen and Charlie McCarthy made their TV debut on another. Two fledgling young comics, Dean Martin and Jerry Lewis, did a routine one night. Gloria Swanson appeared on one of my shows just a week prior to beginning her screen comeback in *Sunset Boulevard*. A leading hat designer had provided a number of his millinery creations for the show that evening, and sent them to the studio in an armored car. He broke off further contact with us afterward because Miss Swanson, enthusiastically following the script, scattered several of the hats across the floor.

Those early days in television were fun. Of course, they were not without their seriousness, but it was seldom comprehended. Some of us were involved in a communications complex which was molding the thought and action patterns of millions of people. This did not, I think, tellingly break into our consciousness. Anyway, we had deadlines, budgets, ratings, guest stars, new formats, and audiences to worry about.

Yet a group of television producers, acting out of a sense of social responsibility, formed an association. I was elected president of the Television Producers Association of Hollywood. We organized a small committee to engage in drafting a self-censorship code. As a member of this committee, I considered it more important to criticize dehumanizing caricatures of a black male, and comic stereotypes of a Chinese cook with long pigtails, than to determine exactly how much of a woman's breast might be revealed on screen.

. . .

One of the independent producers for whom I acted as liaison with the radio industry was Triangle Productions. Its owners were Mary Pickford, Buddy Rogers, and Ralph Cohn. Miss Pickford and her husband were remote, legendary figures to me. Mary Pickford had been Hollywood's first authentic woman star. Her partners at United Artists had included Charles Chaplin and Douglas Fairbanks; their triumvirate represented the industry's best-known personalities. Buddy Rogers had once topped all Hollywood stars in fan mail, after the release of *Wings* in the late twenties, and had later become a noted bandleader. When Mary Pickford divorced Douglas Fairbanks, she married Buddy Rogers.

I first met Buddy at a Hollywood radio broadcast. I had arranged his appearance on it as promotion for a film produced by Triangle Productions. Tom Breneman, a wise showman whose *Breakfast in Hollywood* was a favorite American radio show, took me aside after Buddy received a warm ovation from the studio audience. "You can see how people love him," he told me. "Buddy should have his own show."

I agreed. I got busy lining up writers, a director, an orchestra, even an interested advertising agency. All this required many months. The essential work was done not behind a desk, but over lunch tables at the Brown Derby in Hollywood and beside outdoor barbecue pits in Beverly Hills gardens. Ideas were washed down by hard liquor.

Finally, the time had come to test the proposed radio show. We decided to try it out in San Francisco. I flew up from Hollywood with Mary Pickford and Buddy Rogers. An orchestra with which Buddy had rehearsed was also flown north. The night before we taped the program, I sat up with one of the writers who adamantly refused to stop drinking and stay through the tryout. We needed him because the show was very shaky. He kept picking up a phone in his hotel room to call an airline for a reservation back to Hollywood, and I kept knocking the instrument out of his hands. We wrestled with it on the floor. Mercifully, when dawn finally came, the early sunlight seemed to subdue the writer, who decided to stay and took a nap. Leaving his hotel, I climbed Nob Hill. Milkmen were making their door-to-door deliveries by horse-drawn carts. The sun shone on the milk-white San Francisco houses, and I felt kinship with those elegantly sophisticated, early-morning characters in perfume advertisements.

Back at my hotel, Buddy was trying to reach me. We had work to do, for the show was to be taped that evening. It was a success. Immediately after we finished, Miss Pickford, Buddy and I were sped by limousine from the broadcasting studio to the airport to return to Hollywood. Under all the pressure, I had not eaten all day. Aware of this and worrying about me, Mary had ordered a sandwich for me from room service. But that had been several hours earlier. She had saved it for me in her large handbag. When she finally handed me the turkey sandwich on rye, it smelled like fine leather. I munched on it. Then, when Mary and Buddy were looking out their window at the bay, I stealthily rolled down the limousine window on my side, and shared my turkey sandwich with any seagulls in the vicinity.

When I negotiated a network show for Buddy in New York, Miss Pickford closed her estate, Pickfair (named for Pickford-Fairbanks), for the first time in a quarter-century to join her husband there. The three of us formed a packaging-production firm in New York called P.R.B., Inc., the initials representing our last names.

On the evening before I was to fly from Hollywood to

New York to set up the machinery of our P.R.B. operation there, Miss Pickford gave a large reception at Pickfair for visiting journalists from various parts of the
world. (This was at the request of the U. S. State
Department.) An orchestra played on the lawn, Hollywood celebrities mingled with foreign newsmen, and
caviar by the tray was served along with champagne
by the gallon. Several guests who were close friends of
Miss Pickford decided to go swimming in the pool and
dispatched me to locate bathing suits somewhere in the
great house.

I never got back to them with the suits. For the dura-
tion of the party I sat in a car parked beneath the porte-
cochere of Pickfair. I was talking with one of the
shrewdest, most durable observers of the Hollywood
scene—an elderly lady whose husband had for years
been a dean of motion picture critics. She told me of
past years at Pickfair, which had been known as the
second White House for visiting international figures,
reminiscing about lavish parties and historic receptions
which had been held there. Many names came into our
conversation that night! D. W. Griffith, Fairbanks,
Chaplin, Elsie deWolfe Mendl, Lillian Gish, William
Randolph Hearst, Marion Davies. She brought up to date
the legend of Mary Pickford. She said that now I should
have to take my own place in that legend. When we
finished talking, the party had ended, lights were
dimmed, and all the other guests had gone home.

In the morning I caught a plane to New York.

Once as I was looking from the windows of my pent-
house office over Fifth Avenue toward hundreds of thousands—perhaps millions—of lights spread below me I
learned something about the public. Each light represented people, families. They watched television, listened to the radio, read newspapers and *defined* celeb-

rity. The public may love in one moment and hate in the
next, exalt and reject, offer support for wrong reasons,
and withhold it when help is needed most. The public is
moved by a political candidate's mustache, a divorce, a
bad headline, a good headline, the sound of a voice, the
way a suit of clothes is worn, a haircut, the quality of a
man's shave, an honest answer, a dishonest answer, and
always *images*. The public is won when a famous person
can break through images, even very briefly, with a demonstration of humor, warmth and undeniable humanness.

Mary Pickford had, within this century, stirred millions of people in every corner of the world. Once, in a
city square in Europe, thousands stood expressing adu-
lation by moving their hands in a clapping motion—yet
without making the noise of applause, for they had been
told Miss Pickford felt ill. The Duchess of Windsor once
told Buddy Rogers: "I am married to the best known
man in the world and you to the best known woman." I
was able to see Miss Pickford in action with the public
when, during my seminary days in Berkeley, California,
she visited San Francisco as co-chairman with Mrs.
Dwight D. Eisenhower of a savings bond campaign. I
stayed with her then. She won over any crowd at the
drop of a hat. Television was new to her, yet she was
candid and winning when she appeared on it.

Miss Pickford, a millionairess, was amusingly frugal
about small expenses. I dined with her one night in her
suite at the Pierre. She ordered finnan haddie and boiled
potatoes. She did not feel particularly hungry, she said.
Might we share a single order? And she had a habit of
being *quite* late. On my birthday, she and Buddy were to
take me to dinner. They made a reservation at "21." I sat
in Miss Pickford's Park Avenue duplex, waiting for her
to get ready. The table was held for an hour, but was

gone when we finally arrived. We proceeded to eat my birthday dinner—and it was a very good one—in the Sherry Netherlands bar. A young black pianist, entertaining in the bar, spotted Mary. He played "Coquette," the title not only of a song but of the film which won Miss Pickford her Academy Award "Oscar." She tipped him graciously for his memory.

Miss Pickford's charismatic power with a vast public was fading rapidly, but her economic power was solidly entrenched. It, more than mere celebrity, bestowed enormous social power upon her.

At home over the dinner table, either in New York or back in Beverly Hills, Miss Pickford liked to portray Queen Elizabeth and Mary, Queen of Scots, for us. Remarkably, she presented one role, then the other, as we sat at the table eating our dessert or sipping coffee. Her voice caught the essence of what one felt was the personality of each queen. As Elizabeth, Mary would thunder and rage. As the Queen of Scots, she was soft and tender. I came to know what a fine actress Miss Pickford was, although most people knew her more as a personality. I wished that she had not banished herself so long ago from the screen and, indeed, from life. The waste of such a talent, that burned fiercely even in tragic and self-destructive exile, is incalculable.

I always sensed the presence of wonderful ghosts at Pickfair. The attic itself was stored with priceless mementoes of Miss Pickford's foreign visits. She was showered with gifts by heads of state. Jeweled matador capes in various colors were there. (Later, in my seminary days, I wanted very badly to have them made into chasubles—the red for one church season, the green and white for others—but I never asked.) There was also, locked away in that attic, an Asian tapestry which came from an ancient temple. It was stained by centuries-old layers of smoke and incense. And incongruously, amid the enchanting *objets d'art* hidden in the attic, was a curious bust of Joan Crawford, who had once been Miss Pickford's daughter-in-law, and had long not been personally welcome in that house. Miss Crawford had been married to Douglas Fairbanks, Jr., a union received in chilly fashion by Miss Pickford and her husband, Douglas, Sr., who then reigned over film society as an imperial couple.

Once when I had been overworking and was dangerously tired, the doctor ordered a two-week period of rest. Miss Pickford suggested that I stay in the guest house at Pickfair, which was secluded and quiet. Queen Marie of Rumania had stayed here, so had the Mountbattens of England. The guest house possessed graceful elegance and pastiche; Mary's Academy Award "Oscar" was casually present in it. (During these years I also helped to select the "Oscar" winners as a voting member of the Academy of Motion Picture Arts and Sciences.) I would spend my days at the pool, soothing my tired body and frayed nerves.

The first night, the butler turned down my bed, placed a pitcher of fresh water on the night table and early editions of the two morning newspapers on the bed, and told me that if burglars broke into the house during the night, seeking Miss Pickford's jewels, I should not be alarmed but merely punch a button that would quickly summon the Beverly Hills police. Thanks to this casual warning, I doubt that I slept a wink at night during my entire stay in the guest house, relying on sun and naps by the pool during the days to pull me through.

It is a curious afternoon.

I sit here amid deceptive silence. There are layers and gradations of it. Ideas are whispered and shouted at me. Memories move like riders in my mind which is as fevered as my body. Now I hear a motorcycle, now guilt; a jet races overhead and a compulsion to be free on the periphery of what passes for my heart. I am calm and excited.

Miss Pickford told me one of her favorite stories concerning the colorful royal past of Pickfair. One evening she and Mr. Fairbanks were entertaining guests at dinner when the butler called Miss Pickford away from the table for an emergency phone call. A reporter was on the wire from the Los Angeles *Examiner,* which was owned by William Randolph Hearst, a friend of Miss Pickford's. What was Miss Pickford's opinion of the flamboyant revivalist Aimee Semple McPherson, he asked. The newspaper was on a deadline for an important story about her. Miss Pickford said that she had no opinion. Then would it be correct, the reporter asked, to quote Miss Pickford as saying that she was opposed to Miss McPherson? Certainly not, said Miss Pickford. All right, under these circumstances, might the reporter quote Miss Pickford as being *for* Miss McPherson? No, replied Miss Pickford, she had no opinion at all. She hung up.

But now she was upset. The telephone call had been senseless and disturbing. Miss Pickford returned to the dinner table. Shortly the butler informed Miss Pickford that Aimee Semple McPherson was downstairs at the main entrance to the house and demanded entrance. Mary said that, under the circumstances, she would not be able to see Miss McPherson as an uninvited guest in her home. Then Miss Pickford and Bebe Daniels, another movie star of that period and a close friend, ran up a flight of stairs overlooking the foyer. Soon they heard a woman's strident voice. Miss McPherson had climbed the stairs from the main entrance and was standing in the foyer, surrounded by the other dinner guests. They were embracing Aimee Semple McPherson, laughing and welcoming her. This angered Miss Pickford because it seemed hypocritical in light of derogatory remarks these people had made about Miss McPherson at the dinner table. She and Bebe Daniels strode down the great stairway to the foyer. *They* would see to *this*. They discovered what the other guests had already found out. Impersonating Miss McPherson was Marion Davies, the film comedienne and close friend of Mr. Hearst, one of whose *Examiner* reporters had dutifully quizzed Miss Pickford on the telephone in an uproariously funny hoax. It is a good Hollywood story of that era. It has the "court" qualities of great excitement about a very small incident, and furious flurry and to-do as a distraction and divertissement. It concerns a meeting, both fantasy and real, of illustrious personalities. And it has about it a certain gaiety and immediacy, as if caught in a single moment by a camera.

I saw Miss Pickford, on a vastly different occasion, use the same great stairway winding down from the second floor of Pickfair to the mirrored foyer below. Now I was in seminary and it was two years after our association in P.R.B. had ended. It was either Thanksgiving or Christmas vacation, and I had driven down from Berkeley to visit my mother who lived in Los Angeles. Miss Pickford was receiving a group of ladies making a subscription tour of famous homes for a charity benefit. Her maid was putting finishing touches on her hair and arranging her gown as we stood talking on the second floor of the house. The visiting ladies waited downstairs in the foyer. Then Mary leaned over and kissed me. I started making my exit toward a back flight of stairs. But before going, I saw Mary start her own descent down the winding stairway to the foyer. She was the star. As soon as the ladies below caught sight of her, they broke into applause. It started in an awkward, flighty, even embarrassed way. Then it grew to a sustained crescendo. I could hear some of the women exclaiming in their excitement. A voice cried out "Mary." She would briefly greet them. They would touch her hand or her gown. She would give some of them her autograph.

I remembered then how much I loved her. I partially adored her as the star—how could one help it? This star shone very warmly and seemed to bring people happiness. But I believed that I also knew and felt compassion for the gentle, lonely and driven woman who had wanted to be the star.

I could write a book about Mary. Maybe I will, someday, describing the happy and unhappy sides of her nature, her buoyancy and self-defeat, the bubbling humor and heartbreaking sadness that I found in her. I was young, impetuous and hard-driving; she was a legend who had preceded Garbo, Harlow, Lombard, Monroe, Taylor and Hepburn as the first great Hollywood feminine star: it happened that, across the gulf of years, fame, money and experience, we became friends. This friendship matured me, confronting me with immovable tragedy as well as fondly remembered happiness. It remains an integral part of my life.

It has surprised me to find how many people in the church have wished to make me feel embarrassed about my years in Hollywood or else attempted to write them off as somehow simply unrelated to the church's respectability. What rubbish. For a while, in seminary, I almost started to accept this fuzzy theology with its strong rejection of humanness and life as created in the image of God. The years in Hollywood are a splendid, warm, painful, alive, real part of my life. I am grateful for them.

Yet I moved through them animatedly running at breakneck speed and responding to life with loud laughter and fast jerky mechanical motions, as one already dead. Only in fearfully isolated moments would I let a human being touch me as a human being. Between such moments there was absolutely no connection. I felt that I had a magical, wondrous gift in the seeming fact of my resiliency. I could bounce back from the depths of fear and depression by the automatic function of starting a new day.

Alexander the Great was not my model. He roamed the earth, accumulating kingdoms by extending the map. I laughed at this. I was content with the tight context of my own domain; build high walls around it! I would be absolute monarch here. My despotism was not benevolent. *I* would decide what new ideas might penetrate its borders, *I* would mercilessly eradicate heresies, *I* would dictate the nature and hierarchy of the court.

My goal was not happiness but success on my terms. I considered it essentially moral that I was always prepared to sacrifice myself first, and other people only if it became absolutely necessary. This sacrifice of others, when it had to occur, entailed no sadism or torture, but was quickly and professionally done. I reserved the pains of torture for myself. Yet, strangely, as I now look back, I know I felt virtually nothing during my Hollywood years. I constructed high goals—as one might erect a gigantic set on a bare stage—and accepted the presence of other goals as great mountains hidden momentarily by clouds. I simply pressed forward, with animal strength, to attain these goals. The necessary sacrifices did not need to be agonized over; the decision had already been made to offer them, step by step, to whatever gods one encountered on the way.

Looking back, I can see myself in Hollywood, wearing the correct smile, going through the accepted motions within the context of success (as a student of Zen works within the context of the relationship with his Master, or a Christian seminarian works within the context of the wishes of his elders and the goals of his organization), developing the correct image for life both within my own kingdom and the enclosed world of "the industry."

The time came when I was devastated by the fact of my barren emptiness. Lacking originality, I contemplated suicide. Then I blasphemed the friendly gods of my kingdom: I abdicated. Instantly new ideas ran rampant over the old terrain. I found myself suddenly exposed and vulnerable. I was no longer in control of my life.

Unmailed Letter 1

Dear A.,

This is a hard letter to write. I won't mince words. When you got falling-down drunk in the restaurant and had your public outburst as a celebrity I gave up on you. A moralistic self-righteousness surged up in my throat like unexpected vomit. My reaction has left me terrified of unloving demons which I failed to realize make their not-uncomfortable home inside my otherwise (of course) loving frame.

It didn't occur to me, as I looked in puritanical disgust at you, to ask *why* you were so lousy drunk. Yet, I said to myself in a glimmer of recognition, it wasn't fun and games for you. Bully for me. Chalk up a useful number of merits to help me out of goddam burning hell.

All right. The point is I haven't thought of much else since the Incident . . . when you simply blew up and went to pieces, with a lot of people looking on. Among other things, I realize I had simply not known you before and am now questioning to what degree I've known myself. You broke every piece of china in the shop.

I long ago disposed of you by defining you. Cremating you, I placed your ashes in a neatly labeled box. Loneliness and scars have no right to exist after cremation. But, looking at you the other night, I watched your heart break open when an old, old hurt was suddenly *there* in front of you. No doubt you saw in some supposedly innocent person (was it I?) a symbol of a thing you had held—hating it—imbedded deeply within yourself for God knows how long.

When you exploded, we were all caught off guard. You were as surprised, I'm sure, as anyone else at the table. Suddenly you shattered peace and mutilated people's feelings. But what kind of peace had existed among us? If my own feelings are indicative of other people's, there really wasn't much to mutilate. Looking back, it seems that you were crying out because of what you saw in your own mind and around that table. So for the first time we could really have met one another. The silly, surface half-thing we were all doing could have become one hell of a human encounter. However, we all made a quick, tacit decision not to hear you.

Now I must break that covenant. You are, I see, human. The fact that you are what is called a celebrity is not an insignificant part of the episode. The celebrity thing is so dangerous that it is almost impossible to describe in any rational way. A celebrity is someone who is known, by one advance image or another, without program notes. A celebrity is privileged by being placed at the center of the circle, and therefore also doomed. You were, from the outset of the evening, placed at the center of our circle. When the Incident occurred, it took place in the middle of someone's sentence and everybody else's uninterrupted smile.

It was funky, bitchy and very dirty. You were suddenly paranoid. A killer poised in the circle (a nice guy) was helplessly intoxicated by the smell of unseen blood. Bystanders knew that an uncontrollable sickness had made the circle a plague. There were savage, brutal thrusts. Irreparable damage was done. I thought, in retrospect, how someone might have awakened everybody else in the circle from the nightmare by saying just one word or even walking away, but the circle held firmly. Within the accumulating rage there was no issue which could ever be isolated or pointed to: "There, that's what it was about." But issues there were, having irrational connections with frightening threats to identity. Celebrity itself, by now pure image, was perpetuating and celebrating image while fighting for personhood: so the battle was a lost one except inside yourself.

It was at night, somewhat boozy; the talk would fill many tapes. (An FM station might play the tapes for interesting Sunday night programming, perhaps ahead of the Cleveland Symphony.) One wonders how a good reporter would break it into three paragraphs, give it a lead sentence and sufficient perspective for a headline writer to work on it. The next day, the pain of the Incident was physical. Memory, having been cut, must bleed.

There is plenty of gossip by others who stood in the circle. (Get more tapes; cancel the Cleveland Symphony.)

There was, I think, some particular, crucial need for

you to be drunk in that public place. For the tensions created by your being a celebrity accentuated the struggle in you to assert yourself as human instead of image. One must recognize that the reason for your celebrity is your talent. As an artist, you have channeled it into work which people have accepted, along with you—as image.

The other evening I scandalized myself by so casually yet firmly judging you; I found myself menaced by images which have successfully kept me away from my own humanness.

II

"Please don't call me controversial," pleaded
Malcolm Boyd, Episcopal minister, ex-
atheist, ex-Hollywood television producer,
freedom rider, playwright and twice-resigned
college chaplain . . . Protestations aside,
Malcolm Boyd says and does things that are
controversial. His unorthodox views on
religion, society, and civil rights have brought
him into direct conflict with conservative
elements of his own church. His is a
smoldering outrage, born of the conviction
that the world is awry and must be set right
and that this requires involvement, personal
commitment.

Washington *Post,*
February 6, 1965

The Rev. Malcolm Boyd told 200 members of
the Detroit Women's Division of the American
Jewish Congress: "There's no 'them.' Why
do we always have to have a 'them' to look
down on? The religious issues of today are
the racial problem, the population explosion,
war and peace—not the silly little things
we call religion. The church has been of the
world—with its price tags and buildings
and society weddings—but it hasn't been in
the world, with picket lines and concern
for the poor."

Detroit *News,*
October 13, 1966

PRIEST

I had failed utterly, it seemed, to identify myself as a person. Now I asked: who am I, where am I going, *why*? This questioning caused me to drop out of P.R.B. and end my television activities. I broke the rhythm of the life I had known.

In the winter of 1951 I went away to a place where I could be very quiet, driving from Los Angeles to Arizona. I cut myself off from the people and events in my life. Every day I drove out into the desert, where I meditated. There I read through the Bible. For some strange reason, living as a nominal Christian in a so-called Christian society, I had never done so. I had always assumed that I understood what the Bible said from Sunday-school lessons; but they had really only obscured adult meaning of Christianity for me. Sunday school had, in fact, converted me into an atheist. (A very nice lady had taught Sunday school when I was a kid. She told us childish stories about some people away back then, such as Joseph and his brothers, and kings who tried to kill everybody. We didn't want to hurt the teacher's feelings so we never argued or talked back. I got to college without a real understanding of God or sin or love.)

Now, as a man trying to make sense out of my life, I

cautiously began attending Sunday church services. Always I would walk out during the singing of the final hymn. I wanted no demanding questions at the door: "We have a young adult group"; "Would you give us your name and address?"; "Would you like to sing in the choir?"; "Could you come to an organizational supper we're having Wednesday night?"; "Are you saved?"; "How much would you like to pledge?"

> Time is flooding it is violent, rushing
> But time has left me empty
> I want to be filled. I want to be whole.
> I can see time on its mad rampage, yet this is taking
>   place outside me. I do not feel it.

When I was away in Arizona I struggled to know the will of God for me. I did not want my own will to act as sovereign any longer. I knew I should always possess a free will and that it must always be respected as part of God's creation of man. You see, I had been reading theological works; it seemed as if new windows had been opened up inside my life. I had a different sense of dimension and altogether new views. With my free will I wished to act as an instrument of the sovereign will of God. I had come to believe that the full autonomy of man was nothing but a misnomer and a lie, a tragic misunderstanding of the nature of human life. One is serving; perhaps God or evil or oneself—but one is always serving someone or something. I wanted to come out of the imprisonment of the fantasy of full autonomy which was represented by the shell of defenses behind which I lived. In desiring to become related to God and other persons, it seemed that I should first have to respond with my God-given free will to the will of God for me. How could I find it?

They cast their nets in Galilee
　　Just off the hills of brown;
Such happy, simple fisherfolk,
　　Before the Lord came down.

Contented, peaceful fishermen,
　　Before they ever knew
The peace of God that filled their hearts
　　Brimful, and broke them too.

Young John who trimmed the flapping sail,
　　Homeless, in Patmos died.
Peter, who hauled the teeming net,
　　Head-down was crucified.

The peace of God, it is no peace,
　　But strife closed in the sod.
Yet, brothers, pray for but one thing—
　　The marvelous peace of God.

Hymn 437,
The Hymnal of the
Protestant Episcopal Church
in the United States
of America

Through my religious readings and contact with church people, God was a new and overwhelming factor in my life. During worship services when a priest stood before the altar and people said prayers or sang hymns together, I found that I might unexpectedly be moved to weep. The beauty of the meaning of God's presence, the sense of my own inadequacy and sinfulness, and the absolute fact of God's loving forgiveness: these things pulled me asunder, reducing me to a mixture of repentance and joy.

Holy Communion was almost unbelievable to me. It was intimate, actual contact with God. I was given the body of Jesus Christ to eat. I did not chew it, but let the

wafer disintegrate in my mouth. I was given the blood of
Jesus Christ to drink. I tried not to taste it for it seemed
to me it might really be blood, and then I thought that I
should faint. When I received his body and blood I
prayed passionately that I might be enabled to touch the
hem of Jesus Christ's garment and be healed of all sin.
As I walked up the church aisle to receive the holy
sacrament, I prayed for the blood of Jesus Christ to
inebriate me—to make me spiritually drunk.

Finding humanness in people meant, for me, somehow perceiving the meaning of Jesus Christ's humanness even as he remained divine and the Son of God. He
had remained sinless. I assumed this meant, among
other things, that he had never engaged in sexual inter-
course. It was easier for me to comprehend Jesus' divinity than his humanity. I prayed for Jesus Christ to draw
me close to him so that at the moment of death I might
join him, with all his angels, in heaven forever. This
took on a dread and urgent meaning for me.

When I made my regular formal confession to a
priest, I prepared lists of my sins which I enumerated.
The priest's absolution meant forgiveness and newness
of life. Then when I went to Mass or the Holy Eucharist
it was similar, I felt, to a rebaptism: I was washed clean
once again in the blood of the Lamb. Washed! Washed
clean! Always sin was seen as abstract. It meant sex,
envy, anger, ambition, greed, and sloth.

Blind faith was the essential element—an altogether
new one—in my life. Kierkegaard's image of a man leaping into a pit—not knowing if it contained a rope for
him to hold—had very personal meaning for me. I had
actually given up all of my "security." The life of the soul
possessed as much meaning for me now as the life of the
body. I mistrusted intellectual awareness if uninformed
by spiritual perception.

I read the Bible and prayer books for long stretches every day. I made it a practice to stop in churches to pray. Although I meditated in silence, holding a single thought or image in my mind—for example, Jesus suffering on the cross or Jesus offering the sacrifice of his life in the Mass—I basically used words in my prayers. I said the same words over and over and over, trying to imprint them, as if with acid, on my consciousness. Then, through the communion between my consciousness and the spirit of God, and by means of the sacrifice of Jesus Christ as mediator, the meaning of the words might be received by God within the holy of holies. This process required an almost unbearable amount of concentration as I knelt, hour after hour, on the stone floor of a sanctuary or on a wooden church kneeler.

It was my intention, despite the weakness of my human nature, to use my free will as an instrument which would respond to the will of God. I wanted to make the strong drive of my free will identical with God's will for me. My personality—even in the saying of the Holy Eucharist—should be completely submerged and as unrecognizable as possible. I wished that the Second Coming of Jesus, might happen now, so that my earthly life would be ended as I was taken up with Christ in the glory of the fullness of the Kingdom of God. *This* was a tortuous, painful, preparatory time of trial; it was a time to be got through as sinlessly as possible so that one might enjoy the glories and delights of heaven.

Controversy within the church was unthinkable for me, particularly as related to myself. I could see myself serving in a vine-covered Gothic church building. My life would be restricted to my flock (the people in my congregation)—calling on them, marrying, baptizing, preparing for confirmation, teaching, absolving (God really did this; I would merely act as his intermediary, expressing his absolution by the symbol of my priestly forgiveness and mercy), acting as administrator for God's house (our church building), occasionally representing God in the wider community (an invocation or a benediction before a service club or a school graduation), and burying the dead. This is the life I saw ahead and wanted.

I talked with a priest in Arizona. Then I drove to Denver for conversations with Dean Paul Roberts of St. John's Cathedral there; he seemed a figure of integrity and courage, vivid in my consciousness from childhood days. Soon, after I had met with the bishop and the standing committee of the Episcopal Diocese of Los Angeles, I was accepted as a postulant for holy orders. In September, 1951, I would commence studies for the priesthood at the Church Divinity School of the Pacific in Berkeley.

When I entered seminary, I was preparing myself for the specific duties of an ordained priest: proclaiming the Word of God, and making available the sacraments of the church to the people of God.

I learned many things there—from liturgics to history, from sermon preparation to exegetical study of scripture. I learned how to "do" the sacraments and services, select hymns (and sing them), say my prayers, raise money, construct church buildings, run a Sunday-school class, and keep records of membership. (Shortly after my graduation, the dean of another seminary would ask me to become its instructor in pastoral theology. "We need to tell these divinity students important things they won't learn from textbooks," he said. "For example, how they should wear their rubbers to a cemetery when they are conducting a funeral. If their feet get damp from the fresh soil, they may have a cold on the next Sunday and be unable to do the morning services.")

The public images of a seminary and its realities possess few similarities. "Goddam you, Boyd," an older seminarian once said to me under his breath as we stood outside the chapel door, waiting to enter for the Holy Eucharist. "I may have to love you but I don't have to like you, you son of a bitch." We lived with many tensions, inside and outside ourselves.

It was too masculine a world inside that theological compound. Often I was reminded of my fraternity days in college. There had been a fraternity brother who liked to paddle the naked backsides of pledges. After ordering a pledge to drop his pants and shorts, and assume the correct position by placing his hands around his ankles, he would beat him repeatedly with a hard wooden paddle. He deliberately used slow motion, holding the paddle for a long moment after it had made abrasive contact with a pledge's bare rump. He said that he enjoyed watching a man's flesh shiver and then grow firm again beneath the solid weight of the wood. In the seminary, there was often the heightened tension to be found among men without women. Some seminarians were married and lived outside with their families, but the rest of us ate, slept, worshiped, studied, and lived together. Release from tension could take the form either of violence or laughter, anger or joy.

One night seminarians from two different dormitories had a water fight. It was an orgiastic spring release of pent-up feelings. The incident became something of an issue when water seeped down from the second floor into the dean's office below. Hoses from the garden were run through dormitory rooms and turned full blast on men and walls indiscriminately. One student, trapped behind "enemy" lines, was soaked to the skin and dragged through oozing mud, all the while shouting for help which was not forthcoming. Seminarians were sliding down wet stairs, engaging in hallway wrestling matches, and having a lot of fun.

But a strong sense of protest, or frustration, underscored whatever seemed to be mere horseplay. One morning, in chapel for the Holy Eucharist, I tiredly stumbled into a pew and knelt down to pray. A seminarian was on my left, between me and the stone wall of the chapel. During the creed, when everybody stood up, I noticed that he was gone. His body was no longer next to the stone wall. *But where was it?* He couldn't have gone through the wall and he had not passed by me. I felt that I was cracking up under the accumulating strains of seminary. I was unable to listen to the morning sermon, the prayers, the canon of the Mass, *anything*. It was only after the Eucharist that I found out what had happened. Seminarians immediately behind the student had dragged him by his feet backward, underneath the pew, from his kneeling position in prayer; others had kept pulling him back until he reached the rear of the chapel. At least, my sanity was temporarily restored—although I am not sure the same could be said for his.

What will I feel after I have been burned?

I wonder if my soul will still yearn this fiercely for——

If my body has been taken away, what will be the connecting structure between my soul and mind? Does soul require body? If my legs and feet are gone, who can run errands for the soul? Does mind require body? If my arms and hands, head and mouth are missing, who can transmit messages from the mind?

I am curious: will I still care with this itching and unappeasable passion? Will I still burn after I have been burned?

We had the effrontery to define holiness, yet could be outrageously unholy in going about it. It was fashionable for us, in seminary, to change "the moment" of mystery in the Eucharist. There was a period when we genuflected during the canon of the Mass to indicate the exact moment of God's action upon the elements of bread and wine. Later, we genuflected at the end of the canon, as a symbol of our awareness that we did not know precisely when and how God acted. (A seminary "in" joke singled out Marilyn Monroe as "the girl I'd most like to genuflect with.") Others did not genuflect but bowed their heads, and there were even variations of this: a deep Sarum bow was a kind of anti-Latin reaction, while a short, casual bow of the head was a reaction against overritualization of whatever school.

Before my own seminary days, a "low-church" priest had allegedly refused to consume the consecrated elements at the end of the Mass, and walking from the altar, had opened a door in the wall of the chapel and tossed the wine remaining in the chalice onto a bush outside. This had provoked student outrage to the breaking point. The next time the priest did this, the students were ready. As the faculty and students left the chapel the bush was topped by a burning candle. The bush, burning in zeal, was a reminder of the sacred and the secular.

Also before my own days in seminary, there had been brief liturgical processions through the neighborhood; seminarians wore vestments made out of lace curtains and draperies, and carried incense. Now, however, "high" and "low" churchmanship tensions had eased considerably, so overt demonstrations were out of mode. Yet, on a cold winter morning, one might still sometimes detect the odor of incense seeping into one's room through the radiator. An enterprising "high-church" student, dedicated to his ideals, had been about his Father's business in the middle of the night.

"Religion" and "life" became ridiculously juxtaposed in our day-to-day existence. I remember an athletic seminarian who did rigorous exercises each morning on a board in his room. Covering his body with a black cassock, he energetically pursued his push-ups while loudly reciting the canticle "Benedicite, omnia opera Domini."

In chapel each student drew his turn to read the Old Testament and New Testament lessons as well as to serve as an acolyte during the Eucharist. When, as a new student, my first turn came to read the lessons in chapel, the portion of the Old Testament assigned to me by the lectionary contained allusions to sorely troubled bowels. At this period of our seminary life, more than half the students and faculty were suffering from intestinal flu. Many chapel seats were empty, yet the sounds of the sorely troubled bowels of those in attendance virtually drowned out my reading. Howls of laughter interrupted the Old Testament. My red and burning face remained turned downward to the scriptures; somehow I completed my assigned and terrible chore.

In a course called Homiletics, we learned "how" to preach. This boiled down to listening to one another's sermons, then offering criticism. The criticism was fierce. The theme of my first sermon in the class was "Lift Up Your Hearts." I thought I had preached the greatest sermon to be heard west of Chicago in a decade. "Mr. Boyd didn't make me lift up *my* heart," was the terse, dry comment of a fellow seminarian. Each of us tended to consider himself at least a Phillips Brooks, combining gospel integrity with a near-classic style. While we were preaching in the Homiletics course students often held up small mirrors or reflectors which would blind the novice preacher, who had to somehow continue without letting the instructor know what was the matter.

One day I had a wisdom tooth extracted. That night in chapel I was chanting the "Nunc dimittis" when the student next to me, glancing my way, caught sight of my open mouth filled with blood. I appeared to be unaware of the crisis, chanting, if anything, louder and more assuredly than usual. He grabbed my shoulder; something must be done, quickly, to save me. I told him I was praying and that he should leave me alone and attend to his own soul.

In my senior year at the seminary, I was elected president of the Society of the Celtic Cross. This was somewhat equivalent to being chosen president of a student body. I felt highly honored, yet the distinction was a bad thing for me. I took the position a bit too seriously, developing some grandiose schemes for making it effective. As I was a bit defensive about my Hollywood background, this honor seemed to denote acceptance by my fellows. I would have been far better off if I had felt accepted without it.

A large church in the Bay Area decided to have a Feast of Lights service on Epiphany. Elaborate preparations were made. I was selected to be the preacher, not at all on the basis of ability (I later realized), but as the seminarian from Hollywood.

On the night of the service, several hundred people had to be turned away from the church. Massed choirs of children processed up the center aisle, preceded by acolytes bearing gold crosses. Dozens of clergy marched in their robes. The service assumed Hollywood proportions of spectacle and glamour. A number of Episcopal parishes, representing both "high" and "low" traditions, had come together to sponsor the event. The church in which the service was held was "low," yet part of the compromise called for the use of incense, customary in a "high" church. As acolytes wafted incense over the heads of the congregation, one "low-church" lady became hysterical, indulging in a coughing fit of such proportions that no one inside the building escaped its moral preachment against the idolatry of ceremonial ritual.

As a novice struggling to graduate from my homiletics course, I did my very best with the sermon. I can imagine how corny, and religious-movie-uplifting it must have been. The occasion took on the meaning of a lavish pagan rite. I was suddenly disgusted with myself and everybody else who should have known better, and ready to run outside that ghoulish religious bazaar to freedom.

Run I did, the moment the Christian extravaganza was over. I was joined by other seminarians who were as revolted as I. The night swiftly assumed shape and became a memorable one for us. Many frustrations had apparently been building up in us all—about our seminary life and organized religion. We drove to a low-grade, friendly, smoke-filled and raucously loud Italian restaurant, which we were in the habit of visiting from time to time because it was cheap, and got drunk. The waitress, a devout Catholic, was a good friend who understood us, listened to our outpourings of anxiety and rage, and absolved us by expressions of tough sympathy.

The martinis were like acid. Group suicide was the theme of the evening. A psychoanalyst, had he been present with a tape recorder, could have produced the major religious tome of the decade, entitled "Inside Future Men of God: What the New Religious Are Really Like." The catharsis was heavenly. The dirt of religious spectacles was washed away. The next day, after our hangovers had healed (I healed mine by walking across the Golden Gate Bridge), we were in fine fettle to hold high the banners once again and push on.

My fondest memories of the seminary are connected with the people who were my close friends there. One was the dean, Sherman E. Johnson, a scholar and a man warm and kind in personal relationships. He taught New Testament to our incoming freshman class and inadvertently revealed the gap between his level of scholarship and ours when he told us to read a certain "essential" book, going on to add, "Of course, it is published only in German and is out of print." He asked me to start a seminary newspaper. I named it *The C.D.S.P. Times* (the letters stood for the name of the seminary). I also worked with the dean and Henry J. Kaiser, Jr., son of the industrialist and a concerned Episcopal layman, in developing a fund-raising program for the Church Divinity School of the Pacific called "The Builders." In conjunction with this effort, I helped to produce a filmstrip and signed up Mary Pickford (whose photograph was used in the seminary's publicity) as a member of "The Builders." The dean encouraged me to study the relation between Christian theology and the world of mass communications and very patiently helped me develop my first article on the subject for an excellent, now defunct, magazine *Episcopal Churchnews*. One classmate (who is now a psychiatrist) and I spent hundreds of hours, days—then weeks and months—studying together for our comprehensive exams. He was much smarter than I and helped pull me through.

During the summer following my first year in seminary, I worked as a seminarian-assistant in the parish in North Hollywood where I was a postulant for holy orders. I spent most of my time calling on parishioners and assisting with a summer-camp program. The church was called St. Michael and All Angels. One of the kids in the camp, seeing me approach one day, called out, "Here comes St. Michael!" The rector, who later became a bishop, had been a Navy chaplain and was a severe disciplinarian. He saw to it that my shoes were shined and that I was punctiliously on time for all my appointments. It was also made apparent which members of the parish had money—I was enlightened as to what financial needs of the church might be met by them.

During my second summer in seminary I lived as a guest retreatant in a monastery high in the California hills. I remember the day I arrived. When the people who had brought me there drove off, leaving me behind, the silence became almost audible, a kind of concrete presence, as it closed around me. We had prayer offices early in the mornings before Mass; then we ate breakfast, said another office in chapel, and did housecleaning chores until lunch. A rest followed, then tea on the terrace, then an afternoon office preceding supper. After an evening prayer office in the chapel, we went directly to our cells, where we maintained silence until the next morning.

Our ritual of afternoon tea provided virtually the only opportunity in the day for conversation. Visiting retreatants were especially welcome at teatime. One afternoon I mentioned Carlo Coccioli's book *Heaven and Earth,* alluding to the violence that I found in it. A retreatant from Los Angeles sought me out afterward. Whispering as we stood in a monastery corridor, he explained that he suffered from a nervous disorder. The retreat master had ordered him to read only light novels and had, in fact, given him a book by Nancy Mitford. But he *had* to get ahold of the Coccioli book, he told me. It excited him —enticed him. Where could he find it? I hedged the

question, making my escape, for if I told the retreatant
where to locate the book I might be causing him harm
and would certainly be breaching the discipline of the
monastery where I was a guest. But the retreatant
stalked me the next day, persistently asking me to get
the banned book for him. Finally I took refuge behind a
couch in the monastery common room, where, perched
beneath a window, I read Baron Corvo's *Hadrian the
Seventh.* I could hear the poor man's footsteps as he
walked about looking for me. I evaded him until his
retreat finally came to an end; then I felt that I could
come out of hiding.

The "lights out" rule was, as I recall, for 10:30 or 11
P.M. One night, during a violent wind storm when the
air from the ocean met the hot air off the nearby hills, I
sat in my bed until 3 A.M. reading, of all things, Charles
Williams' *Descent Into Hell.*

Back in the seminary the next fall, in my senior year,
I borrowed from the monastery the idea of having everybody eat in silence, while one person read aloud from a
religious book. As president of the Society of the Celtic
Cross, I instituted this plan. On one or two nights each
week, while the seminarians were eating dinner one
student was selected to read passages from a book on
theology or a more popular work by C. S. Lewis. The
plan did not succeed. Silverware was slid up and down
refectory tables, dishes dropped, and there were occasional verbal outbursts. We switched, then, to playing
records of religious music. The first night the selection
was "The Hallelujah Chorus," played full blast. Combined with hamburger patties and creamed mashed
potatoes, no one could stand it. It was decided that a
more secular type of music might be in order—and,
after all, wasn't the secular really sacred? The entire
plan collapsed during a violin concerto; Heifetz was

soloist. A student accidentally spilled hot lamb gravy in the lap of a classmate. "You bastard!" suddenly drowned out the meditative silence evoked by the concerto. An uproar of recriminations and hoots of laughter followed. When it was all over, we noticed that the record had been turned off. After this we returned to eating meals in our usual secular, noisy style.

Most seminarians did field work on Sundays. For me, in my senior year, this meant acting as seminarian-in-charge of an old mission church which was too poor to engage a full-time priest. Sunday services would be held regularly, along with Sunday-school classes, and, once a month, a priest would visit. The mission occupied an old wooden building. Every Sunday morning, I would drive there, unlock the building, light two gas stoves (very necessary in dead of winter), and don my cassock and surplice. One Sunday, when I applied a match to one of the stoves, there was an explosion. I was hurled back onto the floor. Downstairs from the basement, where the Sunday-school classes were shortly to be held, the seminarians who had accompanied me called my name. I couldn't respond because I was partially stunned. Slowly, reluctantly, my classmates made their way up the rickety stairs—would they find me dead or alive? Alive I was, but my eyebrows and the lapels of my coat had vanished in the blast.

When I spoke to the people in that tiny, very old mission, I was rather inclined to point in the direction of the great cathedral atop Nob Hill, across the city in order to remind the parishioners of their significance in the universal church. "We are related to them," I said. "The whole church of God is worshiping. We are part of a great army." Then the fifteen or twenty people in the congregation would sing "Onward, Christian Soldiers."

In the film *Bonnie and Clyde*, the outlaw pair are joined by Clyde's brother and sister-in-law Blanche, and a young car mechanic, Moss. At one point Blanche and Moss are driving to a nearby town to pick up five fried-chicken dinners. They don't realize they will be detected and that a police attack on the gang will shortly follow. "It must be strange for you— you being a preacher's daughter," he remarks to her. "What kind of church was he a preacher in?"

"Baptist," she says. They drive along in silence for a few moments.

Then he says, "We were Disciples of Christ."

During my first year in seminary, another student and I felt very sinful because we did not love God enough. We wanted the drives in our bodies, minds, and souls to be directed simply toward God. We felt a compulsion to become more holy. Frequent Holy Communion, in addition to morning and evening prayer in chapel and compline said in our rooms, was not sufficient. We decided to pray together during the night. On two nights a week we set our alarm clocks for 2 A.M. We met in the chapel. We knelt down on the stone floor. We prayed silently. At 3 A.M. we returned to our rooms. One night, we prostrated our bodies on the stone floor of the chapel in the form of Christ hanging on the cross. "Body of Christ, save us," we prayed. "Blood of Christ, inebriate us. Passion of Christ, strengthen us."

"Come, I'll walk a mile with you."

"That will be good. I'm not sure I could walk it alone."

"You are alone, then?"

"Yes."

"Have you always been alone?"
"Yes."

"I must leave you now."
"Why?"
"I have walked a mile with you."
"Please don't leave me."
"I must. We agreed, remember? I said I would walk a mile."
"What will I do?"
"You will walk the next mile alone. But it won't be so hard. And then maybe you will walk a mile with someone who needs you."
"I don't want to be alone."
"You won't be alone."

Communion was holy. The bread had been transformed into the spiritual Body of Christ. This moment was separate. It had nothing to do with other moments. Other moments were sinful. They held anger. They held envy. They held malicious gossip. They held covetousness. They held pride. This moment was pure.

"Christ, let me offer myself as a living sacrifice to thee. Lord, I am unworthy. Purify me. Burn me. Burn away the dross. Let pure gold remain. Lord, I will not betray thee. Jesus, I have betrayed thee. Again. And *again. And again.* Let me start anew. This moment. Let it be clean and unsullied by the world."

This separateness of the holy moment from all others was underlined when I was assisting priests one Sunday in a parish in the city. It was before Mass. The priests and acolytes and I were in the sacristy. The priests were getting into their vestments. Suddenly an acolyte cried out. Some older acolytes had the kid down on the sacristy floor. He was struggling. They had his shoes off and were putting gold-covered slippers on his feet. *The sanctuary was holy*—not even an acolyte should walk on it in his shoes. If a layman wanted to enter, he should first ask, "Father, may I enter the sanctuary?" *Jesus was there in the reserved sacrament.* The nave of the church, where the people sat, was not holy. The world outside the church door was not holy.

The fallacy of the separated holy moment was becoming apparent to me. I also learned that it is a Christian commandment that Christians should be in the world but not of the world; this meant, in effect, that Christians are to be involved in the world's suffering and joy, and to be conscious of what the world is thinking and saying; yet, at the same time, a Christian is to live on the basis of a value or priority system that is not worldly. Gradually, as I attempted to develop a life style based on this, I found that I was approaching a condition of Christian nonchalance. I came to understand God as loving, accepting, and forgiving, instead of as a capricious and wrathful God who wished to inflict pain, punishment, and torture upon people. I felt that God, having created life, did not despise it; that Jesus, having lived life, comprehended it.

I graduated from seminary in 1954 and was ordained a deacon a few weeks afterward by the Bishop of Los Angeles. I was ordained a priest by the same bishop in the following year. During the service in the Los Angeles cathedral, the sound of TV cameras almost drowned out, from where I stood, the bishop's words. The Hollywood priest was being ordained.

I was going to be a success. It seems so long ago.
I had an image of myself.
I don't any more.
Can a man live without one?

When I look at myself, I see a stranger among stran-
  gers.
  I'm neither more nor less attractive, it seems, than
  the others.
Am I a failure?
  I wonder if a failure can be a free man.
  Can a free man be a failure?

In seminary we were told by young priests how, on
wearing the clerical collar for the first time, we would
develop boils on our necks. I anticipated this but it never
happened to me. However, growing accustomed to clerical garb was not easy. The effect was often startling. It
changed one's relations with other people, especially
strangers. On a train going to New York, I met the
soprano Lily Pons in a corridor. She said, "Good morning, Father." I turned fiery red. I could not find my voice
so did not say anything to her. I felt unworthy of being
called Father. It established a peculiar relationship for
which all of seminary had not prepared me.
    When I first wore the clerical suit and collar in down-
town Los Angeles, one man knelt on the street to kiss my
hand, and another spat in my face. I will never forget
the trauma of this. What was happening to me? I was
still Malcolm but apparently not to anyone else. I got out
of my clothes and lay face down on my bed. I tried to
comprehend such mistaken, fierce love, and such mistaken, fierce hate. (They seemed to be the same.) Was I
merely the representative of an institution? Did old superstition, and medieval inquisitions, affect my relationships to total strangers? Image had, far more than in my
old Hollywood days, taken over from humanness.

  Lead, kindly Light, amid the encircling gloom,
        Lead thou me on;

The night is dark, and I am far from home;
    Lead thou me on:
Keep thou my feet; I do not ask to see
The distant scene; one step enough for me.

I was not ever thus, nor prayed that thou
    Shouldst lead me on;
I loved to choose and see my path; but now
    Lead thou me on.
I loved the garish day, and, spite of fears,
Pride ruled my will: remember not past years.

So long thy power hath blest me, sure it still
    Will lead me on
O'er moor and fen, o'er crag and torrent, till
    The night is gone;
And with the morn those angel faces smile
Which I have loved long since, and lost awhile. Amen.

Hymn 430,
The Hymnal of the
Protestant Episcopal Church
in the United States
of America

Following my ordination, I was dining with a group of friends who were show-business celebrities. I was wearing clerical garb. A few days before, I had seen Tennessee Williams' play *Cat on a Hot Tin Roof*. It portrays an ineffectual, namby-pamby, sanctimonious Episcopal cleric who, in the midst of just about every human problem taking place right around him, seemed able to do absolutely nothing. Finally he managed to say a very weak, "God bless you." Having done this, he retreated into the night, presumably to the comfort of his bedroom slippers and a nightcap. That honest characterization had shaken me up.

Now, eating with my friends in a hotel dining-room, I

noticed that one member of the party was drunk; I knew he had a serious drinking problem. At last, when dinner was finished, I saw the party to the elevator of their fashionable hotel. In a few moments the elevator would carry them upstairs. Just as the door was sliding to a close—realizing the uncomfortable and sad situation of this drunken man—I blurted out, "God bless you." Everybody in the crowded elevator looked at me unblinkingly, the door closed, and I was standing there alone. *I* was the clergyman in the play. I was incapable of involvement or costly love. I had used these words as a smoke screen—a substitute for any decisive action requiring guts. It was not that I was denying the potential force of these words, or the involvement with the other that saying "God bless you" literally signifies. Instead I was reacting against the undemanding formulas that permitted us, the self-righteous of the religious ghetto, to stay antiseptically clean—removed from raw involvement with life.

Following my graduation from seminary and ordination as a deacon, I departed for England to attend Oxford University for one year to study theology. It was a year that changed my life.

During my Oxford days, I lived in an ingrown community which seemed to prefer life in the nineteenth century, which it had not seen, to life in the twentieth century, which it had not seen either. The pictures and mementoes surrounding us always pointed to meaning and beauty in the past. Every morning we were in chapel early for the Holy Eucharist. (The chapel was so cold, in winter, that most of us wore overcoats, woolen mufflers, earmuffs and gloves to the service, and removed the gloves only when we approached the altar for

Communion.) There was, within that community, a strong sense of proper English as opposed to improper, vulgar, upstart American. I was thrown off guard by being treated as an alien. We *seemed* to speak the same language—yet I found that we really didn't; we only formed similar sounds and words. Once, when tension was high because of a British national election, someone addressed me over the breakfast table, "Boyd, this is an English election. I hope we can be spared altogether your comments as an American." Sipping my scalding hot tea, and looking out over the top of the *Times* (of London), I couldn't resist replying, "I'll try, but of course, we Americans run this country from Number 10, the Pentagon." This did nothing to thaw already frosty relations.

I took to reading three daily morning newspapers, the *Times,* the *Manchester Guardian* and the *Daily Telegraph.* I avoided other American students like the plague, just as they tended to avoid me. All of us wanted new experiences, and to meet new people. When the date of Thanksgiving approached, one American student actually tried to bring together all of his compatriots at dinner in honor of the holiday and "fellowship." The plan became a shambles as everybody frantically hustled to cancel other appointments. Happily, a previous engagement gave me an excuse not to participate in the Thanksgiving togetherness orgy.

While at Oxford, I took wonderful daily walks. Specific trees in specific college gardens became old friends. Often I visited an English friend in London to rail against the English, thereby discovering that there are Englishmen *and* Englishmen, as there are Americans *and* Americans. The theater in London was a splendid experience, but so was the more provincial theater in Oxford. A Brazilian friend, Aharon Sapsezian, and I visited the new coffeehouses which served espresso, and had a continental excitement about them. (I did not realize that this innocent beverage, espresso, would later embroil me in a furious ecclesiastical uproar which would cost me my job.)

Once, at Oxford, I attended an evening revivalist meeting. As an ordained Anglican deacon, I wore my round white clerical collar. As the meeting became more and more emotional the revivalist announced that those who wished to be "saved in Christ" should come forward, while those who did not wish to be "saved in Christ" should leave; this would, in effect, separate the sheep from the goats, so that the remnant could then get on with the Father's business. I filed out with "the damned," strongly convinced that Jesus managed to be present among us, as well as among those who had appointed themselves "saved."

It was during this period that I practiced daily the saying of the Mass. A kind American priest, studying at Oxford, patiently worked with me. I donned all the Eucharistic vestments, learning how to get into and out of them properly. Then I assembled the Eucharistic vessels and marched from the sacristy to the altar in the nearby ornate and historic chapel. And here, every day, I practiced the entire service. One morning, as I stood before the altar, robed in Mass vestments, I noticed a Mary Petty type of cleaning woman innocently enter the chapel to dust the pews and sweep. I was under the impression that she noticed me as well. She hummed quietly, going about her tasks, and I proceeded to practice under my breath, mouthing but not articulating the words. The winter sun, shining on the ice and snow outside, cast warming reflections on ancient life-size stone statues and ecclesiastical flags inside the chapel. At one point, carried away by the meaning of the words

before me, I exclaimed loudly, *"This—is—my—body."*
The cleaning woman evidently had not seen me—on her
knees, cleaning the floor amid statuary and the lingering
scent of incense, she suddenly heard my voice in the
heavy silence. Looking up, she saw sunlight pouring
down on the gold and white vestments of a figure poised
directly before the high altar. She uttered a most frightening scream (but why would an archangel be a source
for alarm?), and scattering her brooms, fled madly.

Sunday is tomorrow
When I was a kid living at home, I used to go to
    church on Sundays.
    I didn't believe it but they did.
Church was a building
    It was a priest
    It was a ritual
    It was a thousand lonely people in that building
    It was a coffee hour afterward
    It was driving home
Why wasn't it real?

At Oxford I had a particularly good friend, one of the
gentlest men I have ever known. He spoke very little,
listened a great deal, and sensitively touched other lives
with his innumerable acts of charity. He was a philosopher who taught in the university. Often he asked me to
share the starkly simple meal he ate in his quarters. After
the meal, sitting before a fire over a cup of coffee, we
would talk. I would speak intensely, letting some of my
pent-up feelings pour out to him. He would listen, and
when he spoke it was with long pauses. Sometimes, over
lunch, he would bring together three or four students
with whom he wished to engage in dialogue. He strongly
disliked strident, overt religiosity. Patiently, unceasingly,
he worked to piece together isolated bits of valid

Christian work being done in the university. He criticized most helpfully the initial draft of what would become my first book, *Crisis in Communication*.

On my way to Oxford, on a Dutch liner sailing from New York to Southhampton, in 1954, I had met Janet Lacey, who conducted refugee work and interchurch aid for the British Council of Churches. She was returning to England from the World Council of Churches' assembly in Evanston, which had produced a pageant she had written about refugees. I had just graduated from seminary in Berkeley and been ordained a deacon. Janet, a stateswoman in international ecumenics, spotted me in my immaculately pressed black suit and stiff round white collar, and took an interest in this newcomer to the church world. When I told her that I wrote, she said she would like to read some things I had done. Later that day, I brought her a large pile of my manuscripts, pointing out that she must be careful with them as I had no carbon copies with me. *Could* she read them that same night? She allowed as how she might. I met her for breakfast in the morning. Had she completed reading all my manuscripts, especially the article on communication of the gospel? I eagerly asked. Janet smiled, vaguely and yet very specifically when her eyes centered on my face. No, she hadn't read everything yet but would report back when she had done so. Meanwhile, would I like orange marmalade on my toast? On subsequent days, as she read my work, she offered excellent criticism and encouraged me to continue writing.

After we docked, Janet bought me my first meal on English soil. It was on the boat train, taking us to London. After I settled at Oxford, I often visited her flat in London. Seated in front of a roaring fireplace, drinking beer, I would tell her how awful the English people were. During this period we often went together to the theater in London—and on those occasions afterward when I was visiting in London, we always managed to see one or two plays. Once Janet and I were seeing the Australian play *The Summer of the Seventeenth Doll.* I could scarcely make out what I assumed to be its heavy English accent. Janet leaned over to me and said, "I can't understand a *word* of this. What are they *talking* about?" For a moment I was absolutely confused—of course the Australian accent had been too much for her, too.

It was Janet who sent me to Sheffield to live with working people there and study the experimental Industrial Mission. Then she arranged for me to live in a parish in Halton, Leeds, which was engaged in the activity of the "house-church," a bold development in evangelism and church life. These experiences would later be reflected in my presence in coffeehouses and freedom houses, and indeed in the whole thrust of my secular understanding of priesthood.

In Sheffield, I visited five steelworks; attended industrial meetings and a conference for steel foremen; spoke to groups of steelworkers in the plants at lunch- and teatimes; went to afternoon meetings of apprentices and evening meetings of men at Church House in the city; participated in a meeting with theological students who worked in the steel mills; was a guest at a session of the Bishop's Committee of the Sheffield Industrial Mission; attended a dance commemorating the tenth anniversary of the mission; and joined a group of clergy to hear Canon (now Bishop) E. R. Wickham speak informally about the industrial work of the church, an area in which he had pioneered. "We are concerned, in the Industrial Mission, less with flesh and blood than with

principalities and powers," he said. "A problem of the
church's mission with flesh and blood in the parishes is
that men are so molded by their institutions, such as
industry . . . There are only the haziest relics of the
meaning of Christianity in about ninety percent of the
general population. We must empty men's minds of a
great many things they still think about Christianity:
for example, the concept of the church as a building run
by men called clergy who conduct sessions called services. There is a great emphasis upon the sermon. The
sacraments are infrequently understood in the context
of a church building at a particular time. There is only
the haziest idea of the Bible; men don't know how to tell
the difference, for example, between mythology and
prophecy and apocalyptic. It is such a relief to men
when they lose their Christian misconceptions!"

Next visiting Leeds, also in the industrial sector of
England, I came upon the Rev. E. W. Southcott and the
house-church. "We do not presume to come to *this* thy
table, O merciful Lord . . ." Canon Southcott told me
how he noted the deeper meaning which he came to
experience in saying these words of the Eucharist when,
instead of celebrating at the altar in the parish church,
he stood by a kitchen table converted into an altar in a
house-church. The first house-church Communion
which I attended was at 6 A.M. in the living room of a
very small home in a slum-clearance area. Canon Southcott had brought me there on his motorcycle. It was dark
and cold outside. Eight of us took part in the service.
The kitchen table was set up before a fireplace which
burned coal. Homemade bread—the same bread which
the family had used the night before—was used for
Communion. The Bible and the last evening's newspaper were close together; "They would soon be in the
same conversation, too," Canon Southcott said.

For the equivalent of an Oxford term, Janet Lacey
sent me to study at the Ecumenical Institute conducted
by the World Council of Churches in Bossey, Switzerland. The institute was a world-wide center of evangelism, study, and Christian nurture. There, I lived and
worked with young men and women representing many
nationalities and Christian denominations. As I noted in
my *Book of Days*, I became alive in an altogether new
way. Ideas, persons, concepts, wholly new equations
rushed toward me; I was consumed by them. My new
friends had come from different corners of the world—
Japan, Latin America, Africa, Australia and Europe. We
examined our own, and one another's, myths about nationalism, religion, sex, society, politics, technology. It
was a long list, and we would talk animatedly late at
night, argue furiously, and alternate between accepting
one another as human beings and as geographical symbols. One night we had been in the nearby village, drinking the cheap wine of the region (a staple for students;
Coca Cola was expensive), and talking. Walking back
through the countryside, we entered an ancient stone
chapel. It was past midnight, and the moon was shining
brightly. There were many feelings buried deep inside
us; so far, we had felt unable to let them out. That night,
standing together in the old chapel, we began—quite
spontaneously—to sing. At first tentatively, finding our
way, then growing in volume, assurance, and solidarity,
we sang the Negro spiritual, "Were You There When
They Crucified My Lord?" Then we quietly left the
chapel and walked back along the moonlit country road
to our school and rooms.

I knew the countryside well. Each morning whether
in winter snow and ice or spring sunshine, I went for a
walk to clear my head between sessions of study and
writing. Finally, in the spring, I wrote a poem. I include

it here not because of its poetic merit, but rather as a clue to my feelings about life, both outside and inside myself.

Spring

The sun glistens on the pane of glass and on the
    brook running by the road.
A leaf lies, unmoving, in the brook.
A red bud shines on the gaunt, black tree in the
    garden.
One hundred birds swim through the sky
While a sparrow perches on a branch, and sings.
A flashing stream of water rushes through the
    earth, passing me as I walk in the field.
A tree beckons my interest, assuming a different
    shape each way I look at it.
Sunlight mixes with a cool breeze;
A single blade of grass stirs.
The earth is alive, life is dynamic,
Something is happening.
Something is happening, too, in my heart, in my
    mind, in my soul.
What is man that thou art mindful of him?
To what do you call me, my Lord?
Blood runs through my veins,
An idea stirs in my mind,
A sin lies, unmoving, in my soul,
And I know the promise of renewal.

I encountered love, finally, as an adult. I learned that looks and actions said more than words, yet that words could provoke great clouds of depression and hostile days of misunderstanding. Afterward came healing and loving again. Communication became fragile—held together by the sheer threads of laughing and crying. It was the greatest happiness to be together and maddeningly painful to be apart. Jealousy! It was muggy and awful. To open up the relationship and share it with others—my God, this required terrible effort. I knew now how closely the body is tied to the mind and soul, for both joy and pain swept through an absolutely total being. Parting. Simply to move away from each other when there was no looking back. I felt mute, numb and dead inside. The sun, which had been a hot yellow mass of tenderness and ecstasy, was not warm any more.

After my stay in Switzerland, I spent several weeks as a guest at Istina, a Dominican study center in Paris. Here I experienced a feeling of unity with Roman Catholics, to match that I had found with Protestants in Switzerland. At Istina, every morning I attended the Mass. Then I assisted the community with work, talked with theologians and students, and generally felt a closeness to Catholics which I had assumed was forbidden.

Once, when I was asked to attend a Protestant service in Paris, I invited a priest at Istina (a brother from Chevetogne in Belgium) to accompany me. Women wore furs and smelled of expensive perfume; men were very, very correct and snobbish. My friend and I became separated. I learned later that he had fled in embarrassment, feeling unwanted and out of place. Then over coffee, a rich American woman asked, "Who was that dirty Roman spy?" "I am his houseguest," I replied.

Before leaving Europe I was invited by a Greek Orthodox bishop, whom I had met at Bossey, to visit Athens, Istanbul and Mount Athos in Greece. I stayed at the Orthodox evangelism center and student hostel, Apostoliki Diakonia, in Athens. Some two hundred theological students attending the University of Athens lived there. I shared their life, my best friends being two students from Cyprus, and one from Ethiopia. The Zoe Movement was known to me, before I came to Greece, as a focus of church renewal and deepening of the sacramental life. I was privileged to talk with some of its leaders. Then, in Istanbul (which the Orthodox still referred to as Constantinople), I was a guest for Holy Week. I stayed at the great seminary of Halki, located on the nearby island of Heybeli. This seminary was very different from my own in California. Only by special permission could a student leave, even to visit the tiny village below the seminary. The locked entrance was guarded. All students lived in crowded dormitories; they were not permitted to study there, but only at assigned desks in a classroom with some dozen others. One occupied an assigned place in chapel, and attendance was required. Discipline was severe and autocratic. The day began with a bell at 7 o'clock, and ended when a bell summoned students to their rooms for "lights out" by 10 P.M. Living conditions were Spartan. My best friend there was a seminarian from Crete, who as a teen-ager had fought hand-to-hand against the Nazis and whose father had been killed in the encounter.

My ecumenical experience, which radically reshaped my entire concept of the church, and ultimately molded me into a post-ecumenical Christian, was being rounded out by my visit among the Greek Orthodox. His All Holiness, the Patriarch of Constantinople, kindly received me for lunch at his table and later talked privately with me about problems of the contemporary church. His eyes burned in his parchment dry, lean face. His passion, he told me, was ecumenism. When I leaned over to kiss his hand, he kissed the top of my head.

My visit ended with a trip to Mount Athos, "the Holy Mountain." To get there, I took a bus from Salonika to the small fishing village of Ierissos, where I boarded a small open boat. Sheep, their feet tied together, were carried aboard and placed in the hold. A donkey was forcibly dragged on, and stood precariously alongside us for the voyage. Early morning mists were closed in tightly around the island as we approached it. They gradually lifted to reveal the surrounding hills as a backdrop for the blue Aegean, and finally the peak of Mount Athos which was called *le petit Everest*.

With my knapsack, my sole luggage, over my shoulder, I traveled by donkey and boat around the island, staying at the various monasteries. Everywhere I was offered the hospitality of *glyco, ouzo,* and Turkish coffee. I made two good friends on Athos, an elderly monk who had once lived in the United States and Canada, but had spent the past fifty years on the island, and a hermit.

For more than a thousand years no woman has been permitted to set foot on Mount Athos, so the story goes, although there have been several celebrated attempts to circumvent this rule. First I visited the aristocratic monastery of Vatopedi, then Coutloumous, Iviron, Great Lavra and Gregoriou. The sea swept right up to the very gates of Vatopedi. I wandered along the beach, with its millions of sea-washed and sun-bleached stones. I climbed a hill which gave me sharply different views in all directions—in one were stone ruins, in another, hills rising higher and higher; then I could see the walled monastery where chimes were now pealing; and I could look out upon the open sea. I stood there in that rare moment following sunset just when darkness is about to fall.

I must write again.
   I must create pattern out of this emptiness.
   Out of this dread nothingness I must mold life, or
      else I die.
Suicide
   Is it to will nothing?

I am killing myself today.

Pattern seems futile. Life is spontaneous and can-
    not be molded.

Being empty, I am light.

But the heavy stone is upon me.

Spending the night in Coutloumous, I found the guest book, which is signed by all visitors, next to my bed. I thumbed through it, reading the old clichés, the monotonous expressions of greeting and appreciation, adding my own. Then I came upon a message written by a Los Angeles physician. "We are gratified with the gentility and hospitality extended by the monks in this out-of-the-way hostel. Because of the teachings of Koch and Lister which have become an inseparable fundament of our cultural training, we feel we must hastily retreat from this haven of refuge provided by the good fathers. The various bacilli and parasites at whose disposal we have placed ourselves must sadly wait for the next visitors to this little haven out of the way from life's stresses. Adieu, you cockroaches and rodents, products of the kindly hand of God, adieu, you lice and flies, little insects blessed by the saints and Holy Mary. We leave you with the good monks in the decadent faecal-smelling confines of this place of prayer and meditation." Underneath, a guest from Cleveland had written, "Why do these men write of food and beds? Have they not found the art and civilization of Athos awesome?"

At the monastery of Gregoriou, my last stop, I stood one night on a wooden balcony, looking straight down hundreds of feet at angry waves hurling themselves in intense and unabated fury against the rock and stone base of the monastery. A few hours later, at 5 A.M., a young deacon awakened me. "To church!" he cried. After church and a last breakfast consisting of a small loaf of wheat bread, two pieces of goat cheese, a hard-boiled egg, *ouzo* and a cup of Turkish coffee, I was at the pier waiting for the open boat to take me in the pouring rain to the port of Daphni.

Daphni contrasted seeming intrigue so neatly with a cultivated appearance of plainness. Sitting in Daphni's country store which had all the mystery of a diplomatic center, I talked with a Czarist priest and aristocrat who was now a hermit at Mount Athos. His English was impeccable, his charm very grand, his manner educated and polished. He had friends in the great capital cities of the world. An extremely old man who had experienced deep tragedy, he waited for the apocalyptic devastation of terrible times to be unleashed upon a sinful world. After my visit with the Greek Orthodox, I returned to the Ecumenical Institute in Switzerland. The director of the institute, Dr. Hendrik Kraemer, a great Dutch figure in the world-church and a kind of ecumenical patriarch, had befriended me and guided my studies. He invited me back to deliver two lectures on the Christian faith and mass media. (Later when my *Crisis in Communication* was published in the United States, he wrote me a note: "My dear Clement of Alexandria: We received with joy your book on mass communication. Our congratulations! Continue in this way. With kind regards from Tertullian minor.")

Dr. Kraemer took seriously both what I thought I was trying to do and what I was unaware I was trying to do. Always a step ahead of where my mental processes had led me, he kindly suggested new ideas, recommended books and courses, and took the time to criticize my work. It was he who helped me decide to study for a Master of Sacred Theology degree at Union Theological Seminary in New York City. While I was in Switzerland, Dr. Kraemer became seriously ill and was not expected to live; when I left for the States, I could not see him to tell him good-bye. However, he made arrangements with Henry P. Van Dusen, then head of Union Theological Seminary, for me to commence studies there at the start of the next term.

I stayed at Union for two years. I lived in a dormitory room and, every morning, walked a dozen blocks to the Cathedral of St. John the Divine to receive Holy Communion. Sometimes I would reach the cathedral entrance at precisely the hour when the service commenced. Since the cathedral is as long as two city blocks, I would be late by the time I had crossed its nave to one of the small chapels behind the high altar.

James A. Pike was dean of the cathedral. I did not know him very well but admired him a great deal. He seemed to possess an extraordinary intellectual capacity —his grasp of issues was at once intuitive and deeply informed; he had great integrity, and a unique ability to communicate his ideas and feelings in a low-keyed way which did not strain credibility. Hearing him preach in the cathedral pulpit was, for me, a rare and memorable experience. I found exceedingly meaningful the controversies in which he became involved, such as his early opposition to racism and his support of freedom in the arts.

For a half-year, while I was a student at Union, it became necessary for me to work for my meals. I took a job at International House, near the seminary. In return for cooking breakfast for two hours each morning, I received three meals a day. I had waited on tables and washed dishes in college, but had never cooked before. Now I poached, scrambled, fried, and boiled eggs for residents of International House; I also toasted white or whole-wheat bread and, on request, English muffins. Often thirty to forty people would be standing impatiently in line, waiting to place their breakfast orders.

From my point of view, the boiled eggs were the best thing to order. There was a timer which sounded for them, so they were fairly easy to cook properly. However, try as I would, the poached eggs generally turned out hard as rocks, and the scrambled eggs resembled cheap leather. Then there were the fried eggs; the fried eggs were something altogether different. I always had at least ten frying simultaneously; some people called out to serve them sunny-side up, others to turn them over, and still others wanted the yolks broken. (There were plenty of times when the yolks broke anyway.)

One morning, an older woman—a graduate student? —requested one fried egg. She made no other immediate specifications. The yolk did not remain firm but slithered into a glob. Her face turned livid. She wanted an egg with an unbroken yolk, she said. A man waiting in the long line promptly took the one with the broken yolk. I began to prepare the lady another egg; its yolk did not remain firm either. This second egg was promptly commandeered by someone else who happily marched off to eat. (The eggs that morning were warm, I thought, which provided the source of trouble.) The lady, now unnerved, half-screamed at me, "I'll have you fired unless you give me the kind of egg I want." People in the line became interested—something unusual was happening. My third egg for the lady was a triumph; the yolk held firm. I looked at her in anticipation of warm gratitude. Her steely eyes met mine. "Turn it over," she rasped. I did. The yolk still held firm. When I served her the egg, I received not so much as a simple thank you.

On another morning, a guy in line asked for whole-wheat toast. All the toast was prepared on a giant rack, which kept it hot. Grappling with some dozen to fifteen orders at once, I gave him his toast. I was amazed to see him turn pale, clench his fist, and rapidly walk way up along the breakfast counter. I left the people in line—some shouting—and followed the guy. Catching up with him, I asked, "What's the matter? Did I do something wrong? If I did, I didn't mean to." He was shaking now with rage.

"Something wrong?" he yelled. "You gave me white toast. *You've ruined my whole day.*" Then he was gone. Wet with sweat, my face burning with indignation and self-pity—I was too harried to appreciate the humor in all this—I walked back to my waiting eggs and waiting people.

During this period a friend of mine invited me to have an expense-account dinner in a luxurious and fashionable restaurant. He felt that his old friend Malcolm, sweating over eggs as well as theology books, needed a bright, fresh change. An executive in a big corporation, he dined out on an expense account. The dinner was sumptuous and our evening's conversation warmly full of recollections. I could not help but note that the bill for the dinner was more than sixty dollars. The next morning, walking along upper Broadway near the seminary, I was hungry. I looked into a breakfast shop, indulging in fantasies of scrambled eggs with bacon and buttered toast, until I realized I had no money. Then the discombobulating impact of the lopsided evening before hit me with full force. It had not been a happy interlude, only a deeply frustrating experience, for one could not make any sense of such savage contradictions.

In my second year at Union, Dr. Kraemer, having made a miraculous recovery from his illness, came to the seminary as a visiting professor. His wife accompanied him. She had a strong interest in the theater, so I invited her to a Broadway performance of Eugene O'Neill's *Long Day's Journey into Night* and some of the off-Broadway Theater of the Absurd plays. At the Kraemers' apartment, the three of us would animatedly discuss the plays over dinner. Dr. Kraemer was always especially interested in our ideas concerning their relevance to implicit Christian evangelism. I remember that we discussed Ionesco's *Rhinoceros,* Beckett's *Waiting for Godot* and *Krapp's Last Tape.*

While I was at Union, my first book, *Crisis in Communication,* was published. (I also completed work on my second book, *Christ and Celebrity Gods.*) A book, I found, is like a child in that it has its own life. It seems deeply symbolic to me that the publisher sends the *first* copy to the author. I held the first copy of my book for a few moments; it was a time of raw awareness of creation—an occasion of combined awe, thankfulness, and anticipation.

Almost immediately, people start relating directly to the book—as to a child. They fondle it possessively; they sometimes punish it cruelly. The writer hovers, quite lost, in the background. He is not a part of other people's emotional involvement with the book. Certainly, they may occasionally be kind enough to write the author a note, in which they detail something of their feelings about the book—I started collecting these—but their affair is with the book. The author, for the book's sake as well as his own, had better get to work creating a new one.

The theme of my first book was communication of the gospel. In it, I argued strongly against mass media manipulation as a corruption of evangelism. At that time, I had no idea what experiences lay ahead of me in this area. For example, several years later I was asked to address a clergy conference on the same theme. I was busily exhorting the assembled clergy to guard against public-relations exploitation when our session was interrupted. A church official important in the field of promotion and publicity had just arrived. He could stay only a short while, so we promptly filed into a hall to hear him. The clerical pragmatist, caught up in a spirit of ebullient exploitative zest, grabbed a handful of matchbooks out of a large paper bag and good-naturedly hurled them at us. (Ironically one struck my mouth, causing my upper lip to bleed.) Then I noticed the words printed on the matchbook cover: "Are You Lonely? Come to St. Paul's Church."

On another occasion, I was addressing rural Southern white clergymen on the theme of communication of the gospel. It was hard going. I stressed the Cross as the basic Christian symbol of "success." But a visiting preacher, who had a thriving congregation of several thousand and a huge church building, took a different view. He stressed material standards of success in churchgoing. He said that intellectual publications had a high "fog index," whereas Jesus' "fog index" was lower than that of comic books. So the gospel was very, very simple. After the successful preacher had departed, I met again with the rural clergymen. "Okay, let's assume that the gospel *is* total simplicity," I told them. "Jesus' fog index *is* lower than that of Little Orphan Annie. So if we really preach the gospel we ought to meet with success in getting our message across to everyone fast—like Jesus we should be able to be crucified within three years."

At Union, I had my first close black friend. He was a fellow graduate student, about my age, and deeply committed to a radical practice of Christianity. It took me weeks, even months, to feel at ease with him. Moving into a shared way of life was like walking on eggs. He was my black friend, not my friend who was black. I watched my language with him, not wishing to give cause for offense. (What did one *say* to a Negro?) I was always on guard. Parts of his life seemed impenetrably mysterious, yet I never asked about them.

One day we had lunch together in the Columbia faculty dining-room. I had not realized, until he told me, that he was the only black present. He became moody and quiet as I grew more talkative, until I was engaging in a noisy monologue while he withdrew into his shell. Later, he told me that as we departed, the black doorman was saying to him in his very proper smile, "Nigger, what are you doing here?"

My friend took me one night to a party in Harlem. For the first time in my life, seated in that apartment, I was the only white present in a room filled with blacks. It was an unfamiliar, threatening sea of blackness—but coupled with a new sense of exhilaration and human possibility. It seemed to me I should be attacked by everybody in the room—but I was grateful when I wasn't. Through it all, I played the white man.

My world was white.
　I must have been aware there were blacks in it . . .
　For some reason, they didn't interest me very
　　much.
　Maybe because all the ones I knew were serving
　　whites.
　Yes, Black had its place in the ordered white world.
No one ever questioned that world.

I went all through Sunday school and never heard it
  questioned.
I was confirmed and attended church and never
  heard it questioned.
I studied in junior high and high school and never
  heard it questioned.
No one ever questioned that world.

My friend and I talked about nothing but race when
we were together. Civil rights. Discrimination. Bigotry.
Prejudice. Housing restrictions. Outrages against
blacks. Our conversation never got beyond "the issues."
Perhaps we tried too hard or not in the right way, but we
were not ourselves with each other. Later, in Europe, we
met and sat up late one night talking. It was only then
that I felt we had finally bridged our own lack of confidence—learned about humanness across ghetto walls,
walls of innate bigotry. If it had not been for our relationship, I might not now have close friends who are
black. Remembering our attempts to communicate, I
wish that black and white youngsters could be placed in
close proximity to one another, and taught how to be
open about their feelings. "Pardon me for staring," a
white youngster, already a bit warped by the prejudices
of his family and society, might say, "but I'm trying to
get used to your thick lips, kinky hair and blackness.
Pardon me for staring."
  And a black youngster might reply, "Pardon me for
staring, but I'm trying to get used to your whiteness. It
frightens me. It seems to mean deceit, betrayal and
death. Pardon me for staring."

Another friend of mine at Union Seminary was Frère
Laurent, a brother in the Taizé Community of France.

Because of him, I lived and worked in the community in the summer of 1957. It is an experience which continues to have a marked influence on my life.

I had taken a train from Paris and it was mid-morning when I arrived outside the small rural village in Burgundy which housed the community. I could see the château, the center of the brotherhood's life, at the top of a nearby hill. Carrying my luggage, I climbed the hill, rang a bell outside the large wooden gate, and was taken in to meet the prior, Frère Roger. My assigned work was in the fields; I would also assist at meals by carrying food on trays from the kitchen into the guest house, where visitors to the community stayed; and for a few hours each afternoon I would act as concierge, answering the bell when visitors rang, and taking care of their needs if I could. After seeing me and hearing my French, most visitors assumed that I was Dutch.

Taizé is a French Protestant monastic community. It comprises men from various countries and maintains close ecumenical ties with the Roman Catholic Church. Many of the brothers went out in twos and threes to live outside the Taizé Community itself, representing it in the world where they took jobs, for example, in industry. According to the point of view of Taizé, when a Christian lives in the world, he represents Jesus Christ simply by being a Christian and praying. This is based on the belief that, in the incarnation, Jesus Christ did not exclude any part of the world, or any man, or any part of society. He came to save all men of all conditions.

It was felt at Taizé that the presence of Jesus Christ in the world cannot be without effect. Therefore, when it is understood that the life of all Christians is the life of Jesus Christ within them, the simple presence of the Christian in the world cannot be without effect. Men do not live like Robinson Crusoes and all thoughts have to be translated into a milieu. The life of a Christian cell is considerably determined by its environment. However, the cell's prayer life will be the determining factor of its very existence.

Before coming to live in the community, I had for many months studied the rule of Taizé. This study, and my own life and work within the community during my visit in France, strongly influenced my own thinking about Christian evangelism. I came to believe that much religious activism, sometimes labeled evangelism, is not really Christian involvement at all. On the other hand, much strategic, patient, unpublicized penetration of culture is evangelism of a high order.

During the mornings at Taizé I was out in the fields. At noon a bell would ring, summoning us to noon prayers in the chapel and to lunch. Making our way into the chapel, we would kneel in silence for some minutes. Then a member of the community would offer intercessions, often for people featured in the day's news. For example, if I heard the name of Eisenhower or Dulles, I would realize that he had figured in some special way in that day's events. (The community subscribed to *Le Monde,* so I could later read the paper and find out what had happened.)

One day after noon prayers we were told that the community was observing a luncheon fast in solidarity with those who, on that same day, would literally starve to death in Asia. Anyone who wished to eat, or was ill and had need of sustenance, could simply go to the refrigerator and help himself to some food. However, the community as a whole would carry out an intention of fasting. I have never forgotten this because it seemed very meaningful as a practical relation of prayer to work, and work to prayer. The fast was, in fact, an intercessory prayer.

One rainy morning I was out digging to widen a narrow path on a hillside near the château. As I slid in the mud, and the rain poured down my face and neck into my boots, I felt almost completely sorry for myself. I could not believe that what I was doing had any meaning for God or anyone else, and thought how much better I might be occupied working in a library or in some nice heated room, studying or writing.

Time is so short.
   I should be writing
   The minutes and hours are falling away
   Another day
   I have nothing to show for anything
I feel that I'm a great stone.
   My mind is a stone
   It doesn't do any good to move my body
   I want to care but I can't
   I can't do anything
I must sit down and force myself to write.
   It won't matter if it's good or bad
   If I can't write, I've died
   I must express this deadness
A great stone is blocking the tomb.
   The tomb is empty
   I am empty—but filled with doubt and pain

Just then, around the top of the hill, a young German brother was moving toward me, pushing a wheelbarrow filled with ashes to place on the mud to cement it. His father and brother had been killed by the Russians in World War II. Following the end of hostilities, he had gone to Israel to learn Hebrew. He did this out of a realization that his people were responsible for the death of six million Jews. On his wall in the community hung only one picture—of Anne Frank. As the young brother approached me that miserable morning, I could see that he was smiling and singing. "Isn't this a wonderful day to offer to the Lord, Malcolm?" he asked.

He had taught me an important lesson. It is easy to offer some days to God—days when the sun is brightly shining and things are going one's way. It is harder, and infinitely more significant, to rejoice in those other days, which seem cruelly difficult—days when one wonders if he possesses the strength to go on living creatively. Years later, I recounted this incident at an American university. I went on to say that one may offer moments of failure, despair, and seeming personal death to God, as well as moments of supposed goodness, virtue, and happiness. A minister approached me later and said this was a new concept for him. He had always told people that they could offer God only the moments which seemed in their own eyes to be "clean and good." I pitied the people who had heard him. I wondered what they did with their unhappy, bad, even destructive moments if they felt these could not be offered to God.

At Taizé, I discovered a new sense of movement in Christian life-style. Jesus runs, joyously and lovingly, to meet us in the world. Our response should be to run toward Jesus. The rule of Taizé states: "Never remain in your place but march with your brothers, running to your goal on the steps of Christ . . . In order that the brightness of Christ penetrate you, it is not sufficient for you to contemplate it as if you were only pure spirit, but rather you must engage yourself resolutely in body and soul in this way . . . Be among men a sign of fraternal love and joy . . . You would narrow your comprehension of the Gospel if, because you feared to lose your life, you would keep it to yourself. *If the grain does not die,* you cannot hope to see your person open up in the fullness of the Christian life . . . like Abraham, you can advance in this way only by faith and not by sight, being assured always that he who will have lost his life on account of Christ will find it."

I had in mind this running image—both of Jesus and of a responsive Christian life-style—when I later wrote my book of prayers, *Are You Running with Me, Jesus?*

After my stay at Taizé I was invited to visit West Berlin, where I stayed at an ecumenical center and later at the home of a theological student whom I had met at Taizé. We made a number of illegal trips into East Berlin—meeting with underground Christian cells there and sometimes taking them money hidden in packages. Risking arrest, I even attended performances of Brecht's plays in East Berlin (I had seen his production, in Hollywood during the forties, of *Galileo* with Charles Laughton). I saw the startling differences between the two Berlins—one desperately poor, with scars of bombings still unrepaired; the other rich and bustling, with smart shops and new signs of luxury. Yet, in the houses where I stayed in West Berlin, we ate peanut-butter sandwiches and boiled potatoes, our coffee was hot water with flavored coloring added, and the affluent, competitive world of businessmen and tourists was psychologically far off from us.

In the fall of 1957 I was asked to be rector of a parish in Indianapolis. I accepted—looking forward with mixed feelings to my return to America. For in a newspaper one morning I saw the report of Sputnik: a new age—science fiction turning into simple fact—had begun. Yet, another morning, I saw a photograph of that small black child in Little Rock, her dress wet with spittle, her dignity a shining vision, as she made her way through a crowd of jeering white children in order to go to her newly integrated school classroom.

St. George's parish in Indianapolis, my first parish, was located in a deteriorating slum area of the city. The congregation was predominantly lower-middle-class. Three truck drivers served on the vestry.

The rectory was an old house located directly next to the church. The night I arrived it was empty except for a single bed, a kitchen table, a chair, and a wall telephone —disconnected. A letter awaited me; it bore a French stamp. It was written by one of the brothers of the Taizé Community. The letter read:

> I hope you have arrived safe and full of joy and courage at your new church. And in the evening, when the day is over, you will wonder every time again that God gave you this church, this holding place for Him. Do not make your own rectory too austere, but not too "easy-corner-like" either. You know how "easy-corners" always remember the easiness they cannot provide! I hope so much you will find nice parishioners, people who know what praying means and who will surround you with Christian responsibility . . . I am sure all will go fine. And when it should happen that at night you are crying in your bed, know that you will get up, in the morning, as that little servant of the Lord and of His people that He wants you to be and will help you to be. I hope that the Lord may reveal Himself to you as He who came to dry faces, to make eyes see, ears hear, lambs walk and to preach the Gospel to the poor. I hope that you and your congregation will, like angels, proclaim the gladness of Christ's coming into our human darkness.

Though I had been told that the autumn weather had been extremely pleasant, upon awakening the next morning I found outside my window a world of snow and ice. It was Sunday and I was to conduct my first services in the parish. But there had been a very old-fashioned blizzard during the night and, as a result, only a handful of parishioners came out to church.

We got the rectory in order. The precarious roof was fixed; although, whenever it rained for the next two years, I had to place tubs under the three most intransigent leaks. Gradually, I moved in pieces of furniture which were donated or loaned by parishioners.

Often I was invited for dinner in parishioners' homes in the evenings. At other times, certain of the ladies left hot dishes or cold salads for me at the rectory door. An unmarried vestryman shared the rectory with me, along with Loretta, a cat (named for Loretta Young) who was fierce, possessive, and had a distinct voice in parish affairs.

I played the role of a ship's captain when I first met with the vestry and other lay leaders of the church. Would my senior warden please stand up? Would my junior warden please stand up? And, of course, the president of the women's auxiliary? No lady stood up. I found that I had *two* women presidents—the result of a political altercation within the group after the annual bazaar. The friction had not healed. When I asked the bishop what to do, he advised me to disband the women's auxiliary for a time, and instead, institute a pro tem women's organization called the St. Mary's Guild; I was to act as its president. All this was very ticklish business for a young, uninitiated priest, but I followed the bishop's advice. The dissension healed after some six months. Meanwhile, brother priests offhandedly referred to me as Madam President.

The toughest assignment during that first winter was

keeping the furnace going in the old church building. We had little or no cash. The walls were full of holes and cracks—in effect, we were heating the great outdoors. Yet I loved the building and especially the altar, free-standing in front of a white brick wall.

When I arrived at St. George's, a life-size figure of Jesus nailed to a wooden cross was hanging over the altar. Indeed the stark emblem of Jesus' suffering reflected the hunger, crime, broken homes, racial hatred and human deprivation which marked life in the neighborhood surrounding the church. Yet I felt that St. George's remained locked within the experience of Jesus' crucifixion, overlooking the joy and fulfillment of his resurrection. The rhythm and symbols of the church year, moving from Advent to Christmas and from Lent to Easter, unite the fragments in Jesus' life. But at St. George's, on Easter, we had no symbol of the triumphant Christ to mark the end of Good Friday's pain and death; the Good Friday depiction of the Lord still dominated every prayer, hymn and ritual within the church. When I sought the backing of parishioners to keep the figure of the suffering Christ over the altar only in the penitential seasons of Advent and Lent, and to replace it in other parts of the year with an empty cross or a Christus Rex, I encountered only anger and resistance.

Finding myself blocked in any effort to remove this symbol of Christ over the altar, I decided to paint the brown wooden church doors a triumphantly bright red. *This* would conjure up visions of the joys and beauty of everlasting life with God. And, within our drab and discouraged neighborhood, the church doors would be an occasion of hope. However, on the Sunday morning following the painting of the doors, there were ugly discussions on the subject. Indignant families were threatening to leave the parish or cancel their pledges. I will never understand the latent feelings inside the people which were triggered to blow up by the dabbing of some bright red paint on those sad old brown doors.

On Sunday mornings there were two celebrations of the Holy Eucharist, with a sermon at each. Monday through Saturday, I celebrated Communion each morning at 7 o'clock. At the time I wrote a short piece entitled "Holy Communion" which explains a good deal of what I felt about this daily service.

> Every morning: and yet, what each time is so different for me, is it the same each time in His eyes and in the divine Heart? This, He ordained; this, His giving of His Body and Blood, He instituted; and—it is quite simple—He comes to us, and we receive Him, and He indwells us and we are permitted to dwell in Him. Communion. So, we live now in eternity. The altar is an outpost of His Kingdom.
>
> We offer before the altar in His Sacrifice the ills, the hurts, the injustices of our society and of all men. He is the Healer; we, kneeling before the altar, are the broken, the sick, the unfaithful. Have mercy upon us—dwell in us—heal us—vivify our God-given capacity to love.
>
> Again, it is over. The darkness of the early winter morning has been suffused by incoming light. The quiet of the street outside has been lost in the roar of car and truck engines going by, and the whirr of many tires. The candles on the altar have been put out. Our Lord—He who has taken our humanity into the Holy of Holies—pleads for us before the Father.
>
> Help us to be thankful as we ought and as we want.

The neighborhood surrounding St. George's was racially mixed—and rigidly segregated. The people were forced to live close together because of biting poverty, but the demarcation was absolute. This enabled the poor whites to look down upon the "niggers." But it took more than a casual glance to see the segregation: *This* street, up to an alley or street light, was black; *that* street, up to a certain telephone pole or corner, was white.

So it followed that any church in that neighborhood was black *or* white. St. George's was white. One Sunday morning a black priest and I arranged to exchange altars and pulpits. There were tortured discussions within my parish concerning this plan. Some announced they would not receive the sacrament of Jesus' body and blood from a black hand. On the Sunday of the exchange there was outward passive acceptance, but I learned that several white Christians had remained in their pews, not going to the altar. Afterward, the Afro-American priest joined my senior warden and his family for dinner, while I remained within the black parish for a meal.

Four inner-city Episcopal churches, including St. George's, conducted a summer program for children in our neighborhoods. St. George's enrollment of black children kept increasing; at the same time, there was a sharp decrease in the number of white children. We were assigned two student counselors for the program —a white woman and a black man. The black counselor stayed with me in the rectory, which aroused great feelings of hostility and resentment among many parishioners.

One day during the summer, as the black counselor was boarding a bus with youngsters for an outing, a white boy of about ten stood on a curb and shouted, "Dirty black nigger, dirty black nigger, dirty black nigger . . ." And I came upon another small white boy, jabbing a pocketknife into a wooden pole. "I wish it was a nigger," he exclaimed.

The jail has white walls
   A white toilet stands in the corner of the white cell
   Guards with white faces look through the bars
   I will take black clay and mold a black jail and
      black guards
Murder
Cool, man
   Anger is a luxury.

Finally, at the end of the summer, there was to be a party in the parish hall to officially terminate the children's program. The art and handicrafts they had done were exhibited. Some hundred and fifty black parents of the youngsters who had participated came to the event. Only five members of the all-white church were present, although the total membership had been urged—begged —repeatedly to come.

I took one long look at the tragic party, slipped out, walked over to the rectory, climbed the stairs, and lay down on my bed. I was too tired and discouraged to try any more. But I had to. In a few moments I was back in the parish hall. The president of the women's auxiliary was pouring punch. I went up to her and said, "Alice, don't pour punch. Anybody can do that. Move around the room, greet people, shake hands with them." She replied that she had been doing that since the party began. She had, in fact, been around the large hall three times. "Keep it up, Alice," I told her. "Keep moving until you drop." And so we got through the evening.

The next morning at Sunday Eucharist not a word was said about the preceding evening. Everybody participated in the sacrament of the body and blood of Christ, sat amiably through a harsh sermon, and smilingly remained afterward for coffee and cakes in the same parish hall that had been the scene of the previous night's slaughter. The parish had thereby announced, that the church would remain a private reserve—a club with restrictive membership clauses. "Damn it, we're going to keep it that way"—one could almost see the handwriting on the church wall—"in the name of the Father and of the Son and of the Holy Ghost. Amen."

Eventually these sentiments brought an inevitable outcome. Many of the members wanted to move into a white suburb. The church was to be closed. It would have happened with or without the summer program. The bishop visited the parish to deconsecrate the church. During the ceremony, I poured water over the sanctuary lamp, extinguishing it.

> I'm finding my way toward freedom
>> Not in society
>> Not in any system
>> Inside myself
>> I hope I can let other people be free when they're
>>> with me, and not stand in their way
>> I'm trying
> It's the only beginning I know
> Freedom has to start somewhere.
>> It passes from one person to another, but can't be
>>> given.
>> You have to claim it.
>> You have to take it.
> Whadaya want?
>> Freedom.
> When?
>> *Now.*

On Sundays, prior to the deconsecration of St. George's, I had to conduct double services: one at the old parish and another in the suburban neighborhood where the new church, St. Timothy's, would be built. Sunday mornings after my first Eucharist at St. George's, the ladies of the Altar Guild would fill an enormous lunch basket with vestments, the chalice and paten, bread and wine—everything needed for the second Eucharist. People living near the rectory would see me going off late every Sunday morning in my car, carrying this immense picnic basket, filled to the brim. It was a private joke within the parish that the neighbors who were not members of our church obviously thought St. George's priest was living high off the hog.

We always needed money at St. George's. In summer, attendance slumped way, way down. (I sometimes thought that the "god of churches" died around the first of June and rose again at Labor Day.) Pledges dropped to a disastrous low. There were diocesan assessments to be met. We held rummage sales, at which some ladies who did not have jobs spent most of the day drinking coffee, gossiping, and greeting our very few customers. We had an annual bazaar. At one of these, I worked hard to get some wealthy Indianapolis socialites to visit our humble parish hall in the way of charity. But the rich weren't spending that night. In an auction, items such as hand-painted tiles were going for five and ten cents each. I had donated my childhood stamp collection —worth a fortune to me in the love and concern I had invested in it—and it went for ten dollars. (A good buy for a sharp investor that night; it turned out to be worth three hundred dollars.) Finally, near despair, I mounted a chair to berate the people who were forgetting this was a fund-raising occasion, not a bargain sale. As I spoke —heatedly, using earthy words—the rich fled. Only the poor remained; at the close of the evening we drank coffee, speaking to one another in low voices.

The ladies of St. George's were fine cooks, so potluck

suppers seemed a natural way to raise money. The suppers were popular, family get-togethers. For a dollar,
you could have a delicious roast, cream-whipped potatoes with gravy, two or three vegetables, casseroles, salads, hot breads, dessert, and unlimited cups of coffee.
Needless to say, we seldom made much money this way.
Once I visited a wealthy Episcopal parish on the other
side of town when it was holding a fund-raising luncheon. The meal consisted of a bowl of chili (no refills),
soda crackers, and a cup of coffee (no refills) for $1.50.
The rich get richer . . . At least we had our dignity—
and ate some good suppers.

One night, during a meeting of ladies inside the parish hall, word came by telephone that a tornado warning
was out for the neighborhood where many of them lived.
Everybody rose to go into the church and pray for their
families and homes. One of the ladies held back. She
was crying. I asked her why she didn't join the others. "I
want to," she said, "but I don't have anything to put over
my head." There is an old custom that women in church
must have a covering on their heads. I gave her a Kleenex. (Now she would be acceptable in the eyes of the
Lord.)

I remember well my first meeting in the ancient
parish hall with this group of ladies. The women, most
of whom were old enough to be my mother, sat in a
circle. They had placed a single chair in the middle.
"That's for you, Father," I was told. The System was
suspended heavily over us like Damocles' sword; it
dictated the nature of our relationship and, indeed, our
identity.

Once I invited a newspaperman who did not attend
church to conduct a series of discussions on Sunday
mornings about the relation of faith to the kind of

human questions he faced in his job. He was terse, objective, highly idealistic beneath a cynical exterior— and terribly threatening to the people in the congregation. One lady walked out on him, deeply angered, for he had stabbed easy piosity with hard truth.

My sermons were long. I became deeply involved while preaching them, exhorting the people furiously, pacing back and forth at the top of the chancel steps. One Sunday after I had been holding forth for a long, long time, I noticed a lady parishioner looking at her watch (God knows, understandably). "That won't do you any good," I shouted at her. Heads swiveled around to look at her. "I will preach the Word of God until the Holy Ghost stops me."

Now the day is over,
   Night is drawing nigh,
Shadows of the evening
   Steal across the sky.

Jesus, give the weary
   Calm and sweet repose;
With thy tenderest blessing
   May our eyelids close.

Grant to little children
   Visions bright of thee;
Guard the sailors tossing
   On the deep, blue sea.

Comfort every sufferer
   Watching late in pain;
Those who plan some evil
   From their sin restrain.

Through the long night watches
   May thine angels spread

Their white wings above me,
   Watching round my bed.

When the morning wakens,
   Then may I arise
Pure, and fresh, and sinless
In thy holy eyes.   Amen.

Hymn 172,
The Hymnal of the
Protestant Episcopal Church
in the United States
of America

There was an orthodox synagogue across the street. Orthodox Jews are forbidden to do any form of work on the Sabbath, so every Saturday morning I used to turn on the lights for the rabbi. He lived far away, but since he could not drive on the Sabbath he would start walking along and by prior arrangement be picked up in a car driven by a gentile. When he arrived at the synagogue the lights (by a strange chance) would already be burning.

A prominent lawyer and his small son drove in from one of the remotest suburbs to attend the early Saturday morning Eucharist, unavailable at their church. We became friendly. At least once a week I had lunch with the lawyer in the business section of the city. One noon as I started to order I remembered it was Friday—when I, like many Christians, used to eat fish instead of meat. I asked if the lobster had been flown in fresh from Maine and if the shrimp were being served with rémoulade sauce. My friend Claude didn't bat an eyelash when he told the waiter, "I'll have a hamburger—I'm fasting."

When I was serving at St. George's life became intense and demanding for me. I was exploring human relationships that were sometimes painful. Frequently I

felt torn apart, for while I had great affection for many
of the parishioners, I detested our corporate sin of bigotry. But I did care what happened to St. George's, its
parishioners, and the people in that neighborhood: for
the first time I was making a commitment. I was moving
outside the ghetto of myself.

And, happily, I was not alone in my concern. Every
Tuesday morning at 7 o'clock, the priests working in
inner-city parishes met at the cathedral for Eucharist
celebrated by the bishop, and for breakfast and discussion following. The bishop, John P. Craine, was an ex-
traordinarily faithful man who never missed one of
these mornings with his men. As the months passed,
this gathering assumed great significance. A feeling of
solidarity emerged. Through our discussions, we lived
through one another's crises and came to know inti-
mately the problems of the various inner-city parishes.

A social worker told me that no matter what efforts we
might make, a high percentage of the neighborhood kids
would end up in reformatories and prisons. Many of the
major crimes reported in the daily newspaper occurred
within a half-dozen blocks of the church and rectory.

> I look into a kid's face out here on the street and want
>   him to be free.
> I want the system to work for him.
> I want him to have an education.
> I want him to be able to find out who he is
>   To know himself as a man.

Outside St. George's ran a major thoroughfare for
huge trucks; one could hear them going by, from early
morning until night. The bodies of dead dogs and cats
on the street simply reaffirmed something we all knew
about an impersonal, massive force outside our very
doors. There was only one small area with green grass

for kids to play in the neighborhood. Then a large firm (with a liberal reputation fostered by an active public relations department) bought it, stripped the grass, and built a new plant. Yet, in the city's prosperous suburbs, I saw expensively maintained, lushly beautiful parks in the midst of areas which already had block after block of fine lawns and immense yards.

In spite of our slum locale, St. George's doors were never locked. Episcopal churches in the exclusive parts of town usually were closed at 5:00 P.M. Members of those churches often came to St. George's to pray at any hour of the night when they felt personal stress. I told the parish that if someone were starving and stole our crucifix to hock it for food, Jesus would understand.

> That guy who used to run every morning in the playground over by the community center.
> I saw him sometimes
> Once I talked with him
> He was out of work
> He was trying to keep his body in shape
> He couldn't just sit in the house all day, looking at TV while his wife was at work
> He dropped dead in the playground on Thursday.
> Yesterday his wife came over
> She asked us how he died
> Andy told her that he had been running in the playground.
> He fell
> Andy was there
> Andy tried mouth-to-mouth resuscitation
> Did everything he could
> Somebody said it was an okay way to die
> *Running*

I was sound asleep in the rectory one night when a woman rang the bell. She was a prostitute who had just made her third suicide attempt. We smoked many cigarettes, drank black coffee, and talked for hours. When I drove her home, I met her young daughter. She was in bed and did not speak to me, but her eyes could not hide her rage, her contempt for all men. To her I was simply another man waiting in that apartment to go to bed with her mother for a few bucks. Many times I have remembered the girl's eyes and impotent rage when, on a university campus, I have seen women students who have been given unlimited opportunities and lavish expressions of their parents' concern.

One morning at St. George's the telephone rang. I received word that my father was dying in a New Jersey hospital. In a short while, the telephone rang again. He was dead. Divorce had shattered the family and kept me from seeing him as a growing child, but I had gotten to know him in more recent years. His courage and humor had endeared him to me as a friend. I wanted to perform what seemed to me the final act of love and respect for him; I would conduct the burial service.

I took the train east from Indianapolis to East Orange, New Jersey, where he had lived happily with his third wife. Many of the Boyd family gathered for the funeral rites. I decided there should be no music; I did not trust myself to hold up under the emotion of a funeral hymn. I read the burial office for him, standing above the closed casket at the foot of the chancel steps. Then we drove to the Brooklyn cemetery where his father, an Episcopal priest who died as a young man, had been buried many years before. I committed his body "earth to earth, ashes to ashes, dust to dust." My father's body was placed beside that of his father.

Unmailed Letter 2

Dear B.,

I know it will not surprise you that when I think of death my thoughts automatically turn toward you. It is because you live on a paper-thin sheet of ice separating life from death. Perhaps the transplant will be perfected in time to save your life. Meanwhile you live only thanks to that machine that keeps giving you fresh blood.

Because I am very close to you, and because blood is such a strange symbol of life and death, I learned much that morning I spent with you in the hospital, watching as your blood was pumped through the machine. I found that you are more intensely a friend than I had ever before been able to realize. I discovered myself breathing oxygen with you, being conscious of the flow of blood in my body as well as yours, enjoying life (yes!) with you.

What is it like, being so close to death? You tell me that you appreciate life each morning with an almost fierce gratitude. Since life and death are both so close to you now, what would you describe as the substantive difference between them? Is it the difference between the known and the unknown? (Yet is life "known"?) As life and death are almost inseparably close now within your own life, how can we presume they will be irreparably splintered *afterward*?

Your struggle to live is a drama which I have watched from the vantage point of my own life. I am sure that I would, under similar circumstances, lack your courage, patience and humor. With the numerous operations to place new tubes inside my arm, my capacity for humor should likely give way to despair or bitterness. Yet the reserve of humor within you is a basic part of your spirituality.

I realize you do not have "faith" in any traditional sense. The "God" of the past which we shared is, by common assent, dead. (He always was.) Superstition and mere optimism have been burned out of you. Your spirituality is deeply humanist—rooted in the mystery of Jesus' humanness.

May I tell you that your style of life, developed in the close tension between life and death, is one of the great things I have seen in recent years? You have let go of lives close to you—let them simply bloom in an unbelievably clean freedom. You quit making demands on them which would inhibit their own growth; you let them know that their justification did not depend on winning your favor, to be bestowed or withdrawn at whim. How did you achieve this victory over self?

It is linked, I suppose, to the audacious, splendid absence of self-pity in you. Confronted by death, you have looked outside your own life and squarely into other people's lives. Is it possible that death is a liberating force? From watching you live in dialogue with it, I tend to think so. Maybe the word "death" is altogether meaningless. However, for the present, we seem to be stuck with it. Maybe death, like anything else in life, can be confronted and dealt with in a right or wrong way. Could it be that fear of death is really a denial of life; that to understand death as a creative part of living indicates affirmation of life? You seem—with your amazing combination of hard discipline and spontaneous joy—to be affirming it.

All I know is that just as my thoughts turned to you when I thought of death, so they do when I think of life.

III

In the late 1950s, after a brief and conventional parish assignment in Indianapolis, Father Boyd became a campus chaplain at Colorado State University where he initiated free-wheeling coffee-house discussions of civil rights, poverty, war, sex— well, that's what was going on in the world, and why limit your ministry to doctrinaire religion? As the students gathered 'round and as the folk guitars strummed, wire services clattered out his name. Father Boyd was known as "the espresso priest" in those days when "espresso" had the sort of fuzzy connotation now reserved for pot and LSD— bananas, even. He was not that sort of a pusher, of course, but he was asked to change his style. Instead, Father Boyd quit and took a similar, and similarly colorful, position at Wayne State University in Detroit. While there, he was one of the first clergymen in the country to take part in civil rights demonstrations down south, and he was a familiar sight around local picket lines and poverty cores in Detroit.

> Chicago *Tribune*,
> April 29, 1967

Boyd is a full time disturber of the peace, a jarring blend of Luther and Lenny Bruce, who is attempting to shock religion into being relevant, to get back to what he calls "armpit theology."

> London *Evening Standard*,
> March 22, 1967

CONTROVERSY

On a winter night I can remember very well, I found myself in a converted garage near Colorado State University where I was called from Indianapolis in 1959 to be the Episcopal chaplain.

The lights were low; abstract designs were painted on the walls. More than a hundred students sat on flat cushions on the floor, and drank espresso coffee or cold punch. We were listening to folk singing and watching an interpretive dance. In a few moments I would be speaking—seated on a high stool on the small stage, lighted by a single bright spot.

I would read some lines of Tennessee Williams' *The Glass Menagerie* and *Sweet Bird of Youth;* that part of Truman Capote's *Breakfast at Tiffany's* where Holly Golightly leaves her cat behind in Spanish Harlem; some lines of dialogue from *The Sun Also Rises* (but Hemingway doesn't seem to read well now, the sound doesn't come off as one remembers it used to); a speech from Camus' *The Plague;* Eliot's *The Hollow Men;* something of Ezra Pound and Dylan Thomas. Then I would close by reading, without music, the lyrics of Cole Porter's *Love for Sale*—very immediate, threatening, close to contemporary man's questioning of the meaning of love and sex.

I can't shake this feeling sad.

It started yesterday. We were laughing like kids, re-member? You know how freezing cold it was. Like idiots, we walked along the street looking in store windows. Then we went into the record shop, and I bought a Nina Simone album. (I've been playing it today. She didn't make me sad—just kept me com-pany.)

After that we found that psychedelic shop we were looking for, only it wasn't quite as good as we'd ex-pected. On the funny balcony of the overcrowded paperback store, you got the first Tolkien book, and I the second. We had a three-hour lunch with two drinks—decadent! fun! the clock stopped.

It was all a high. Way, way up. Now I feel so low my barnacles are scraping the bottom of middle earth. I want you to be all right. I'm sure you know that—and also how I apparently can't ever help you to be. I somehow rocket you into fantasy, which is the worst possible place for you. Maybe a high like yesterday gives you a great shove outside that rotten prison you've been living in. Does it? But I'm so sad now. I wonder if you are too.

At the very end I would read the beginning of the Gospel according to St. John.

Many of the students and faculty members who came to this place, The Golden Grape, were among the most imaginative, stimulating and promising people on cam-pus. This former garage filled a need: creative writings could be read, original work shared, offbeat and noncon-formist ideas presented to others who were sensitive and concerned. On a visit here I might talk for well over an hour and a half, and my audience would remain silent and almost totally attentive. Certainly, I did not "preach" in a traditional sense. Instead, I engaged in give-and-take dialogue. A church congregation used only to a set sermon would have been restless after thirty minutes. Much of what I had to say here could not, in fact, have been said to a church congregation. Yet here, in an unconventional way, I could often impart more of the gospel's inherent message than I could in church. Why? Because here, in this place, I could speak without pretense or accommodation about sex and love, the role of the rebel historically and existentially in society, the meaning of individual and social freedom; because here I related the gospel to life. Even those who might not accept the gospel would accept the fact that belief in it necessarily involves the believer in the social implications of that same gospel. My method was adapted to—indeed, grew out of—this rather unusual environment. Mine was in no sense a traditional mission situation (I sometimes wonder if anyone's is) and strategy had to be altogether altered in order to permit the gospel to be heard here.

I'm twenty-one—without much faith in anything, and totally aware of the double standards this world lives by. Why can't life be beautiful like when you were five—everything great—blue skies, snow, green grass and toys —and a faith in your world—Why do we have to outgrow our faith in this world? And God? Why do things have to hurt and pull and break and rot? Why can't you always keep a child's faith in God and life and people? I want to believe in something—help me???? I need some basic, strong foundation for my life, and I can't find it. I see people with tons of faith and belief and it hurts me and makes me almost physically ill that some people are so secure and I can't be. How can you have faith in something that is unreasonable? How can you be expected to believe something just because you are supposed to? Why

can't people help each other, and care and love for each
other?

(From a letter written by a college student)

Fort Collins, the town that housed Colorado State University, had a Main Street out of any Hollywood movie.
Mexican-Americans lived in a rural slum and their segregation was an accepted fact of life. Their women
could work as maids in Anglo homes, but they were
supposed to worship in separate churches.

In Fort Collins I had my second, and final, cat. (I
have now moved my allegiance back to dogs, though
a recent dog in my life was, I must admit, strangely
catlike—possessing a certain introspective quality,
inscrutable eyes, a sense of untold mystery, a streak
of mischief straight out of a reincarnation, and a
quality of drama which Duse might envy.) My Fort
Collins cat walked simultaneously into my life and St.
Paul's House one day, from across the street. We tried
to get the cat to return home but he refused. For
ecclesiastical reasons, we named him Lucifer. The
little girl whose cat he had been wrote a short poem
which she delivered to me personally.

Lucifer

My cat is as black as night,
    not one spot of white.

He followed me around like a dog,
    Always right behind at his cute jog.

When Father Boyd came along one day,
    A very great man, if I do say,

My cat must have liked him too.
    Oh!! What can I do?

Across the street my cat went,
    Although he was really not sent.

Now my cat lives over there,
    I guess he likes the fulfillment of prayer.

It was both amusing and sad how many people in that small Western town fiercely resisted the existence and the work of that espresso coffee place where new ideas —in the form of poetry, drama, the novel, the dance, contemporary design, folk singing—could be presented. All this was somehow strange, foreign and new, to such people. Therefore, they felt threatened. Opposition became vocal. What had "the arts" to do with religion? The Golden Grape smacked of the avant-garde and allegedly had overtones of "beatnik"; it must be closed, they said. (Finally it was—because the rent could not be paid.)

My experiences in the place forced me to ask myself, What *is* a sermon? Was the stream-of-consciousness investigation, the free exchange of ideas as much a sermon as a tightly controlled monologue? I concluded that the honest, searching, open dialogue was *more* of a sermon than what was preached from many a pulpit—for it involved "outsiders" to the church in a contemporary evangelism.

The morning after a visit to The Golden Grape I would find "outsiders" flocking into the Episcopal center across the street from the campus to ask frank, serious questions. They would come alone, in twos, or in small groups. "What, in your opinion, is immoral?" "Who is Jesus Christ?" "What is sin?" "What do you mean by salvation?" "What about other religions—are they false?" "Do you really believe in God or do you just do this for a living?" I became the close friend of several students whom I would not otherwise have known.

I'm groping. I have been involved for the longest time with myself. I know that to a certain extent you must find isolation. You have to really first feel the pulse of your own humanity—and that's the trip I've been on.

But now I need others with the same bag (but that's a real trauma out here in suburbia). Social change—it can tell you a lot about yourself, and that's where I need help. I'm grabbing, laughing and crying for some outer involvement—beyond, yet not alienated from, the alternative world of being completely free to find *me*. Yet I fear that any deep social involvement could easily slip into an obsession, a real hang-up.

I just want to survive as a whole human being. I want to give my confused world something beautiful (made and articulated out of my own confusion). I know that society and I need each other. We've got to get on human terms: need and capacity.

Still, I don't know. The closer I get to an understanding of me and all of this—the more absurd it seems. I just don't know.

But then maybe that's something of what "life" is all about. I mean, existing in terms of something we're not really sure we are. And groping, always groping. And just being beautiful (human) about the whole thing.

(From a letter written by a student)

I was now putting to use in the college chaplaincy my experiences in Hollywood and Europe, as well as what I had learned in my first parish. A sense of the theatrical was clearly linked to the coffeehouse involvement, as was the theology of the English industrial missioners, the outreach of the house-church, and the concern for modern evangelism that I had learned at the Ecumenical Institute in Switzerland.

For several months, after coming to Colorado from Indianapolis, I had sat inside the expensively outfitted Episcopal center, seeing only the denominational students who came to see me. Their questions basically concerned sex or faith. Then, in an effort to relate my belief to my actions, I literally forced myself to move into the give-and-take of student life on the campus. Students welcomed me warmly, and we began communicating. My participation in The Golden Grape developed naturally.

When the next semester got under way, I decided that St. Paul's House, the Episcopal center at the university, must try to continue the spirit and work of The Golden Grape after it closed. A student suggested using the name Expresso Night. The phrase had recently cropped up in an English film, *Expresso Bongo*. "It captures the feeling we have of wanting to express ourselves, of needing a way of expression which is uninhibited and free," the student said. (Later, when controversy was lashing at us, this name caused seemingly endless newspaper confusion. The names "espresso" and "expresso" were used interchangeably.)

No Expresso Night was in any way related to any church service. No sacrament of the church was ever administered at one of these events, nor did such an idea even remotely occur to any of us who were involved. Yet this absurd charge was soon to be leveled at us.

At one typical Expresso Night, the evening opened with dancing by a student from the Near East who was accompanied by bongos played by a student from New Jersey. There was folk singing, followed by a student's short original monologue. Espresso coffee and mulled cider were prepared and served by a committee of faculty wives. Everybody was seated on the floor of St. Paul's House. The room was dimly lit and all the furniture had been moved out.

Then a student and I combined various folk songs with readings. We called our offering "Songs and Words about Life and Love." I concluded our presentation by simply saying, "In the name of the Father and of the Son and of the Holy Ghost, Amen." There was a deep and long silence until someone started up some folk singing again. Afterward we talked together—everybody in the room—for nearly an hour about conformity and nonconformity on the campus and in American society. Unknown to us, this was to be our final Expresso Night.

The Denver *Rocky Mountain News* headlined a story:

Minister Sanctions Religion With A Cool Bongo Beat

and went on to say: "Flickering candlelight in a dim, smoke-filled room, the throbbing beat of bongo drums, the melancholy words of poets loved by the avant-garde set, the haunting rhythm of the blues. This is 'expresso night' at St. Paul's House on the edge of the Colorado State University campus . . . It is the 'out group' that Father Boyd is attempting to reach, as well as to serve the others through more ordinary church activities. . . . 'Christ came not to save the church but the world,' is one of Father Boyd's favorite expressions and he puts it into practice by putting himself into some unorthodox situations where he is available for those needing help."

Controversy erupted. In the April, 1961, issue of the *Colorado Episcopalian*, the official publication of the Diocese of Colorado, the Rt. Rev. Joseph Minnis wrote:

One of the signs that one is getting old is the degree of shock one feels when one is informed about some new, secular practice being injected into the worship of the Church, particularly in the administration of the Sacraments. "Beatniks" comprise a group of young people who seem to have a language comprehensible only to themselves and who are given over to the non-practice of bathing and the wearing of beards and black leotards! These beat the Bongo drums and mumble meaningless words, which, by the Beatnik, passes for poetry . . .

One thing I do know and that is that Bongo drums and the playing of them with doleful countenance or enraptured twistings of the body have no place in the worship of the Church. I suppose there might be a way of playing a Bongo by which the tones coming out of such technique might be called worshipful. What I am trying to say is that I have no objection to a Bongo drum as a thing, but that is all it is, a thing, and its association has been certainly in the past few years with the jungle, and those who tried to transport the jungle into cafes and drinking halls. Therefore, the drum suffers by association, and therefore, it has no place in the worship of the Church . . .

I believe that there should be joy in religion and that the words of the Prayer Book as they are used in our service can be inspirational, and make for happiness as one faces the problems of one's life.

> If the Beatniks get to heaven,
> They will find that harps are there,
> And they'll find their drums forbidden
> As they climb the heavenly stair.

You might like to sing this lovely poetry of mine to the tune of the Marine hymn!

None of us should ever forget that we are created in God's image and that dignity is a precious attainment. It comes as a result of a man's having self-respect and appreciation of his position as the highest of God's creatures. You can't think of yourself as a beloved Son of God and at the same time go around with matted hair, dirty bodies and black underwear. I think that of these three probably the black underwear is the least objectionable. . . .

Heaven is your home. Don't allow the puny minds of modern intellectuals to rob you of the great truths revealed to us by the Holy Spirit through the ages.

The fat was in the fire.

Fling out the banner! let it float
    Skyward and seaward, high and wide;
The sun that lights its shining folds,
    The cross, on which the Saviour died.

Fling out the banner! heathen lands
    Shall see from far the glorious sight,
And nations, crowding to be born,
    Baptize their spirits in its light.

Fling out the banner! sin-sick souls
    That sink and perish in the strife,
Shall touch in faith its radiant hem,
    And spring immortal into life.

Fling out the banner! let it float
    Skyward and seaward, high and wide,
Our glory, only in the cross;
    Our only hope, the Crucified!

Fling out the banner! wide and high,
    Seaward and skyward, let it shine;
Nor skill, nor might, nor merit ours;
    We conquer only in that sign.

Hymn 258,
The Hymnal of the
Protestant Episcopal Church
in the United States
of America

The bishop's newspaper comments were particularly surprising because I had not received a telephone call, a letter, or communication in any form asking questions or expressing concern about my work. I agonized for several days, driving my car in the mornings north of

Fort Collins toward Cheyenne, then parking and just trying to think. *You can't think of yourself as a beloved Son of God and at the same time go around with matted hair, dirty bodies and black underwear.* To me this was absolute heresy.

Finally, I offered my resignation in protest against the bishop's views. "I find myself in fundamental disagreement with the bishop concerning the nature of Christian evangelism," I wrote in the letter which would sever my relations with St. Paul's House and the diocese.

"If a Christian church would ever express contempt of, or self-righteousness toward, any segment of the population racially, religiously or socially, it would forfeit its claim to be the Body of Christ," I continued. "A Christian church would deny its dynamic and reason for being if it ever would bar anyone because of a label, be it 'negro,' 'Jew,' 'wop,' 'dago,' 'Catholic,' 'Protestant' or 'beatnik.' Underneath the confused and stereotyped images which comprise the popular image of beatnik, there is a valid element of protest as well as an honest searching for fundamental values rooted in truth. The church cannot turn away from this or any other manifestation of social change or unrest.

"Jesus Christ is the Lord of the whole of life or He is not Lord of any of it. We must remember that in His earthly life He identified Himself with the publicans and the frequently socially outcast more than with pharisees and the self-labeled 'nice' or 'best' people. . . . Acting out of a deep conviction rooted in doctrinal orthodoxy, I am merely trying to relate the Gospel of Jesus Christ in a challenging, radical, demanding way to contemporary life where modern man is living."

Within the next six weeks I received more than nine hundred letters, four hundred of them from Denver, with all but around a dozen endorsing my stand. On

April 9, 1961, the *New York Times* gave me a new identification in a headline:

BEATNIKS' PRIEST
QUITS CHAPLAINCY

The irony was that from the beginning I had simply
been making a protest against stereotypes as a form of
dehumanization. Now, maddeningly, I was the "beatnik
priest"—stereotyped as a result of this very protest.

> Maybe this time I'll crack up
>> I don't fear it as much as I once did
>> If it's got to happen, then it's got to
>> In a way there's nothing I can do about it anyhow
> Would a single split tear my mind apart?
>> Could I hear the split and know it was happening?
>> Would there be an awareness of it in my mind
>>> afterward?
>> (In which part?)
> It's odd, at this moment I appear to be well
>> My eyes look normal, at least, to me
>> (What is normal?)
> I am on the edge of a high wall
>> I don't want to fall off
>> The pieces would be so scattered
>> All the king's horses and all the king's men . . .

There could seemingly be no communication between
the bishop and me. A priest who headed college work for
the diocese wanted to arrange a meeting between us. I
consented. A morning was chosen and, the night before,
I drove to Denver and stayed in the priest's apartment.
The next morning he asked the bishop to see me. The
bishop refused. I felt that I knew something of his terrible mental and spiritual pain, for I knew my own.

Daniel Corrigan was in Colorado as Suffragan Bishop

during my first year there. He and his wife Elizabeth were unusually compassionate, sensitive, warm, courageous and honest—we tend to use the word "saintly" to describe such men and women. I drove to Denver on Friday nights when my spiritual wounds needed to be cleansed and bandaged, and stayed with them until late Saturday when I had to return to Fort Collins for Sunday duties. There was good talk, quiet understanding, Mass on Saturday morning with Episcopalian nuns nearby, excellent food, laughter, an appreciation of silences, and a strong sense of friendship shared. When the Corrigans left Colorado for New York, I sorely missed them.

I was prepared to stand by my convictions even if it meant leaving the active ministry. At this moment I ceased to be an organization man. Henceforth I would place Christianity ahead of institutional loyalty; I would honor Jesus more than I would a bishop. Some would argue that I should have kissed an episcopal ring and shut up. Instead I resigned amid public protest and uproar. I found that there are no clear, precise, neat guidelines; no explicit maps with instructions drawn in red ink so that the Abrahamitic journey can be conveniently divided among comfortable inns, and the Way of the Cross eased by stops at clean restrooms and recommended restaurants.

With our church I feel only alienation. I'm coming to detest the minister and pity the people. He is the pompous shepherd herding his flock, and is the epitome of self-righteous, insensitive, stupid great white father. I'm finding myself becoming progressively less loving towards him every Sunday.

I teach Sunday School. So I'm stuck and therefore bitter. I have no spiritual strength to try to help them. I'm too lost myself. As a Sunday School teacher I am a total failure. I don't believe or care about the junk I'm supposed to teach them (the Church Seasons) but have found all other attempts, except games, complete failures. They hate the church and the problem is so do I.

(From a letter)

Yet people can make a serious mistake if they walk away from the church because of its imperfections. All institutions and movements are laced with ambiguities. If one walks away from an institution, having discovered its imperfections, then to what other one can he go? Does he assume that he is moving away from ambiguities, either outside or inside himself? Though I had felt forced to leave the active ministry, I had no intention of departing from the church.

What does obedience mean? To whom is it given? If Christ is the head of the church, doesn't obedience have to be given to him? I agonized over these questions. I knew that the church is a basic social institution and not only a movement. Yet institutions can so easily fall into self-serving organization and stifling authoritarianism; their relationship to society can be open and receptive, or rigid and oppressive. How to be part of the church, and steer clear of these institutional pitfalls.

I kept reading, at the time of my resignation, about the worker-priest movement in the French church. I found it a beautiful example of men struggling in obedience to an authentic vision of the church as the Body of Christ. Not a comfortable, conforming bureaucracy. Not a dispenser of cheap grace and sacraments misunderstood as magic. Not a substitute for tranquilizers, outfitted with a plastic Jesus who is anti-revolution, and likes business-as-usual so that endless new buildings may be raised "to glorify God."

We're in trouble here in our church. Someone has done something wrong. He has been sinful and now it would be best if we do not offer our friendship. He will lie to us, he will hurt us, so yesterday we were friends but today leave him alone. Let him sink or swim. Jesus sat down with sinners (I hope it didn't upset him) but we know better in our supreme wisdom. I'm an active church worker (I'm beginning to despise those words) and have reached my mid-thirties. In our church we are so damn hung up on talk. We talk a great ball game—but oh brother. It hurts when these "Christian" people just seem to despise everybody who is human.

(From a letter)

Many letters I received during the controversy in Colorado commented on the church's exclusivity and rejection of its own true function. "We wish to convey to you our intense admiration for your stand against the tendency to make Christianity a religion for gentlemen," someone wrote. "The Apostles must most certainly have smelled of fish, Job was at his best when sitting on a dung hill, and it is to be presumed that Stylites had no bathing facilities on top of that pillar. Our best Christians have been an odiferous and malcontented rabble, and you are to be congratulated for reminding us of that."

A priest in New York said, "Hunger and thirst are hunger and thirst wherever they occur, and those who seek to give food and water in what appears an unconventional manner will always be misunderstood and feared as enemies of the institutional church. My prayers are with you." Yet another clergyman asked this question, "Blessings and all good wishes—*but*, where do we go from here, we who have a stake in what you stand for?" A woman in Ohio noted in her letter, "We, as a group, deride and use social pressures to exclude from parish life those who 'do not fit.' There is so great a need to give life to this great hulking corpse we call the church."

Can the present-day church—racist as it is, class-bound as it is, fearful of the gospel as it is—say no to honest expression, open dialogue, and confrontation of issues? No, it cannot—because of *respect for persons*, which is inseparable from what the gospel is all about. ("Beatniks" are persons.)

Why did I give a damn about this controversy? Why didn't I stand shoulder-to-shoulder with the organization? I could have moved up within its ranks to a position of leadership marked by predictable behavior in public, honorary degrees from Establishment-controlled educational institutions, and "togetherness." What happened?

When I came into the church, I meant it. I was not playing games, establishing a successful career, running for bishop, looking for financial security, or shallowly seeking a new activism to replace an old. Active I had always been. I sought a commitment which would drive my life.

I have always had two intensely strong drives. One is the drive toward a life of leisure, hedonism, and self-preoccupation; the other is the drive to serve people—a sense of commitment to social justice.

There was a night in a Midwestern city when I experienced such pain that I still cannot comprehend it, talk about it rationally or even work through the blocks which I have placed between it and myself. I was speaking to a group of whites who were rejecting me along with what I had to say. Finally a man in the audience stood up and shouted at me, "*I* didn't kill six million Jews. *I* didn't lynch any blacks."

"Yes, damn it, you did," I replied. "So did I. We all

bear responsibility." It was a tense and angry exchange; I was ostracized by the group. I ate supper
alone in my hotel room. Then I telephoned two
friends; they asked me to come by their apartment.
He was black, she was white, and they were married.
We were joined by the sole black reporter on a major
newspaper, who was in the city to cover a race story.
He had to play a house-nigger role at the paper,
usually being assigned only stories with a racial slant,
and not the most important of these. We all felt, that
night, many frustrations and pains. We drank and
talked compulsively. We alternately struck at one
another with savage blows coming from self-doubt
and self-hate, and then held one another with an intense loving which grew out of our acknowledgment
of a common fate. We cried and shouted, and then we
went to sleep on the floor.

Again and again, I have been propelled outside my
private life—that wall-to-wall carpeted ghetto—into involvement in battles outside. I have not been able to
enjoy leisure while I knew somebody else was suffering
poverty or ill-treatment. I could not pursue hedonism in
an imperfect world which required my participation in
the work of healing. I was not able to condense the
meaning of life into a symmetrically perfect career of
my own because, on the next corner, I met my brother
who was looking for a brother. Life as an exercise in
personal success or private pleasure has always rather
quickly bored me. I don't want to forget, but rather to
find out and remember; I don't want mere activism, but
rather involvement.

As I look back, I can see that the single great war of
my life has been against fragmentation and for whole-
ness, against labels and for identity. As an American, I

am not for my country right or wrong; the concept of one world commands my loyalty. As a Christian, I have struggled against the temptation to mold God in a Christian image and to believe in homogenized salvation for Christians only. As a white man, I want to think and feel black, yellow or red, and I know this means placing my body and mind in actual situations outside the white reservation. In the heat of the Colorado controversy, all these feelings found expression in action.

Once I was made a member of a key policy-making committee, comprising priests and laymen, which met monthly in Denver. I had been elected by an immensely large lay vote at a church convention. To my disgust, I found that it was a rubber-stamp apparatus. One night, after a meeting of this committee in Denver, I channeled my contempt for the committee and myself into the act of getting drunk. Then, as I was driving back to the university town where I was a chaplain, my car had a flat tire. I was speeding and it was a close call. I saw that I could not go on lying much longer; this dishonesty with myself was eating into my life; an awful corruption was going to spread through my mind. I could not survive in a world of neat papier-mâché facades covering up spiritual filth underneath. Casual Christianity was unacceptable to me.

I knew then that just as my belief in God was a strong belief, my love for the church was a strong love. I had come out of atheism and indifference into a confrontation with Christian belief and commitment. It was not for nothing that I came into the church and was ordained. I felt that I could not now be fed pablum, fantasy or lies.

Here is my prayer for today: Goddamit, God, I don't like the way you are running things. You know I often really think it would be a better world if you would let me run it. And then I get knocked about a bit like last week and whimper.

But, on the other hand, thank you so damn much for being who you are—the real God, not my own image. Thank you for being the one Person who is not threatened by a priest saying "God damn," thank you for being Big enough to take my arrogant hostility. Thank you for me having to face the fact that I am worth something, even though it is usually so easy to say I'm worthless. I'm worth something because you make me your child, you become a guy and then die for a shit-ass like me, and then, you say, "Come on, let's go feed sheep." So I'm not worth it; you say, let's go anyway. You're all right, Jesus, thanks for picking me up. Just stay with me when I move into that particular situation that is rough and has no answer. Help me not to chicken, or, when I do, pick me up.

(From a letter written by a priest)

In my chaplaincy at Colorado State University, I had tried to serve and relate to both an "in" group and an "out" group of faculty and students. The "in" group—those who had come to commitment to Christ in the past, either by nurture or personal crisis—were served in my campus ministry by daily celebrations of the Holy Eucharist before the altar in St. Paul's House, Sunday services, regular Canterbury Club (Episcopal student organization) functions, and special events with guest speakers. The "out" group—including non-Christians, atheists, agnostics, lapsed and non-practicing Episcopalians, Methodists, Roman Catholics, Presbyterians and others—were brought into contact with me by the Expresso Nights and similar approaches, where mutual openness replaced mere overlapping monologues. I strongly believed that we must come to people with the gospel wherever they are—not where we might wish they were. This is what Christ did.

However, there was a serious flaw in the Expresso Nights. In the move from The Golden Grape to the church campus center, an authentic quality was lost. I realize now what it was. We had moved from actual mission to playing church. Inside the church-sponsored coffeehouse, one faced no overt hostility or rejection; there was a supportive "in" group on hand to dull the tension of real confrontation; a claque to applaud, laugh or cry—in other words, to respond on cue; a crowd was always guaranteed, even if "outsiders" to the self-consciously evangelistic circle-of-the-saved did not wish to visit.

Since then I have visited and spoken in coffeehouses throughout the United States, Canada, Europe and the Middle East. I have found the same challenge to authentic Christian witness and mission, as well as the same temptation which can lead Christians into "in-group" activity. Visiting Toronto, I spent an evening in a secular coffeehouse where I was received openly, without props or built-in advantages, and where I spoke without an agenda. A real confrontation occurred, which ended after 4 A.M. Then six of us, who simply would not have met under ordinary circumstances, sweated out what we thought and felt, sitting in someone's bedroom, drinking coffee and talking without any program—or any distance between us.

Back in 1961, it could still be an occasion for raised eyebrows if a chaplain sat in a tavern talking with students late at night. Once a policeman entered a beer joint near the Colorado campus around midnight, and was confused to find me sitting and talking with a group of students. "What's he doing here?" the policeman asked one of the students somewhat angrily.

"Well, sir," the student replied, "I think he's saying good night to his parish."

Three months before the Expresso Night controversy exploded in Colorado, there had been something of a furor when I spoke at Lehigh University, in Pennsylvania. I had joined students afterward at their local tavern. The Bethlehem *Globe-Times* reported that I heard a half-dozen confessions over the jazz. "For the modern priest, confession is not heard so much in confessional booths and in rigid form," the paper quoted me. "It is over the oatmeal or martini that people, without form, express themselves. They need to speak and be heard. They need to have layer upon layer of guilt taken away . . . The church must go to where people are. The theological point is that Christ is there—where they are —not confined to the church, but in the Lehigh Tavern, in Bethlehem Steel."

Incredibly, this story received national attention. It was headlined this way in Boston:

PASTOR FINDS
SINNERS AMID
DRINKS, JAZZ

The images set up by the story were quite false—I was not being a modern Carrie Nation, striding through smoke-filled bars to wreck them; nor was I calling people "sinners," exhorting them to church membership. In the Lehigh Tavern, I merely engaged in pastoral counseling (informal hearing of "confessions"). To my astonishment, this was "news." The Denver *Post* even commented in an editorial: "Father Boyd doesn't believe in what he calls 'dollhouse Christianity,' or lace-curtain religion. It must be real, lived every day, the motivating force in life. But to the Pharisees, when religion breaks out of the arbitrarily assigned confines of time and place, it becomes a threat. Father Boyd needs no defense. Religion could use more, not less, of his kind."

A number of people did not agree. I was accused of having heard formal confessions in the Lehigh Tavern. I wonder if my accusers pictured me sitting there wearing a stole while students, one after another, knelt beside me, and shouted over the noise of the jukebox. I hastened to state that I had not heard formal confessions in the tavern or given formal absolution, and the wire services duly clarified this matter for the public.

The pain of such experiences grew out of the age-old dichotomy between "church" and "world." (It is akin to the dichotomy between "religion" and "life," or "priest" and "man.") A European theologian told me: "In meeting with church officials, you find a profound suspicion of the fact that God is not only in the church but is present everywhere in the world as the Lord of history. These officials think and live on the basis that God is present only in the church, with perhaps some dim idea that he is somehow remotely involved in the world." This is a false dichotomy; I have warred against it.

There was a night in New York City many years ago.
An old man lay moaning in a doorway.
Was he drunk?
Had he suffered a heart attack?
The night was very cold. It was snowing. A fierce wind blew.
I held the collar of my heavy coat around my neck with gloved hands.
I saw the old man. I heard him cry.
I passed by.
The old man moves through the curious labyrinths of what conscience I may have, late at night, crying.
He obliterates the sense of jazz or scotch, lights on a street at 3 A.M., or someone speaking.
Did I see him at all or merely look into a strangely misplaced mirror on the cold city street?

Unmailed Letter 3

Dear C.,

I thought about you today when I was taking a long, long walk in the city. I seemed to brush up against every kind of life. Rich, poor, black, white, young, old, lonely, happy, terribly respectable, terribly unrespectable: name it. But all I could do today was brush up against it. There could be no actual involvement.

In fact, I got mad at a guy in a restaurant where I stopped for lunch. He had had a couple of drinks, and then started talking to everybody around him. He was loud. He was funny and unfunny. It was superficial, of course, this small talk—all about how bartenders have a tendency nowadays to make Manhattans too dry. Everybody was seated at separate tables wedged close together. People *wanted* to be alone, really, for a few moments in that restaurant. It represented a break between contacts with other humans. But this guy kept talking. It was threatening and disagreeable and sad and a lot of things. Mostly, it was a bore and absolutely futile. Camaraderie in a damned restaurant over clam chowder! It couldn't be involvement, even if it had surface earmarks. (Or could it? Busy people over lunch weren't about to find out.)

Later, on the street, a little kid came up and handed me a crazy circular. A piece of paper with an announcement about some meeting or other. *Communication.* I tried to smile and managed to say thank you. The kid was away and running to the next pedestrian. I looked at the circular. It simply didn't concern *me,* that announcement about that particular meeting—not in a million years. But why were some people making kids hand out circulars about it to absolute strangers?

So this made me think, right away, about our telephone conversation. You said that you are going slowly crazy because you're not involved. You have a husband who goes away all day to work. When he's at home, you're both on different wave lengths. You look at everything differently and can't communicate with him (in your opinion) except occasionally in bed. You have children. They're at school. You have a big house and a servant. You're so bored and fed up you screamed at me over the telephone.

You want to be *involved*. But you're a veteran of past wars and don't want any more liberal organizations, study groups, or obvious causes. You would like to meet some humans. You would like to feel you can still learn something new that might matter. You want to grow instead of vegetating inside a way of life which has become meaningless for you.

You know that I can't give either of us, you or me, a road map neatly marked: "Involvement—go *this* way twenty miles, turn left at the second stop light, and then turn right . . ." However, I believe that one is either open or not open to involvement. One can be prepared for it, go out of the way to find it—and then, recognizing it, seize it and not let go.

IV

Father Boyd agreed with Dr. Martin Luther King Jr. that the problems of poverty and war—the ghetto at home and the Vietnam war abroad—are "totally linked." He feels the American society is faced with two alternatives—in effect, life or death. "One alternative is in the area of holocaust and a deterioration of relationships," he said. "The other alternative is an open society—the walls coming down."

Chicago Sun-Times,
May 1, 1967

"Those who are concerned with the underground church are not vitally wrapped up in arguments over the Trinity or the Virgin Birth, But napalm, black-and-white, the population explosion, the ghettos," said Father Boyd.

Los Angeles Times,
June 8, 1967

BETRAYER

"Nigger Malcolm Boyd," said the scrawled postcard in my morning mail. It was September, 1961. I was back in the North, having returned to Detroit from a freedom ride in the deep South. I had become a chaplain at Wayne State University in Detroit after I left Colorado.

At first I had been called a "nigger-lover," inasmuch as I was a white man involved in many civil rights demonstrations. Afterward I was often called a Negro. Some whites and blacks alike simply came to this conclusion on the basis of my ideas and my activity in the freedom movement. "You've got real thick lips and, because of the things you've done, we just kind of always took it for granted you were colored," a white woman once told me. When the Jackson, Mississippi, *Clarion-Ledger* (January 29, 1963) identified me in an editorial as "colored" and "Negro," I wrote the newspaper that personally I would be happy to be both. Yet I wondered why it was found necessary to bestow racial labels on people mentioned in the news. I asked if it were not sufficient, from a journalistic standpoint, to belong to the human race.

Finally I was being called a "nigger." When one is called a nigger, his identity as a person is being called into question. ("We got to make him a nigger first. He's got to admit that he's a nigger," William Faulkner has a white Mississippian say. And one of Faulkner's black characters apologizes, "I just a nigger. It ain't none of my fault.") In this sense the term can be used for anyone whose human identity is being questioned, in the context of sexuality, work, education, artistic creativity, race, religion or social protest. There is no person who is a nigger. The name can accurately be applied only to someone who, in a given moment or situation, has been so utterly opened up to dehumanization by another or himself that he characterizes or knows himself as a subhuman, a digit, a thing, an object, a category, a label, *not a human being.*

    Goddam nigger, I hate your guts.
    Crawl, coon.
        Don't stand up to me, boy.
    Work, nigger. Move your black ass. Faster.
        I can't even see you.
        All of you look the same to me.
        Your blackness is like dirt.
    Hustle.
        Your existence is disgusting.
        Must you breed more of you?
        I'd sterilize you.
    Boy.

My world is insane.
How can I still be breathing in it?

Then came the freedom ride in the deep South; traveling together, blacks and whites, we could not get off the bus to eat, visit a lavatory, or drink from a water fountain if these functions required the use of public facilities. At the end of each rural stretch of road, we knew there might well be a gang waiting to attack us. In 1962, along with nine other men, black and white, I took part in a ten-hour sit-in at a segregated restaurant in Tennessee. After dark a flaming cross exploded terrifyingly on the lawn outside. We watched the window as an angry crowd milled about restlessly, drinking more and more, getting noisier. In 1963, I marched in Medgar Evers' funeral procession through the streets of Jackson, Mississippi. I have marched for hours in a snow storm outside a segregated apartment house in Detroit which would not rent to a black student; carried a picket sign on a chilly, gray morning outside the fashionable Lovett School in Atlanta when it rejected the application of Martin Luther King, III, among other young black students; stood on the steps of the Dearborn, Michigan, city hall—surrounded by egg-throwing, booing hecklers—protesting a de facto system of all-white real estate; marched around the General Motors Building in Detroit, a symbol of the pinnacle of the U.S. economic power-structure, to demand increased black employment; integrated (along with another white man) a black motel in Natchez, Mississippi, as a half-dozen black men and women simultaneously integrated two white motels; marched with CORE in a Los Angeles suburb to protest the existence of a segregated, all-white housing tract; joined black students in Virginia to picket a movie theater in protest against a segregated-seating policy; marched outside the Syracuse, New York, police department to protest alleged police brutality; worked in rural Mississippi and Alabama during the summer of 1965 with the Student Nonviolent Coordinating Committee; picketed the City and County Building of Detroit to protest discriminatory housing practices in the city; assisted in the work of black voter-registration in McComb, Mississippi, in 1964; stayed with black people in Watts during the 1965 revolt; was arrested in a civil-rights demonstration in downtown Chicago; picketed the Episcopal cathedral in Atlanta to protest commencement exercises held there for a segregated school; and explored racial justice with thousands of university students, white and black, in every section of the United States.

Why?

The main reason is people—and what I have seen of their dehumanization. Personal experience breeds involvement. My protest had been building up over the past several years. In Indianapolis in 1957–1959, there had been the head-on conflict with certain members of my parish as we tried to relate the worship of God to living in a racially mixed slum neighborhood.

One illustration of the dehumanization of blacks was provided when I was leading a student conference in a small college town in the rural South. Some two hundred students attended. Four were black. I asked these four students to have dinner with me, and was promptly informed there was no place in the town where we could be served together. After I threatened embarrassing publicity, permission was granted for the five of us to eat together in my motel room. A waitress carried trays in from the public dining-room. The food was cold. We ate in my cramped quarters. I recall that there was no door on the bathroom; seated at the makeshift table, I faced the toilet and discussed Racial Equality, U.S.A. The white students who were in attendance at the conference denied any kind of solidarity with the problems of their black peers, no doubt went home to announce they had participated in an "integrated conference." White racists, angered by my small dinner party, spread a rumor that I had celebrated Holy Communion using beer and potato chips. This malicious and totally false story, I was later told, led to my exclusion as a writer from a prominent church magazine for two years.

Another deeply affecting personal experience with segregation grew out of a visit to Louisiana in 1959. I was asked to be the convocation speaker for Religious Emphasis Week at Louisiana State University in Baton Rouge. At that time, while I would probably have described myself as "extremely concerned" about the "Negro problem," I understood little, if anything, about black culture, the realities of second-class citizenship, or the dynamics of the freedom movement.

Nevertheless, I knew enough about race relations to be frightened as I reached the L.S.U. campus: This was a bastion of white segregation and I knew I must use the platform given me to say something about Christian doctrine and race relations. So, in my opening address before a large number of faculty and students, I made a clear, unequivocal statement opposing segregation. It was not meant to be inflammatory. Afterward I was accosted by only one person who disagreed.

My comments about race did not appear explicitly in the report of my speech in the *Daily Reveille,* the university's student newspaper, on Tuesday, February 24, 1959. The lead headline on the front page read:

CONFORMITY CRITICIZED
AT REW CONVOCATION

However, the story did contain a strong implicit reference to discrimination when it quoted me as urging students to become angry at the society which would have them be anything other than human beings. "Boyd attacked the conventional definition of sin. Most people, he said, think of sin as being only individual and do not realize that there is such a thing as cultural or social sin of which everyone is guilty."

An unusual feature of my visit was participation in a Religious Emphasis Week panel discussion on the topic "Prejudice and Exploitation in Our Society." The other panelists selected by the university were Prof. Robert Root of Syracuse University and Dr. Paul Young of the L.S.U. Psychology Department. The *Daily Reveille* report on the event included the following: "Presently the eyes of every country are turned toward America, Boyd said, and he explained that our solution of the problem [of race] will either 'make or break' us. Representing the theological viewpoint, Boyd said that racism is a continuation of exploitation and it is the Christian duty to ignore the viewpoint that certain races are inferior. He explained that there is nothing in Christian theology that suggests God created man unequally. 'We are not Christians because we want to be,' Boyd said, 'but because we are called to be. One of the hardest things to do is stand up for the Christian beliefs and let society crucify us if they wish.' "

My visit to Louisiana State University was rather hurried. In my week there I crowded in a number of speaking engagements, running the gamut: reading a paper to an art class, talking informally with fraternity men at dinners, meeting with dozens of dormitory residents, addressing a large faculty group. The editor of the student paper told me he had received one or two negative letters about my visit, but that they were too vulgar and inflammatory to publish. On the whole, though, there seemed to be an unusually good response from the students. In fact, they asked me to return to Louisiana several months later for an Educational Spring Conference at Silliman College in Clinton, under the sponsorship of the Student Christian Council of L.S.U. I accepted the invitation.

Several hundred brochures were printed announcing

the conference for May 8–9. My picture was included in
the brochure as conference leader. The text mentioned
me in the following way: ". . . [he] is no stranger to the
students of L.S.U. for many will remember his outstanding contribution in the 1959 Religious Emphasis Week
program. He is well qualified to lead a study on the
problem of communicating a relevant Gospel in today's
changing world."

In light of subsequent events, I find an unparalleled
irony in the announced "Purpose of the Conference"
included in the brochure:

> This conference seeks to assist the professed Christians
> on the L.S.U. campus in making a realistic survey of
> the meaning of Christian discipleship in the non-Chris-
> tian world that surrounds us. It will in no way attempt to
> avoid an honest, straightforward appreciation of the dif-
> ference in the various traditional concepts of the content
> of the Christian message, while it is hoped that many
> areas of agreement will be discovered . . .
>
> This conference is for you . . . if you have felt the need
> for a relevant application of Christian insights as to the
> nature of man in a world which is confused; if you believe
> that though our society, as limited as this campus or as
> wide as the world, needs a realistic appreciation of ulti-
> mate values as they pertain to daily life, yet the Church
> speaks with uncertain voice; if you yourself are an un-
> willing captive of a culture which is fragmented in its
> thought and you seek a unity of purpose and ideals for
> your life and of those about you.
>
> Now as never before the Church must speak prophet-
> ically to our age. This conference will seek to help you
> see what is involved in bringing this great need into a
> fulfilled reality in your life as well as the Church as a
> whole.

The brochures were destroyed.
The stencils of preliminary reports which I was as-

signing as preparatory reading for the conference never reached the Mimeograph—they were burned. It would have been meaningless to duplicate them, for the conference was canceled. The lofty idealism of the brochure was buried deep in the mire of racism.

I was told of the cancellation in a telephone call on April 19, from Baton Rouge. I was informed that, if I returned to L.S.U. for the conference, the university would not receive a million-dollar grant in state funds. A formal letter would be sent about the cancellation, but would not deal in specifics, its purpose being simply to confirm the telephone call.

The letter, signed by the coordinator of religious activities at the university, arrived on schedule, dated April 21. It noted that the staff members of the University Religious Council "deeply regret that the present situation makes it inadvisable to have such a conference at this time. . . . This is to confirm our telephone conversation of April 19 in which I related the circumstances that have necessitated our cancelling all arrangements for the Educational Spring Conference on May 8 and 9 at Silliman College."

A typist's notation on the letter indicated that a copy had been sent to Troy H. Middleton, president of the university. In a telephone conversation with the *New York Times,* Mr. Middleton declared that there was no truth in the charge that the university would have lost financial support if I had come. He said that he had not spoken to either the coordinator of religious activities or me, and declined further comment.

Mr. Middleton said a bit more in a telephone conversation with the Indianapolis *Times;* he termed my charges "ridiculous," but went on to add that "some people down here can't agree" with what he described as my anti-segregation stand.

I never heard again from the university. The *New York Times* reported the incident under the headline:

NORTHERN CLERIC
BARRED IN SOUTH

The *Times* also reported a second cancellation of a scheduled speaking engagement I had accepted in the South. Mississippi Southern College (now the University of Southern Mississippi) had invited me to lead its next Religious Emphasis Week. The Rev. John F. Nau, described as chaplain of the school's Student Christian Federation, wrote to me:

> . . . In the meantime, however, we received word of difficulties you met at Louisiana State University. We inquired into the nature of the difficulties and now feel that it would be an injustice to you and to the great cause of our program to have you appear as our principal speaker for 1960. Should the climate of our society change in the coming years, we will not only be proud but happy to present you as a main speaker of our Religious Emphasis Week.
>
> We pray that you understand fully the position in which we find ourselves doing the work of the church and of the Lord in an atmosphere that is filled with various tensions, which if unduly excited, will bring harm to the essence of our entire religious program.

I could only marvel at the perpetuation of Religious Emphasis Weeks devoid of religious emphasis. Hypocrisies such as those in the Mississippi letter on "doing the work of the church and of the Lord" seemed to be dreadful skeletons proclaiming the post-Christian era and the death of God in the lives of men.

From Greenland's icy mountains,
    From India's coral strand,

Where Afric's sunny fountains
    Roll down their golden sand,
From many an ancient river,
    From many a palmy plain,
They call us to deliver
    Their land from error's chain.

Can we, whose souls are lighted
    With wisdom from on high,
Can we to men benighted
    The lamp of life deny?
Salvation, O salvation!
    The joyful sound proclaim,
Till each remotest nation
    Has learnt Messiah's name.

Waft, waft, ye winds, his story,
    And you, ye waters, roll,
Till, like a sea of glory,
    It spreads from pole to pole;
Till o'er our ransomed nature
    The Lamb for sinners slain,
Redeemer, King, Creator,
    In bliss returns to reign.

> Hymn 254,
> The Hymnal of the
> Protestant Episcopal Church
> in the United States
> of America

In commenting on the two cancellations, I told the *New York Times:* ". . . when one becomes involved in such a situation, one must make a choice either to condone evil or stand up and fight for truth. . . . It is saddening as well as frightening for me to see such an example of fascistic tendencies, thought control, irresponsible slander and campus McCarthyism."

One extremely encouraging incident that emerged from these events was a student action taken a few days later. Smiley Anders, then editor of the L.S.U. *Daily Reveille,* denounced the university's move in an outspoken interview with the New York *Post.* He courageously criticized what he termed "the secret cancellation of a scheduled speech," pointing out that not even he, although editor of the student paper, was aware of the cancellation until notified of it by me nearly three weeks later.

"This incident shows a great lack of courage on the part of so-called religious leaders who have maintained silence about the news event," he told the *Post.* "When the racial problem can no longer be discussed, a great evil has been allowed to take hold in the south." Anders continued by saying that, in my February address, I had shown "a great deal of compassion and a desire to create much-needed understanding between men. This is something in the south we desperately need."

The incident was closed, but because of it the course of my life had taken a different turn. I started to examine what it means to be a human being and, conversely, what it means to be dehumanized. This episode, more than any other, led to my serious involvement in the freedom struggle.

I remember an elderly black priest, now deceased, whom I knew rather well. We were having drinks and relaxing late one night. He had been addressing me as Malcolm, so I quite naturally used his first name. "Please, Malcolm," he said, "call me Father. It's all I've got."

It was 3 A.M. in McComb, Mississippi on October 1, 1964. I was standing guard in the shadows alongside a freedom house, keeping the night watch to prevent a recurrence of the dynamite explosion three weeks before that had threatened students' lives. Seventeen "hate" telephone calls had been received from the preceding midnight to 7 A.M.—eight of them death threats. Since the start of the summer sixteen bombings had rocked McComb and, to date, there had been no arrests in connection with any of them. (The F.B.I. would, in fact, order the first arrests a few days later.) Now, standing by the freedom house in the middle of the night, I tensed when I heard a sound—a dog barking, footsteps, a car approaching. I was forty years old, white, and Establishment. I learned something in McComb, Mississippi; I learned how fragile a thing is security.

In another Mississippi town the black home I stayed in had eight bullet holes in the front screen door and another dozen imbedded in a front bedroom wall. Angry whites, deciding to punish a militant black whose son had enrolled in a Northern university, showered bullets into his house one night without warning. They barely missed hitting the man and his wife in their bed. Although many whites in the community knew who made the attack, there were no arrests. Thus I came upon the question of violence, not academically, but firsthand.

I had just returned from a tour of the black communities in eight towns in Mississippi, two in eastern Arkansas and four in Alabama. Blacks lived "across the tracks" in conditions which made "God Bless America" seem a sad joke. Whites drove the new cars, lived in the nice, air-conditioned homes, held down the jobs that mattered, went to the drive-in movies, controlled the news printed in local newspapers, ate in the pleasant restaurants, relied on the cops to harass blacks and keep them down, told most ministers what they could preach in church pulpits, and, in countless ways, made the lives of blacks a literal burning hell *here*. The black youths I met were articulate about black nationalism and hatred of everything white. Malcolm X was deeply imbedded in the consciousness of this Southern black generation. I found a determination to meet violence with violence, if necessary, to defend family and home from unprovoked attack.

Violence was always present—whether overt or lurking just beneath the surface—in the South during the summer of 1965. In Selma, Alabama, I was in a car with seven black men and women. The driver asked a white filling-station attendant to clean the window shield. "I can't," the white man said. "Don't you have paper towels? Don't you have water and soap?" the black driver angrily asked. "I can't," the white man repeated, coldly resisting offering anything but strictly minimal service. "We won't pay if we don't get service," the black man said. "You'll pay or I'll call the sheriff—there's a police car right over there," replied the white man, his voice going out of control. We paid and left, having shared just one more galling encounter in Selma, where, after the previous spring's marching and publicity, the lot of the blacks was grimly unchanged. In Natchez, Mississippi, stopping at a filling station to get gas, we were confronted by signs reading FOR WHITES ONLY over the drinking fountain and restrooms. Two days later, driving to McComb, we visited another filling station. A young black SNCC worker in our group had stopped by the drinking fountain when a white attendant told him, "Boy, you can't drink water out of that fountain. If you want a drink, use a paper cup."

During the summer I was in Mississippi and Alabama with SNCC, I lived and worked—shared my life—with four young men, all of them black and long-time veterans of the freedom movement. One had been sentenced once to a chain gang for a civil rights offense, and all had long experiences of jails, police brutality and rejection by white society. They told me at the outset, "We can't make it with a white this close and for this long a time. You're not Negro. So you're going to have to be a nigger with us." In the eyes of White Power, we were niggers together. In practice, we lived as niggers: sleeping on shack floors, eating (if we were lucky) one meal a day given us by a poor black family, harassed by the police, our safety threatened many times.

One July morning, driving between Selma and Marion, we had a flat tire. We realized our jack was broken. Asking for help at a filling station across the highway, we were told there was no jack in the place. Within a half hour, several trucks filled with "crackers" (as poor whites who hate blacks are called by blacks) drove into the filling station. All had shotguns. Then two crop duster planes started flying over our car, swooping low over treetops, examining and frightening us. We suddenly realized we were in real danger, yet there was no way for us to help ourselves. No white car passing would stop to help us; two black cars drove by, but if they were locals the whites surely would not permit them to assist us. Then a car filled with black civil rights workers happened to come along. We borrowed a jack, put on a spare tire and got out of there. But it had been a highly unpleasant situation, ominous in its potential danger.

The first Sunday morning of that summer I got up and planned to go to church. The white church was over *there* somewhere, a part of the power structure which oppressed blacks. Living with black youths who expressed their hatred of whites in dozens of ways each day, I constantly had to remind myself where they had learned their hate, and how. Being with them, I learned to see things more clearly through their eyes. What was I to do on Sunday morning? Leave my brothers, with whom I shared life and the fear of death, and go to meet "God" in a building which was angrily closed to them? Did Christ come only to the whites in their private club, in the rigidly prescribed form of bread and wine administered by an ordained priest? Was Christ not also with *us*, the four young men of SNCC and I, in the broken-down wooden shack in which we had spent the night with an impoverished black family? Eating bread and drinking coffee together, did we not "receive" Christ? At such a moment, I could see the distance I had traveled inside myself, from the days when I worried about chewing the Communion wafer.

Violence is so much the more cruel when it strikes those dedicated to nonviolence. Some of the men and women I knew, who had been working for freedom in a peaceful way, were murdered. Sammy Younge, Jr., was the first black college student to die in the black liberation movement; our lives came into contact when I was asked by SNCC to join the Freedom Singers for a mass meeting at Tuskegee Institute in Alabama in 1965, to assist in a community movement of which Younge was a leader.

A telephone call from United Press International awakened me in the middle of the night Viola Liuzzo was shot. We had known each other at Wayne State University. Did I have a comment for the press? She had been influenced in her decision to go to Alabama, the reporter said, by something I had said in a talk.

Jonathan Daniels, a white seminary student, was murdered at Hayneville, Alabama, on Friday, August 20, 1965. Three weeks before Jon's death, he came to Brown's Chapel in Selma for a performance of a play I wrote and afterward we drank beer and talked very late.

Then I went to Los Angeles when the Watts revolt began. The day I left Los Angeles, I purchased a newspaper before boarding the plane; after the takeoff, I opened it. The headline announced Jon's murder.

I remembered my last night in Selma when he had dropped me by the home of a black family with whom I was staying. As he drove away, he waved good-bye from the car window. I recalled, that morning on the plane out of Los Angeles, his buoyancy, freshness, determination, faith and idealism—but he was *not* the plaster saint some people later made him out to be. He was vital, human, and made life a celebration; his murder was illogical, rapacious and mad. I could not, in that moment, accept his death. (Why was *this* student killed? He had held within his life such vigorous hope for the life and work of a renewed society . . .) So I put down the newspaper, and, placing earphones over my ears, listened for an hour to taped jazz on the plane. I found that I was weeping. Then I faced and accepted what had to be faced and accepted. Within a few days, I joined others—including Stokely Carmichael, James Forman and the Rev. John Morris of the Episcopal Society for Cultural and Racial Unity—to be with Jon's mother at his funeral in Keene, New Hampshire.

Stokely shared with me some notes he had made, during the funeral ceremony in church, on the back of the printed program: "Jon was not a religious man. He lived a religious life. Jon did not die for us all. His life was taken from him. Jon lived for us all. Jon did not get his strength from rituals. He got his strength from people. From whence cometh my strength? My strength cometh not from the hills. My strength cometh from men like Jon. Jon was not a follower of Christ. He lived like Christ."

My involvement in the freedom movement has often

meant fearing death—even as word has come that friends have been murdered in the struggle. I have known the fear of death in a Mississippi town, bunking with a black freedom fighter in a black home—and the whites in that town knew *just* where I was—listening to the stillness of the night outside, the wind blowing through the leaves which sounded like paper; shadows seemed to move across the window and my heart pounded: what would they do to us if they dragged us out underneath the trees? I didn't want to die. I didn't want to suffer. Yet I had to be *here,* because not to be here would be worse than merely dying.

I have known the fear sleeping alone in a big house in the middle of a small, rural Southern town where I had that day spoken publicly in favor of racial intermarriage and denounced white injustice; I lay in bed listening to creaking old wooden stairs, watching the moonlight try to shine through heavy green foliage outside my window.

I have known the fear riding alone in a taxi from the airport of a Southern city, through a desolate, abandoned stretch of land, to a black downtown hotel—feeling that the white driver of the cab probably recognized me as a freedom fighter (from publicity in that day's newspaper and on TV) and I, not knowing who the driver was.

I have known the fear when I was the only white in a car filled with blacks, driving at midnight through Sunflower County, Mississippi, when we were suddenly followed by a car filled with whites. We were civil rights workers; were they Klanners, police (perhaps police *and* Klanners?), members of the White Citizens Council, or simply some people out for a drive in the cool night air? The car stayed behind us for many miles, then abruptly sped past, vanishing into the night ahead. Then, as we passed a lonely fork in the road, the car was waiting for us, its motor and lights turned off. In a moment the car was behind us again on the isolated, dark road. We could not know whether a roadblock was waiting on the highway ahead, and whether we would be dragged from our car and mercilessly killed. The rest of our journey was sober and tense because we remembered Andrew Goodman, James Chaney and Michael Schwerner had been driving on a Mississippi road like this when they were stopped, beaten, and murdered. We feared a sudden attack by gunfire because we remembered how Lemuel A. Penn had been shot to death in his car. As we made our way through ghostlike towns, with the lights of TV sets flickering behind half-closed windows, we feared local police almost as much as danger on the highway.

In the North, sometimes the fear has been taut, cruel, and just as maddening. I have known the fear in a nice house on a nice street in a nice suburb. I rented the house one summer—it was located in the metropolitan area of a great Northern city—in order to complete work on a book. A black friend drove me to the house, stayed for supper, then departed. I was to be alone for an entire week, working in isolation. Then the telephone rang. No one I knew had the number. When I picked up the receiver and said hello, I received no response—only heavy breathing. Was this a joke? I talked to the caller. Only the same heavy breathing came through the receiver. After quite a while I hung up. The telephone rang again. I said hello. The heavy breathing again. I hung up. It rang again. I said hello and listened, longer now, then hung up. Again. I let it ring for one, two, three, four, five minutes before picking up the receiver. I pleaded with the caller: What had I *done,* what was the *reason* for this persecution? (I knew the reason; the reason was a nigger driving into this neighborhood in the liberal North and stopping for supper at this house.) I was terrified by the unknown person who could permit himself to be so driven by hate and possible madness. The calls continued. One, two, three, four, five, six times. Then I realized that he *must have seen my friend* —so the caller must live nearby, might be looking right now at this house.

Not long before coming to this house, I had attended the funeral of Medgar Evers in Jackson, Mississippi. Arriving early on the morning of the funeral, I had stood outside the Evers' home. It looked like a house on a Norman Rockwell cover for the *Saturday Evening Post,* clean, friendly, pleasant. Only it had a bullet hole in a windowpane. Across from the Evers' home was a field of tall grass; the murderer had crouched there with a gun, stalking his victim. *This* house, so neat-looking on the nice street in the nice suburb, looked like a Norman Rockwell home too; *this* house (the telephone was ring-ing again) had next to it a field of tall grass, extending all the way to the next street. Answering in despair now, I shouted into the phone: Leave me alone, what do you want with me, what's the matter with you, why don't you tell me who you are, are you sick, why do you hate me . . .

I tried to sleep at night. I felt a cold breeze coming in through the window from the field of tall grass. My room was in inky blackness; if I put on a light, it could show someone where I lay; if I did not put on a light, I would wait here in terror until sleep came from exhaustion. (The telephone rang.) Morning brought no relief, for light without cheer can be a mocking thing; the morning light was flat and stony. (The telephone rang.) I stayed on inside that house. I did my work. And from time to time the telephone rang. One, two, three, four, five, six

times. I let it ring. After several weeks, when I had
finished my work, I left.

A white man cannot know what it means to be a black
man in America. But he can know what it means to be
rejected by other whites, and at the same time be unacceptable to blacks except on the basis of a particular
friendship or else on a "celebrity" basis as a freedom
fighter. In other words, *a white can learn what living in
limbo means.*

A long time ago I had to ask myself how I could
straddle the two "worlds," finding that I was not exactly
welcome in either. Black nationalist friends told me I
should work not in the black society, but the white, in
order to accomplish basic objectives that only a white
can. (Agreeing with them, I have followed their advice.)
I could get along superficially with "Negro society," I
found, if I would stick to variations on a white liberal
role; but I couldn't do it, so the formal arrangement of
my Negro-white relations was toppled. I was no longer
the "safe" white man to serve on distinguished inter-
racial boards which implicitly adhered to certain approved hypocrisies. But I was in strong demand as a
one-shot "hot" speaker, expected to say things others
would not say. (It was tacitly agreed these things *should*
be said.) After I had left, the pieces would be picked up,
apologies made, certain "truths" publicly affirmed, and
the speaker forgiven—with damningly polite smiles—
his eccentric gaucheries.

It's time for the news.
  The first Negro conductor performed brilliantly last
     night
  The knee-gro novelist explained his position
  The ne-grow jurist addressed the women's club

The nee-gro priest said Mass
The ne-grooow basketball star drew an ovation
The nigra jazzman made the audience weep
Do you have a place for a Negro on your TV series?
No. We've got one. We've already got our knee-gro.
Mr. President, do you believe this great democracy is
    ready to have its first Negro Vice-President, sir?
No. I believe we must first have our first Jew, and
    secondly our first woman.
Thank you, Mr. President.

I simply could not be counted on, by anybody, to
adhere to a defined line, wear a mask as if it were my
face, and avoid trouble by staying within the stockade
of predetermined ideas. I thought and felt white; I
thought and felt black. Richard English, a friend who is
black and with whom I shared an apartment in Detroit
for several years, looking at me in a moment of mutual
suffering in the racial dilemma said, "You've just
changed your color." But, of course, I hadn't. This was
just another way of saying that I had obliterated roles
and their concomitant emotions.

It was at a tiny, segregated all-white church that I first
realized many people thought I was black. I had
preached there that Sunday morning. All the people
present were parishioners, with the exception of two
visiting women, one white and one black. Afterward,
at the coffee hour, I was chatting with them when a
white lady approached the black woman and asked,
"Do you take cream in your coffee, Mrs. Boyd?" She
was taken aback at the question, and made only a
perfunctory response. Later, she wished that she had
replied, "I'm not his wife. I'm his sister." On another
occasion, at a church social following a talk I had
made in an all-white parish, a lady came up to me

somewhat belligerently. I remember she was carrying a pot of coffee and wearing long earrings. "What *are* you?" she asked. "We have a right to know." I said, "Honey, I'm Black Irish."

After leaving Detroit I moved to Washington, D.C., where I served as assistant to a black priest in a black church (in addition to acting as a field director for the Episcopal Society for Cultural and Racial Unity). It was Christmas morning at 2 o'clock in this black church. The midnight Christmas Eve Eucharist had been celebrated and now several members of the parish were seated around a table, enjoying late supper. We were talking about our reactions to a public event. I broke in to say, "As a white, I feel . . ." A black lady interrupted me, "*You're* not *white!*" I replied, "Of course, I'm white. You know I'm white. What are you talking about?" She said, "No, I never think of you as white." We laughed. It was considered very funny.

More than a year later a black priest told me, "Everyone in the church considers you black." I replied, "But they can't. They know I'm white. Everybody *knows* I'm white." He said, "No, they all think of you as black. It's because you're a part of the family. And it's because of what you have shared with them." We had shared a lot. I had been so outspokenly in favor of Black Power, in fact, that one black lady was overheard telling another at a coffee hour, "I like Father Boyd, but don't you think he's *pushing* too fast?"

I shall always remember the Requiem Eucharist I said in that church for Jon Daniels. Tired out after a summer's tense and grueling work in the deep South with SNCC and grieving deeply at the death of yet another friend in the movement, I had nearly broken down as I stood before the altar.

I was the sole white man inside the black hotel in a Mississippi town. Some of us were looking at the TV in the lobby. A commercial came on the screen. "Bleach white," the announcer's voice said. Then as the voice went on and on the effect became Kafka-esque—"Bleach WHITE." "Bleach WHITE." "Bleach WHITE."

Friends of mine, who are black, were purchasing a goldfish bowl and some goldfish. I accompanied them to the store. "We want *two* black ones," they told the clerk who was taking the fish out of a large tank. "That way, we won't leave a black one all alone."

It amazes me that whites feel betrayed when a white man speaks the truth about racial injustice. I have seen the tense, hurt looks in the eye of whites, telling me I am the betrayer. But they assume a race loyalty which I long ago renounced. They assume that I will honor a fundamental immorality, and that my religion is only a matter of personal piety.

Several years ago when I was asked to preach in a great cathedral, I looked out over a sea of white faces. I knew from past experience that resentment would change smiles into frowns when I began to repeat—again—the teaching of Christianity about humanness and social justice—especially as applied to blacks. At the cathedral door, when I waited to shake hands with them, people would act out their anger and disturbance in different ways: some would hurry past, averting their eyes; others would comment, "It was a very enjoyable sermon"; a few would look into my face, hard, making no comment, then abruptly turn away. (Once, at another cathedral door, a lady had smiled, pulled her furs about her, and said simply, "You son of a bitch," then walked outside, still smiling.) I have felt fatigued to the point of physical weakness and spiritual numbness in such confrontations.

Another time, during a church service, I was outraged to come upon a line in a hymn referring to "white angels." Who has captured an angel to give it a color test? What madness is encased in our revered traditions? (Many hymns were written at the time the slave trade was flourishing; many bishops owned slaves.) I like what a European artist created, in reaction to a Negro spiritual which asks why all angels have white faces. He made a stained-glass window for a church, with a panel in it depicting a black angel—playing a saxophone.

Opportunities to be the "betrayer" among whites crop up less in relaxed black-white social situations—there are very few of these—than at the average mixed get-togethers. These annual community-relations talkathons usually boast an immense dinner complete with head table, a mayor, religious leaders, awards, a chief of police, corsages, and an atrocious musical ensemble or singing group. It is here that one can betray with a vengeance. I have always sensed the futility of these slick, managed conferences on "race" or "poverty," where people drink, talk, dine in luxury, and issue press releases together. One finds their manipulation of news as rigid as their control over discussion outside defined limits. Virtually nothing happens in the mysteriously important areas of human relations and grass-roots social change. At one such conference, a white professional woman finally turned to a black woman seated next to her, and glancing at her watch, said, "Look, it's getting late. It would save a lot of time if you people would just tell us what you want."

Invariably some token blacks are sprinkled about the

head table at these functions. On one occasion, however, I recall that the head table was snow-white, with black attendance primarily to be found in the upper-right-hand corner of the banquet hall. The white audience had been brought to the brink of hysteria by my remarks as betrayer. A black lady coolly walked the length of the hall, came up to me at the segregated head table, and in full view of the nervous assemblage kissed me on the mouth. She said the truth had been spoken publicly in that town for the first time in the thirty-five years she could personally recall. The other people at the head table seemed swiftly to vanish into thin air, the clergymen were suddenly nowhere to be seen, and I was efficiently whisked away to a car which drove me home, two hundred miles away, through the night.

Once I was to speak on the announced topic of "Civil Rights" to a group of upper-middle-class, suburban whites. I was accompanied by several black students from a nearby university who wished to hear the talk. The meeting was precipitated into a mood of sullen hostility when a white person openly asked, "How can we talk about civil rights with Negroes present?"

A very different kind of gathering of whites and blacks was a series of informal conversations held in my Detroit apartment during the winter and spring of 1963. The sessions were intended to explore the lack of communication between the races—a problem that was often felt at the sessions themselves. About seventy-five people sat around, on the carpet or in the few available chairs, sipping coffee and chatting in small groups; they were jammed close together, for the apartment was small. A Black Muslim might find himself in a group with a still very tentative and shy white moderate, a middle-class Negro active in the NAACP, a black militant holding membership in CORE, a Jewish student working with SNCC, and a Negro clergyman belonging to the Establishment.

After a while the various small groups would all join together in a single large group. One night we listened to a tape recording of speeches by Malcolm X and William Worthy. A clinical psychologist working in the Detroit Public School System, also editor of a black nationalist journal, then gave his views. Immediately everyone was caught up in a discussion lasting for more than seven hours. A group of black youths belonging to an organization called "Uhuru" expressed their opposition to whites, speaking bluntly and without pretense. They seemed not to have had a previous opportunity to say these things to whites. They became impassioned, describing their feelings and recounting their experiences. This part of the evening took almost four hours. Gradually their anger subsided; they spoke less vehemently, fewer of them had incidents to relate, and quite suddenly they had finished. There was silence in the apartment. No whites were waiting to jump in with a rebuttal. There was no element of racial face-saving.

Soon some whites—quietly and tentatively at first, because of their guilt and fear—picked up the discussion with the black youths. Again the exchange reached a peak of tension. There were angry shouts. A white student, nearly crying, stood up. She was ready to go. "I do not intend to remain here any longer to be insulted by these Negroes," she said to the group. "But before I go, I want to say to them, that despite their rudeness, I shall continue giving my life to underprivileged Negro youth." A black woman, seated on the floor, said "Sheeit." Everybody roared. After a moment, the white student laughed and sat down again. She later told the group that she learned more about American blacks during the course of that single evening than in four years at the University of Michigan. She became a regular at the apartment conference sessions.

A black social worker, present at that meeting, said the discussion made her realize how she had suppressed her real feelings and played a false role in order to accommodate the white world in which she had to earn her living. Then a black man started telling about his experiences as a G.I. in World War II. As he fought to save democracy he had had to eat in the kitchen of an American restaurant, while white Nazi prisoners were served in the dining room. "I hate whites," he said. His arms were around his blond, white wife.

During the course of a radio interview in New York, I mentioned the need for black and white dialogue, and said I believed it was necessary to hear the Black Muslim view as well as that of the white suburban home-owner, the middle-class professional Negro, the black student, and so on. My hate mail from that single broadcast represented an incredible mixture of epithets. I was "a Black Muslim," "a communist," "an s.o.b.," "a nigger-lover"—but who had *heard* me? Or perhaps this very hostility indicated that a great many *had* heard.

One day at a black rally in downtown Detroit, I met Wilfred X, who was the leader of the Black Muslims in the city, and a brother of Malcolm X. We had a pleasant conversation and made plans to have lunch together the next Tuesday. When we met neither of us really wanted to eat lunch. Instead we went to my apartment, and I made coffee. We talked for four hours. I was impressed by his kindness and apparent lack of any pretense or desire to impose barriers between us.

He did not fit my image of a Muslim according to the gospel of the mass media. That is to say, he was not an angry, lean man with a mustache, wearing shades to cover his eyes, garbed in a tight, Italian-cut suit, carrying a mysterious black brief-case (with a gun?), and accompanied either by a counterpart or a police dog. Wilfred X was amiably relaxed, his loose-fitting suit might have been worn by an insurance salesman in Dearborn, his glasses permitted a close look at his eyes, and he was alone.

We spoke candidly and easily. When he was leaving, I told him that he fitted my picture of one of the early Christians: deeply committed to his beliefs, remarkably kind in relationships with nonbelievers, and trusting more in the efficacy of personal witness than in hard dogma or hard sell. That day Wilfred X promised to return to my apartment for a session with a group of whites and blacks. He kept his promise, and the result was an empathetic and creative confrontation.

On another occasion in my Detroit apartment, a group of blacks and whites engaged in a discussion about Black Muslims. The conversation went like this:

"They're not really a hate movement at all," someone said. "This is altogether a false image."

"Not a hate movement!" someone countered. "Why, all they stand for is hate of the white man. They hate any kind of integrationist. All you have to do is listen to a Muslim if you say they're not a hate movement."

"No, they don't preach hate," the first man replied. "All they preach is separation of the blacks until we have enough strength to stand up against the whites as equals. When we're finally really equal, then it will be time to talk about any relations with the whites."

Someone else piped in. "The Black Muslims want to set up a separate state somewhere in the U.S. with an outlet to the sea. All the blacks will be invited to live in this new state."

"That's ridiculous," came a rejoinder. "The Muslims aren't talking about any separate geographical state.

They want a psychological separation instead, with blacks living isolated from the whites socially and economically, yet maybe living with whites in the same city."

"I don't understand any of this at all," a white man in the group said. "Isn't it of fundamental importance for all of us to be human beings first, and then worry after that whether we're Negro or white or something else? If we place ourselves or each other into neat racial categories, it will be too late for us to make it as human beings. To understand ourselves as human beings is the most important thing of all."

"But you can't stand there claiming to be a human being," someone retorted, "if you're a Southern black and a white cop is beating you over the head with a police stick."

"It could be a Northern black and a Northern white cop just as easily," a voice chimed in.

"Of course," came the reply. "But what's a Negro or a white man, anyway? I mean, after several hundred years of integration after dark, who can talk about purity of race?"

"That's all well and good," somebody across the room opined, "but if the color of your skin isn't white, then you're black. At least in this society."

"Okay, okay!" Someone else was speaking. "But it's impossible at this stage to separate one American from another American. We're all in this thing together. We have to share the guilt and the hurt and the possibilities for change. None of us has any choice at all but to do this."

"How can you as a white man say that to me as a black?" came the fast reply. "What's this American jazz all about, man? You talk about sharing guilt and hurt with you. Man, that's all I *can* share with you. You sure as hell aren't sharing other things with me. Are you? Tell me what!"

A new voice was heard. "What bothers me is the corrupting self-righteousness of the Muslims or any segregationists who feel they are better than anybody else. I am suspicious of anybody who feels he has a corner on purity and righteousness. That, in fact, is the most corrupting sin of all."

"But the black man is better than anybody else. He has preserved his virtues. He is more moral than a white man."

"What! More *moral?* Why, that's ridiculous."

Another man joined in. "There is a culture lag in the Negro community. This accounts, in great part, for a certain moral quality still found in the Negro culture which is not found in the white society. Whites are more competitive, aggressive, and they're colder."

"Blacks have soul," someone said. "Whites can never have it."

The talk went on and on. Some said they welcomed the Black Muslims as a protest movement, others claimed the Muslims were not a protest movement, and still others expressed agreement with much of the Black Muslim code of racial separation.

Shortly after this discussion I visited Beirut, Lebanon, where I spoke at the American University under the sponsorship of the Friendship International Club. I was temporarily banned from the American University because of a talk I gave about racism in the United States. The following morning a policeman approached me as I was seated in the student union and asked, "Are you Malcolm Boyd?" I said yes. "Do you want to walk off the campus or be carried off?" I allowed as how I would walk off. The incident remained a mystery to me. The ban was soon lifted, and I received a formal written letter of apology along with full permission to visit the campus whenever I liked.

Afterward I was invited to address several hundred African students at the Sudanese consulate. As I entered into conversation with African Moslems in Beirut, I was told they were in natural sympathy with the American Black Muslims and their cause of freedom with its emphasis on "the black mystique"; yet these Moslems pointed out to me that Islam welcomes white as well as black members. They worried that the Black Muslim emphasis on segregation of the races might tend to distort or tarnish the image of Islam in the United States and elsewhere in the Western world.

I traveled eleven hundred miles through rural Mississippi in December, 1964 with William Jacobs, a writer. We co-authored a series of articles for *Ave Maria* which won an award from the National Catholic Press Association. Jacobs and I drove down country lanes at night, talking to black people living in the shacks of rural slums. (Several years later, walking in "Resurrection City" in Washington, D.C., during the Poor People's Campaign, I noted that the temporary shacks along the muddy streets there were no worse—and in Washington there were three meals a day and good volunteer medical care.) Then I realized that the "moral leaders" of Mississippi—including church officials—had decided not to know what was happening. For we came upon horror story after horror story of degradation and misery. Church leaders fifty miles away remained blind and deaf, *and did not know*. This reminded me of the church leaders in Nazi Germany who did not know.

Would I be nonviolent if I were living in Nazi Germany?

I wonder how Jews felt when the real pressure
started.
After they were attacked by people in the streets.
The cops didn't help them.
The cops were their enemies.
The cops hated them.
Then the laws began, and Jews couldn't have tele-
phones or ride buses or subscribe to newspapers
or eat in restaurants.
They had to wear a public identification.
Of course, a black face provides that in America.
I can't tell a black man to be nonviolent.
How nonviolent was Jesus?
I can't tell.
The Pasolini film showed him as a radical.
He wasn't like the Sunday-school stories. That's for
sure.
Gandhi used nonviolence.
Not as a technique or a gimmick. I despise that.
He tried it as a way of life for himself.
Gandhi broke up an empire, didn't he?

In 1965 when I was in Watts during its "riot," which I
prefer to call a revolt, I realized that the hopelessness of
the black people in Watts, and the causes underlying it,
were not comprehended by people who did not know the
ghetto conditions firsthand. *But why didn't they know?*
Communication had been virtually nonexistent between
poor blacks and the white power-structure including the
chief of the city's police and state congressional representatives. *Why?* With few exceptions, the churches of
Los Angeles had failed to provide moral leadership in
race relations. "Good" people had been hiding behind a
facade of religion devoid of prophetic utterance or social

involvement. *Why*? These people had virtually isolated themselves from personal confrontation with oppressed blacks. *Why*?

Sanctimonious pronouncements judged the rioting harshly but failed to examine the malaise that made it inevitable. Those same white Christians who had withheld freedom from blacks, whom they refused to know as neighbors and friends, were lost in fantasy concerning the real causes of the revolt. There were attempts to explain it away as the work of hoodlums or communists. There was a deliberate refusal to confess that perpetuation of black ghettos caused the outbreak. A community center in Watts summed up, ironically, and quite unintentionally, the problem of black second-class citizenship. Posted on its bulletin board was an advertisement for Avis rental cars, cut from a magazine. It read: "WHEN YOU'RE ONLY NO. 2, YOU TRY HARDER. OR ELSE. *Little fish have to keep moving all of the time. The big ones never stop picking on them.*"

"Separate but equal" education had not proved equal for the blacks I met in Watts. One high school offered only one language course, Spanish, and no drama instruction. Some black students had been told by teachers, "All you need is a shop course." (This is cruelly reminiscent of an incident recounted by Malcolm X in his autobiography.) One black youth told me, "I went all the way through high school without contact with any white person of my age. How can a white kid know me? We can't get together to know each other." A middle-aged Afro-American told me that on one occasion he was walking in the Watts area when two white policemen called out to him, "Come here, boy. Where are you going?" The Afro-American complained, "If we can't go here in Watts, where can we go?" A teen-ager told me that he was told by white cops, with no provocation, "Jump the fence, you black nigger. We're going to make you straighten up, boy."

A full-page advertisement appeared in the Los Angeles *Sentinel*, a Negro newspaper, signed by a white church group. It was in the form of a confession of guilt and wrong. (I wondered why the advertisement was not also placed in the Los Angeles *Times*, so that whites might be able to read it.) The word "freedom" appeared several times in the text. A black student stood behind me, reading the text over my shoulder. When we had finished, he commented, "I don't understand what they mean by freedom. Why do they talk about it at all? They've been free so long."

Notes of an Afro-American
White snow
> Lovely, pure white snow turned filthy black when people trampled it in the city streets.
> When I came up to Cleveland from Atlanta on the train as a kid, I could eat in the dining car. It was screened off from the white people in their dining area.

When I went to a state university in the North, there were less than ten black students and no blacks on the faculty. We were expected to play our black roles, keep in our place, work harder than whites, and expect less.

I couldn't have dated you then, Diane.
> I wouldn't have been lynched, only sent home.
> I didn't even have white male friends.

Once I sat in the Student Union for three hours without anybody seeing me.
> They spoke to each other but not to me.
> Finally I got up and walked out.
> Nobody saw me.

I even tried going to a church at the university, for
    company and that well-known Christian love.
I wasn't welcome.
Black Jesus, remember this.

Late one night in 1966 in a black nationalist coffeehouse in Atlanta I had a curious experience. A few years
earlier, I would have been greeted there as a brother and
fellow activist in the freedom movement; now I met a
solid wall of hostility. "Why did you ever mix with
blacks?" someone asked. "Why didn't you stay with the
whites and do your work where it's needed?" "I know
you. You were in Selma. Who asked you to go there?"
These questions overlooked the fact that, if I had not
mixed with blacks—shared food and jail, housing and
the fear of death—I would have been an unchanged
man with nothing to tell the whites. In that coffeehouse
I sat on a small stage, surrounded by young black men
who wore impassive, contemptuously cool expressions,
but were inwardly seething and furious. For nearly two
hours we maintained, they and I, jagged-edged monologues. Inside that room we shared, without acknowl-
edging it, our condition as cripples and deeply wounded
people within an abrasive, ailing, but still creative and
hopeful society. In that stifling room, packed with young
blacks, I was a bug impaled on a pin; I squirmed, tried to
get my breath, felt my face burning with frustration and
rage, and stayed. Not wanting to interfere with the dynamics of the situation, I waited for the experience to
play itself out. Finally, when there had been no toe-hold
gained, no ally who revealed himself, no grace given, I
stood up to leave. No one would shake my hand. In
microcosm, I was all the white men and women in the
world.
    Outside, the middle-class black priest who had accom-

panied me took my arm and said, "Thanks for sharing my crucifixion with me." The next day I learned that the group in the coffeehouse had remained there for hours after I left. Immediately after my departure I was drawn and quartered. But when the ritual slaughter was completed, someone in the back of the room—far away from the tight circle which had hemmed me in around the stage—asked, "Why didn't you let us hear him speak?" The group was then gripped by debate for hours into the night. Perhaps the most important part of the experience, in my opinion, was what I can only call its redemptive aspect. I had endured, for a brief stretch of time, what blacks have endured for centuries, lifetimes, years, months, weeks, days, and hours. In a museum of horrors, my finger had only been scratched.

On another night, in a city with a particularly bad record in race relations, I asked a group of middle-class Negroes and whites to steer me to a conversation with local black nationalists. They said they didn't know any. "You've had what you call a riot here," I told them. "Do you suppose if we look under a rock, maybe a black nationalist will crawl out?" Finally, they made some phone calls and located a contact for me. Soon I found myself inside a slum bar in the black ghetto.

"Hello, white man," a large black man shouted at me over the deafeningly loud jukebox rock. "What do you want to know, white man? What can I tell you, white man?"

"Nothing, man," I replied. "I just came by to get acquainted. Let's put our white ass and black ass down together and get acquainted."

We did. I found that he was a leader representing dozens of ghetto black people, yet middle-class Negroes and whites who worked in "civil rights" in that town had never heard his name. We had a rewarding conversation. Like me, he felt the futility of the damask-table-cloth approach to race relations—those luncheons in smart hotels where hand-picked, predictably safe Negroes and whites "discussed" race under the watchful eye of an Establishment chairman, hemmed in by a time limit and an eight-point agenda.

More Notes of an Afro-American
Blacks were here before the Kennedys.
> I want to know about us. Where we came from; who we were; what we did. I want to know about Africa.
> Look at white beauty contests.

Black is beautiful.
> They want blacks to fix their hair white.
> Talk white Think white Feel white
> I dressed up to please whites and get along with them.

Only they were all the time thinking nigger.
> Nigger, you did that job real well, also your suit is clean, your hair is neat, and your shoes are shined.

Nigger, you can carry on a pretty good conversation and you don't smell.
> Nigger, you don't seem to be carrying a gun and you went to college.

Nigger, you sure do impress me for a nigger.

All the while my stated concern was to "help Negroes," I didn't realize how much help *I* needed. Dwelling in a nation where freedom was not yet a reality, I myself could not be a free person. I had graduated from high school and college, and had earned two graduate degrees, but was just beginning to find out how much I had to learn about life in America and, consequently, my own life. Unfortunately I was far from alone in being the victim of inadequate education and cultural isolation.

I found a tragic situation of racial discrimination and ignorance in a distinguished Northern prep school for boys run by, of all things, the church. One of the country's best small liberal arts colleges is a short distance away; it imports, throughout the school year, some of the best-known Negroes in the country to address and meet with its students. Not a single black guest speaker had ever been invited, however, to address the prep-school boys—including a prominent clergyman of the same denomination as the prep school. So the boys, all of whom are future leaders in their communities, were inadequately prepared for the world into which they must soon move. They were kept ignorant of black history and culture and deprived of personal contact with black men and boys. (Such an everyday embarrassment as a white barber's not knowing how to cut a black man's hair would be unknown to them.) Their image of "Negro" was out of the American middle ages. One wondered what the church assumed was involved in providing these white boys with a "moral" indoctrination. Morality at the prep school seemed, in fact, to mean just one thing: relations between the boys and girls of a similar age in a nearby female academic institution.

When I met some of the boys at the school, I was confronted with two basic attitudes toward race relations: first, a hungry desire to become informed, coupled with an anger with the school for providing an amputated education in this matter; second, an erratic hostility toward the outsider who was introducing alien ideas about human relations which could disturb the status quo a number of the young men obviously intended to maintain, along traditional lines of class, race, and success.

At a well-known, highly reputable Northern preparatory school for young women, also church-run, a top administrative official told me how she had asked the girls—all whites—to place their heads down on their desks. She then directed two questions to them, asking them to raise their hands by way of response. The first question was: "Would you object to having a Negro student in the school? If so, please raise your right hand." Approximately one-third raised their hands. The second question was: "Would you object to having a Negro student as a roommate? If so, please raise your right hand." This time one-half of the girls so responded. And yet nothing was being done in that school to inform the young women about black culture or introduce them to initial personal contacts with black people.

The headmaster of a well-known private elementary school—again, located in the North and run by the church—told me the bishop had asked him to "integrate." He had replied to the bishop that if he had to get along without the white money which would obstinately oppose such a move it would be necessary for him to close down the school. "The bishop hasn't mentioned integration to me since," he said, smiling. As I saw it, the students at these exclusive, prestigious schools were actually "underprivileged."

Like these students and most other whites, I was ignorant of the most elementary facts of black life in America. For example, a black friend of mine had a brother who had not advanced successfully in terms of employment. Using a favorite white phrase, I remarked that I felt the brother "lacked motivation." My friend looked at me closely. "No, you're wrong," he said, "his problem is that he *has* motivation." Motivation, without an opportunity to do anything about it.

In the operation of The System I could perceive only tacit justice. After all, wasn't it the best the world had ever known? Violence was only something ugly and vicious in the streets, pitted against "law and order." It had never occurred to me that violence might be found in The System, as well as on the streets. Law and order really meant *white* law and order to me.

When it finally came, my awakening was abrupt and —yes—rude. My learning experience was a careening, fast-moving ride. In the process, I became—as a white man—something of a black nationalist. And remain so —I still think blacker than white, and probably always shall.

As I looked out on the world with fresh vision, I was particularly stunned when I perceived the white rationalization for the whole demonic process. At the core of this, I saw a perverted Christianity, stressing private morality and blotting out public morality; with its white Jesus, and its caesaropapist whoredom to local power structures.

Old myths had made me blind to the beauty of black. Now I learned about black culture and history, from books, but more importantly from people. Embarking on a freedom ride, and taking part in various other demonstrations, I was still acting paternalistically. I learned now that the freedom movement existed not simply to incorporate black people into an unchanged American way of life, but to restructure that way of life itself— away from the threat of dehumanization toward accentuated humanness.

Black Power became for me a symbol of breaking out from behind bars, human defense against inhuman violence, and an offensive for social, political and eco-

nomic rights. I felt that it included elements of Booker
T. Washington, W. E. B. DuBois, Malcolm X, Martin
Luther King, Jr., and Eldridge Cleaver.

Strangely, as I look back over the years, I cannot
recall much hullaballoo about White Power. I do not
remember agonized editorials and sermons, angry coun-
tenances at cocktail parties, and ecstatic rumors. No,
White Power didn't even exist by name; nor did Black
Power—that convenient reservoir of energy tapped at
will by white society.

How can a white react to Black Power? Precisely by
working to achieve it as an historical necessity and a
moral right. There has been entirely too much naive,
do-gooder talk about "integration" and a glaringly insuf-
ficient practice of it on the basis of genuine equality. A
number of whites are now working with blacks as fellow
humans to achieve that psychological, political and economic power (Black Power) which is a prerequisite for
the social equality necessary for *true* integration. What
many whites seem not to understand is that a highly
sophisticated form of integration can be found in a tacti-
cal separation, in given situations, for the sake of a
mutually accepted goal.

A film called 5½ depicts a boy, five and one-half and
black, looking at himself in a mirror: "I don't like me—I
don't like my black face, kinky hair and thick lips." How
spiritually rotten must the society be which could teach
this child self-hatred. How can he be healed, and relate
black to dignity, strength, and beauty, if a white man
(no matter how good his intentions, for this is irrele-
vant) is standing there as the symbol of dignity,
strength, and beauty for the young boy? A black man
must stand there instead. So whites must reexamine
working definitions of "love." (So must blacks; so must
everybody.) Often, "love" has been oppressive, demand-

ing, exploitative, binding; at best, paternalistic. Often, a missionary held a gun and a dollar, as well as a cross.

Another revelation for me during these past few years has been that freedom and peace are inseparable. Wisely and courageously, Martin Luther King, Jr., told the American people—when it was not fashionable, when he was attacked for doing so by the Negro Establishment as well as the white—that the war in Vietnam was linked with poverty in the urban ghettos. Racism and nationalism have a way of going hand in hand; each sets up walls between people.

For many of us who feel that America's actions in Vietnam have been hideously immoral and mistaken, it has been difficult to know how to communicate this feeling to other Americans in honest and creative ways. Sometimes the effort has been very discouraging. When I was speaking against the war at a teach-in at the University of Oregon, a baseball was hurled at my head from the rear of the crowded auditorium, grazing my scalp.

Despite marches, signed protests, teach-ins and demonstrations against the war, the nation's policy remained essentially the same. The bombing continued (sometimes in different locations), napalm was still used, the pacification program went on its tragic way, casualty lists still appeared weekly, poverty in the United States could not be dealt with adequately because billions of dollars were poured into the military effort, there loomed the specter of new "Vietnams" elsewhere, and young men continued being confronted by hard, grim alternatives: prison? exile? killing in war?

It is past midnight in a men's dormitory room.
"If you go to Canada, you can't ever come home again," one college senior says.

"They take your passport away if you go to prison, and won't ever let you practice medicine or law," says another.

"I want to stay in America as long as I can do anything creative," says a third. "But, if there's to be a police state, I want to get out before I'm put inside a concentration camp. I'm Jewish. I want to be able to get out, across a border to Canada or Mexico."

"Would whites really want to kill us?" asks a black student. "You know whites because you're one of them. *Would* whites let this happen to us in America?"

All these young men come from well-to-do homes, and attend one of the greatest American universities.

It is getting later.

In Detroit, in late 1961, I fasted for one week to protest nuclear tests and militarism and war in general. Fasting is an extremely personal act in that nothing overt is done to anybody else. It is a passive, not aggressive, act. Yet my week's fast aroused more animosity and outrage than any other "demonstration" in which I ever participated. I was either ignored (only when I was present, needless to say) or shouted at. The fact that one man was simply not eating food seemed to rudely touch some deep-lying nerve in people.

In 1967 I joined some forty other Americans to spend a week in Bratislava, Czechoslovakia, meeting with a group of Vietnamese men and women representing the N.L.F., the National Liberation Front of South Vietnam, and the D.R.V., the Democratic Republic of Vietnam. The meeting was arranged by Dave Dellinger of *Liberation* magazine, Tom Hayden, a founder of Students for a Democratic Society and author of *Rebellion in Newark,* and Nick Eggleson, a former president of SDS, with the cooperation of the Czechoslovakian Peace Committee.

All Americans paid their own travel expenses. We held our discussions and lived in a trade-union hostel on the outskirts of Bratislava. The American delegation included black representatives of SNCC and the Afro-American Association in Newark. One American at the meeting criticized other members from the United States for treating the Vietnamese with what he termed the same kind of gratuitous guilt-ridden mixture of dishonesty and illusion which characterized American white liberals working with blacks in the deep South during the civil rights period.

Nguyen Minh Vy, head of the D.R.V. delegation at the meeting, explained how, after opposing Japanese fascism and French colonialism, the D.R.V. stated in its Declaration of Independence that "all people are born equal." We grasped the complex amalgam of nationalism and communism in what we heard, this at a moment in history when U.S. foreign policy seemed to have difficulty differentiating varied nationalist movements —so easy to file under the monochrome "communist" label.

"Our people are prepared to fight for five, ten, twenty years or even longer if necessary," we were told by another D.R.V. delegate. "Our national economy consists of a scattered culture," Nguyen Minh Vy said. "This, totally unlike the U.S. Our industry is already scattered in small centers. We are prepared for Hanoi and Haiphong to be destroyed and not harm our effort . . . How can such a small, underdeveloped country defeat the U.S.? We have a strong determination. The present generation will not enjoy the fruits of what we are now doing, but our children will. We are changing from a colonialist to a free society." A detailed picture was given of daily life in both North and South Vietnam. Members of the N.L.F. (whose delegation was headed by a woman, Mrs. Nguyen Thi Binh) said the fact that peasants in liberated areas were now owners of their land involved them in a struggle to defend their own vital interests, and represented a form of society completely new for them. The Vietnamese told us that they expected no single decisive military Dienbienphu kind of victory over American forces; their awareness of what they should have to endure in a continuing war [the intensity of U.S. bombing had already surpassed that employed in Europe in World War II] seemed to be free of illusions; yet they stated they would continue their struggle until the U.S. government discontinued bombing attacks on North Vietnam and withdrew troops from South Vietnam.

En route back to the States, while stopping at the Prague airport, Bronson Clark, Vietnam program associate of the American Friends Service Committee, said: "Although they insist they're winning, it's obvious they are paying an enormous price to do so. We're running the bellows of a gas chamber. We're eliminating countless Vietnamese." Russ Johnson, international affairs representative in southeast Asia for the American Friends Service Committee, went on to say: "The possibilities of our policy are almost genocidal, in terms of the destruction of people and land. We threaten the dissolution of the whole moral and social fabric of their society. The N.L.F.'s strength is less in guerrilla tactics than in moral character, giving the Vietnamese a sense of dignity and self-respect. The Nazis always said, 'We didn't know.' For us, there is no similar excuse. We've permitted ourselves to assent to one horror after another. Our own morality is eroding and now facing destruction, step by step." It was this haunting thought that prodded me—and many others—to continue our protest against this war and all war.

. . .

The last time I was with Martin Luther King, Jr., was in a nonviolent protest against the Vietnam war. A number of times I had been with him in the deep South in various demonstrations. He had sent men to instruct twenty-seven of us who were commencing a freedom ride in 1961 in the philosophy and techniques of nonviolence. I had chatted with him in St. Louis on the day before he was named recipient of the Nobel Peace Prize. Now, on February 6, 1968, Martin Luther King, Jr., was among several hundred people from various parts of the country—Christians and Jews, men and women, blacks and whites—who had convened in Washington, D.C. in response to a call from Clergy and Laymen Concerned About Vietnam. We stood together, all of us, inside Arlington Cemetery, directly below the Tomb of the Unknown Soldier. A federal appellate court had rejected an appeal for permission to hold a formal memorial service for the war dead; so we were simply, silently, praying for peace. In the distance, two men could be seen, one carrying a Torah and the other a crucifix.

When we had been called to pray, I was standing next to a young Roman Catholic seminary student. He faced five years in prison and a heavy fine for refusing, in line with his Christian belief and conscience, to participate in the war. Prayer for me at that moment was defined as the agonized concern—and hope—I shared with that seminarian. The silence was broken by sounds associated with the changing of the guard at the tomb above us: spoken commands, heels clicking, the clattering of rifles. A jet zoomed by in the sky. A woman laughed in the distance. As we left, a carillon chimed a hymn.

In Christ there is no East or West,
  In him no South or North,

But one great fellowship of love
  Throughout the whole wide earth.

In him shall true hearts everywhere
  Their high communion find;
His service is the golden cord
  Close-binding all mankind.

Join hands, then, brothers of the faith,
  Whate'er your race may be!
Who serves my Father as a son
  Is surely kin to me.

In Christ now meet both East and West,
  In him meet South and North,
All Christly souls are one in him,
  Throughout the whole wide earth.

Hymn 263,
The Hymnal of the
Protestant Episcopal Church
in the United States
of America

I heard a young black nationalist say: "For America it's clearly either the Fourth Reich or democracy. It will be concentration camps or gas chambers for blacks if it's the Fourth Reich. If it's democracy, it will be freedom. I can see no middle-ground. Present civil rights organizations are neither leading nor functioning on a rational basis." In Harlem, yet another young black man told me: "I see the possibility of extermination of blacks by whites in America within a few years. The black masses aren't being heard at all. Middle-class Negroes, speaking with whites, reflect white and not black values or feelings. Communication scarcely exists at all. White people believe the Civil Rights Act helped and even that blacks are pushing too fast. But the black masses have not been affected at all."

Two black teen-age youths were fighting each other in

a street in a Northern American city. One attacked the other with a big stick, hitting him across the back. A social worker acquainted with the boys was driving by the scene in his car; he stopped and ran over to them. One of the two youths looked at him with hatred and said, "Leave me alone." Two white men were watching. One told the social worker, "You're crazy to get mixed up in this. There's nothing you can do. There's nothing anybody can do. Just let them alone." Did the man who said this *really* believe there was no hope for these youths? Did the man realize that if this hopelessness were to prevail the alternatives could include incarceration of such youths in concentration camps? Would the man acknowledge the relation between his words and the Fourth-Reich fears of the young black nationalist? A rabbi, only too aware of the way genocide has been polished and well-nigh perfected in this generation, was telling me that he is terrified when U.S. black leaders say, "Free us or exterminate us."

On a visit to a great American metropolis not long ago, after speaking in the heart of its black poverty area, I felt a strange fear as I was being driven away after the end of the meeting. I looked back through the car window and saw the black ghetto, blazing with lights, set high on a hill: How little it would take to transform it into a stockade or concentration camp —just barbed wire and guns.

Following the experience of a freedom ride in 1961, I wanted to make a dramatic statement about humanness. At the same time bail money was needed for arrests in connection with the freedom ride. As a result I wrote a short one-act play called *Boy*. In its premiere performance I played the part of a black shoeshine man, wearing a black mask; while a black actor, Woodie King, Jr., played a white man, and wore a white mask. The drama was performed on a small stage area in the center of a coffeehouse, surrounded by a dense crowd.

> Just don't you go gettin' into no trouble, black boy. Damn it, boy, spit on that shoe . . . Make it shine like your face, black boy . . . Spit on it, damn it. Where's your spit? . . . You ain't gonna get nowhere in this white man's world if you're so damned lazy—if you won't spit.
>
> (From *Boy*)

Boy has since been performed in every section of the United States by university, civil rights, and religious groups. It was presented in 1964, on a tour of Eastern university campuses, and in April, 1965, in the National Cathedral in Washington, D.C. NBC-TV televised excerpts from it.

The play was given its most exciting production at the Concept-East coffeehouse theater in Detroit. The Concept-East was originated and run by black artists, actors, directors and playwrights. A number of young men who would later become celebrated—including Ronald Milner, Woodie King and Cliff Frazier—were driving forces in its life. The theater was housed in a converted store in the black poverty ring which circled the inner-city. The first time I saw the building it was filthy with great piles of refuse and layers of dirt. Soon it was transformed into one of the most attractive theaters in-the-round that I have seen. Its importance as a vital testing ground for young black talent—which would otherwise have had no outlet—simply cannot be estimated.

I next wrote three plays, contained in a trilogy: *Study in Color, They Aren't Real To Me,* and *The Job.* When the plays were first presented in Detroit coffeehouse theaters, in 1962, I told the *New York Times* "I've written these plays because I believe that the most powerful sermons of our time and culture are to be found in the theatre, the novel and occasionally in the medium of film. I have something to say about race—or, as I prefer to call it, human—relations. Many people do not attend a church or synagogue; some persons who attend seldom listen in depth to sermons, or are seriously moved by them." I pointed out that the plays represented a frank attempt to disturb audiences and puncture smugness about human injustice.

All my plays have the same theme: affirmation of humanness in the face of powerful, sophisticated forces which try to break a man, compelling him to settle for less than personhood, and become a stereotype, a "nigger," "boy," a thing. (Though written during the civil rights period, these plays have recently been rediscovered in this day of Black Power and emphasis on peace-liberation, and performed in various coffeehouse theaters and on television.)

In representing the confrontation of a black shoeshine man and a white man who brutalizes him, *Boy* has proven to be a painful experience for both blacks and whites. In a number of situations, it has been banned or angrily attacked. When a tape-recorded performance of it was played in a high school social-science class, the teacher was reprimanded by the principal. The manager of a radio station, who played a tape recording of *Boy* on the air, told me this was a contributory factor in his subsequent dismissal.

> Difficulties, hell. I get sick and tired hearing about the difficulties of the whites. Why do they want to integrate with us? If they'd keep in their place I wouldn't care about their existence. But, as my father has always said, give a white man an inch and he'll want to take a mile . . . Stepping on my toes? Let him try, let a white man

try stepping on my toes and you'll see one less white man
in this man's world. They aren't . . . real . . . to me, I
can't really see them on any individual basis, but I hate
them, Frank. I just don't like whites. I can't stand their
lack of color.

(From *They Aren't Real To Me*)

The trilogy was given its premiere in the spring of
1962 in an experimental theater located in an upper-
middle-class, all-white suburb of Detroit, with an integrated cast and racially integrated audiences. Again, I
appeared in two of the three plays during the initial run
of several weeks.

You must acknowledge that you have image problems to
overcome. It will be mandatory for you to appeal to the
Negro dollar without losing the white dollar. You will
wish to try arousing Negro hate without arousing white
hate. When you may seem to be attacking the power
structure, you must do so without getting it mad at you.

(From *The Job*)

My last play in the antibias trilogy, *Study in Color*, has
always aroused strange and paradoxical audience reactions. It opens with two players seated on high stools on
the stage. One player, a white man, is dressed in a black
T-shirt, black trousers, black socks and shoes, and wears
a black mask with Caucasian features. The other player,
a dark-skinned black man, is dressed all in white, and
wears a white mask which has Negroid features. The
white player in the black mask is reading *Ebony;* the
black player in the white mask is reading *Town and
Country*.

The player in the white mask speaks first: "I become
so bored with color. As a matter of fact, I wish I had
some. (He self-consciously stretches and yawns) All
this race jazz. I mean, what *is* color: Well, you know, on

a human being. Is it like being a painting, you know, walking around like a painting among a lot of non-paintings? What is a non-painting? It's so complex, it's hard to talk about intelligibly."

He tosses the magazine on the floor. "Nig-ger. Nigger. Ne-gro. Negro. I wonder what it's like to be a Negro. What it's like to be a nig-ger. Would I be different? Would I feel different?" Later he says, "My God is a nigger. Jesus Christ. Nigger Christ. Christ nigger."

After each character delivers several monologues, during which they show no recognition of each other's presence (they are lighted by separate spots on a dark stage), one puts on a small mask of colored stripes while the other puts on a small mask of colored polka-dots. The overhead light comes on and the two men talk together. But they do not truly communicate or reach each other.

FIRST MAN   I've wondered what it's like, what it must be like, to be colored. You know, in a white society. I hate all this race prejudice. . . . It embarrasses me a bit, even makes me angry, when I realize that I have all the advantages of being white, and I just wear this mask when I *want* to, but you, you're colored all the time, you can't take a mask off or put it on when you want to. It makes me really angry.
SECOND MAN   Why?
FIRST MAN   It's . . . it's so unjust.
SECOND MAN   (*Abruptly removing his striped mask*)   I'm not colored. I'm black.

The conversation continues, involving each man more deeply in the encounter than he had wanted to be. The play ends in a theatrically violent treatment of the question of the absurdity of color.

When involved in a performance of one of these plays, I sometimes thought I would orbit away in an explosion of memory or fantasy. Both as author and actor, I profoundly felt the plays' statement about life. In addition, my relationship with an audience was sensitive and intimate. It seemed that we were openly exposed to each other—unable to hide any feelings or responses. For I *knew* these people seated before me—in laughter or silence, in a nervous cough or the sound of a chair scraping the floor—and they *knew* me, vulnerably standing on the stage wearing a white mask, a black mask—or my own.

During this period, I lived in a dilapidated apartment house in Detroit's inner-city. Stores on our deteriorating street charged more money than their suburban counterparts for inferior food and merchandise. Outside the window, cars raced by day and night on a busy highway leading to the suburbs; the cars were coming from somewhere and going somewhere, but they never stopped *here*.

Looking out the old window
Past midnight
                          So bright, the neon hotel sign
                          (I hear jazz)
It is red
Lively
                          Even so gay
Presumptuously alive.
          Lights shine on the streets
They are wet
                          oh, the traffic lights
Red, Red,
It is a jagged bleeding wound in the street
          Turn Green, Yes!
                          cool, cool
Christmas Tree Green
                          oh, in the gutter
                          Blaze!

Dirty, Dirty
      cars roll past
      Tires hiss on the wet
             order in white-marked lines
             stability and order in white-
               marked lines
    I am so hot
           flash cool
           Rain, fall
(do you extinguish the fires burning underneath the pave-
ment?)
I am so hot
           gently, quietly
(I can't hear the rain for the hiss of tires)
           in cracked cement
           under a bright white light.
I am in a concentration camp, it is 2 A.M.
I am in a supermarket at 4
I am washed in the incandescent brightness of a clean
dawn
           God
I am restless in a beating light
           Christ
I see the tired, tired, tired light of a street
long, long,
hot red, cool green
water falls in a cement crack
I can't hear it for the hiss
           in an alley.
    Lightness
    Lightness
The brightness
           out of the old window
The brightness
    has killed the night
           murdered it
O Easter.

The old building (I loved it) had no elevator, so I climbed up and down its creaking stairs with their faded carpeting. In this apartment, the actors met who would appear in my plays. We read poems together or acted out scenes from plays (*The Zoo Story* was a favorite). I wrote my plays, and had first readings and rehearsals in this apartment.

Reactions to my plays differed sharply from one audience to another. My favorite audiences combined blacks with whites—but not when they were seated in color blocs (a black theater party on one side of the aisle, a white theater party on the other, with no communication or interaction between the two). The best audiences have had blacks and whites seated close together in a polka dot: whites, tensely waiting for a black response in order to feel free to react, have been able to sense and pick up this response, somehow uniting it with their own feelings to form a "white reaction"; blacks, being sufficiently dispersed among the whites to alleviate social fear of a monolithic white bloc, have felt free to respond spontaneously and naturally—thereby breaking through the racial tensions that had initially been present.

Are you self-conscious about being too light or too dark? Would you like to try new skin tints or shades, to vary your whole personality make-up, make new friends and bring out hitherto unknown facets about you? Now you can feel *free*, now you can change the *old* you into the *new* you you have dreamed about. Did you dream about it in black and white? Now you can make your dreams come true in technicolor. Now you can be as stark white or jet black, as rosy-cream or golden-brown, as you have secretly always wished to be. Liberate your secret dreams. If you feel washed-out and pale, *think* color, *feel* color, *be* colorful. If you feel more colorful than you want to be, *think* white, *feel* white, *be* white. Use Bleach *or* Tan —get *both* in the giant economy package. Get integrated . . . today.

(From The Job)

One such night, when the audience was mixed and responding warmly and naturally—with considerable gusto—to the plays, a prominent white reviewer and his wife left their seats in the second row and stood for the remainder of the show at the back of the theater. "Those Negroes were sick," the reviewer later informed me. "They were laughing at things that aren't funny."

When Lorraine Hansberry's play *A Raisin in the Sun* was playing to Negro-white audiences in a major American city, another prominent white critic admonished Negroes, in his review, for laughing at lines which were "not funny"—a most revealing sign of the lack of understanding between white and black cultures.

Whites have a smell. I can't describe it, but in a crowd sometimes I sense it. Weren't they better off as slaves? They were treated well, especially under the late paternalistic movement . . . Did you notice that report over the weekend on the increase in white teenage crime? Whites breed like rabbits. They are destroying the moral foundation of our whole society. I even wonder if the white race isn't biologically inferior.

(From They Aren't Real To Me)

One night I noticed a clerical collar in the audience when we were playing to an all-white audience that was responding with icy reserve. Afterward I stood at the door to shake hands with members of the audience on their way out—after all, these plays were my sermons, and it is customary after giving a sermon to stand at the church door to shake hands with people. I noted that the white collar did not pass by. Later I was informed that the clergyman had simply jumped out of a ground-floor window in the little theater, rather than shake hands with the author.

> *Each* audience—even on successive nights in the same theater was different. A laugh would not emerge at all where, the night before, the rafters had shaken with laughter. But, without warning, a laugh would suddenly crop up at a place where a laugh was *impossible* before. So I would ask myself—what did the laugh mean, what precisely was the audience expressing?
> And then I discovered how useful laughter can be as a means of focusing soberly on a serious question. Laughter is a common acknowledgement of the absurd. An experience of the absurd, shared openly by a vulnerable audience, permits a storyteller to work in a dimension of truth which would otherwise have remained hidden. Now the chips are down. Now people are compelled to focus together—even if only for a moment—on a single shared experience.
>
> (From *Malcolm Boyd's Book of Days*)

Out on tour, the cast would be housed in the homes of people generous and kind enough to take us in. An encounter with our host or hostess might reveal either deep-seated racial prejudice, well-masked but clearly focused in a brief moment of clarity, or a sincere desire to become engaged in the struggle for human freedom.

During a brief Eastern tour of *Study in Color,* a black woman in the audience extended a blanket invitation to the cast, and those local whites who had been involved in the production, to come to her home after the performance. This marked the first time the whites had ever been inside the home of a black family. The conversation that emerged seemed almost an extension of the play itself.

FIRST BLACK   Exactly what do you propose doing with the national constitution? The white man now possesses equal rights under the law.

SECOND BLACK   Equal rights to touch my daughter? Equal rights to marry my daughter?

FIRST BLACK   It's impossible to discuss any of this rationally with you, Art. It's just not possible.

SECOND BLACK   Then let's not talk about it, Frank. Let's not talk about it at all . . . Damn whites. Dirty whiggers. Dirty whiggers.

FIRST BLACK   I've asked you not use that term in speaking about whites, Art. I find it offensive. After all we've got to try our best to get along with them.

(From *They Aren't Real To Me*)

In 1962 I wrote a play called *The Community*. Its second act takes place in a darkened apartment; a segment of the church has vacated its public buildings and gone underground in the society. Throughout this act the telephone rings intermittently. Someone in the underground says: "They have somebody just calling the number nearly all the time. I have to let it ring. It's a very steady testing of my nerve that will never go away. I have to live with it, day and night, as a condition that does not change or go away. It tests my faithfulness and my hope."

The ringing of the telephone was intended to be "a thorn in the flesh"—just as the whole play was written to disturb nominal Christians out of complacency concerning the church. I tried to reveal some of the church's false and distorted images and to state what, in my opinion, constitutes its authentic nature. The theme is revealed in this speech: "The church will never be a building again. For a while it was apartments but that was something like being a building too. Now it won't be even that. But it gets stronger all the time. It moves to essentials. It becomes itself, a body, a community of persons in love with God and in a tight, close communion with its Lord . . . but the very closeness springs it loose, out of the tight body, back in dispersion into the city. So the church is wherever each of us is. The church goes out into the city with each one of us. The church is like the salt of the world there. It is alive, it is active, it is in danger, it is in ferment."

In *The Community*, a white man tells a black man: "I know all the Christian answers on race. They've been fed me like pablum and they've been force-fed me by an ugly tube run down my throat when I didn't want it there. But I still don't want you to live next door to me, or go to the altar rail with me to drink from the same chalice, or kiss my daughter on the mouth . . . And so, in living, I am dead in the ways of false death and false life. Why can't I learn to live by dying to the things I ought to die to?" The black man responds: "Where was the white Christ when I was crucified by white Christians? *Where*? The white Christians respectably praying to the gentle white, blond-haired, blue-eyed Jesus with caucasian features, while I felt the black lash on my black back . . . and was forced into a black, black cloud without light or hope? And then I found the black cloud was a vision of light. And then I found the black was beautiful and the white was ugly, and the light was black! . . We are alive and dead, dead and alive. The church is not dead. Only the church I see is dead. It is a part of my sin that I see it in this way. I have faith that there is a newborn, a reborn, church. I cannot see it but only know it is here. I feel its life. But when I look to see it, I see only the church which is dead."

We had a performance to give at 8:30 that night, but as we speeded along the highway toward our destination, the odds seemed to be moving against us. It was 7:30, we weren't even within miles of the town, and four cops were tailing us.

Those headlights shining back there on the dark, menacingly swamp-lined highway seemed to be out of a romantic, very old Bogey movie. But, we realized with clammy discomfiture, they were indeed as real as any other part of our incongruous situation. We were in Mississippi, and it was July, 1965.

If we were stopped, on a real or an imaginary minor violation, it would probably mean at least one night in jail. In this part of Mississippi, white and black workers in the freedom movement had learned to anticipate incarceration instead of a traffic ticket, along with a likely beating and a very high bail—for people inevitably short on money.

Miraculously, there *was* a performance that night as scheduled, for we were not picked up by the gendarmes. After tailing us for an interminable length of time, they had either had their sport for the moment or were called to better pickings, and without warning, they zoomed ahead of us and swiftly out of sight.

In the town, an audience awaited us in a haggard, flea-bitten cavern which was the "Negro theater." The owner, of course, was white—and was on hand. He had, in fact, been told by local civil rights workers that our performance would be "a cultural event" without racial connotations. So, instead of the usual innocuous B film, we were present that night inside the seedy hall which, with its ancient red plush seats, seemed to be a huge mouth from which all the shiny clean teeth had been extracted, leaving only empty space and blood-red cushy holes.

Youngsters under ten years of age completely filled the first row of seats. Men and women were scattered throughout the house, and wishing to create as intimate a setting as possible, we asked them all to move down and fill up the seats near the front.

It was hard to tell who were the actors or where was the stage; indeed, this was true of the whole experience.

Under the sponsorship of the Student Nonviolent Co-ordinating Committee, I was touring Mississippi, Alabama and eastern Arkansas, giving readings from black writers and my own plays before rural black audiences in freedom houses, churches and community centers. Four young Afro-American veterans of the movement, the Freedom Singers, were traveling with me. The audiences seemed as integral to the program as we actors. We were all part of the Mississippi drama, the deep South cycle, the Alabama passion play.

Everybody in the deep South seemed to be playing a role, speaking given lines, responding to cues; every so often when the dramatic action seemed to lag, one instinctively knew this was pure deception; suddenly there would be a new shock, a thrust in the movement, drawing very tight again what had momentarily seemed to be a slack in the plot. (The blood was real.) In our drama, stage lights could change, in a flash, to hard headlights of a car cutting through a lonely stretch of highway late at night. We never forgot that we were performing within the context of this greater drama of the South—this life-and-*death* reality.

Now I was on stage before the all-black (with the exception of the white owner) audience. The Freedom Singers had sung four freedom songs, and the wary, weary crowd had begun to respond to them. "Oh, freedom." "*This . . .* little light of mine." "Whadaya want?" "Freedom." "When?" "NOW." The white theater owner was becoming visibly agitated. He stood up, walked to the back of the theater where he used the phone, and then remained standing there, smoking in an unrelaxed way, observing the rest of the performance with the air of a Madrid censor. Time was golden; we breathed and worked in it.

I explained to the audience that I am a white man. "Or a white devil, if you see it that way." There was a warm hum of appreciation from the people; the white theater owner took a long drag on his cigarette. "Yet white blood has been shed along with black. Viola Liuzzo . . . Jimmy Lee Jackson . . . Jim Reeb. No white man is free, despite what he may think, so long as anyone else in the society is not free. We're here for freedom." I explained something of what it has meant to be a white man in the movement: one has the seesaw experience of being called, in one moment, "a white nigger," and in the next, "a white devil." There were laughs in such a situation, and tears, I said. I attempted to share some of both with the audience. Suddenly, all of us in the theater seemed to have acknowledged relationship. The theater owner was fighting it, but I felt he had nonetheless experienced it, too.

"How many of you know the name Richard Wright?" Just a few hands went up. "He lived here," I said. "Do you know what a freedom school does? One thing is teach black culture and history. It's important for us to know black writers . . . Richard Wright, for example . . . and to understand what is their experience and what they are saying." I read Wright's short story, "The Man Who Went To Chicago."

After another freedom song, I asked: "How many of you know who Ralph Ellison is?" Hardly any hands were raised. I told them about Ellison. Then I said I felt it was important for Mississippi to know about Harlem, and for Harlem to know about Mississippi; and I read the Harlem funeral scene from *Invisible Man*. A pin, had it been dropped, would instantly have been heard inside that old theater; the youngsters in the front row seemed not to breathe or move. This reading is a long one, and not uncomplicated, but the people heard it and shared its meaning. (Later, over a urinal in the men's room upstairs, I would see scrawled these words: "The Peoples Wants Freedom.")

Now, we would perform my one-act play *Boy*. This required me to don a black mask, for I would play the role of a black shoeshine man; a black actor would play the white man. Here the audience had to work hard and try to make difficult adjustments. What *right* had the white man (white nigger *or* white devil) to become a black? How could he *know* what an Afro-American feels? Was there any *justice* in such a performance?

No audience before had ever laughed at any part of *Boy*, but, when the white man, wearing the black mask, knelt on the floor to shine the shoes of the Afro-American wearing a white mask, appreciative and joyous laughter swept through the theater. "Shine my shoes, nigger . . . No, dammit, *spit* on the shoe, boy. Spit. What's your spit worth, boy? Make it shine like your black face, nigger." The audience roared. The white owner tried to stop the performance, but the people decided that *Boy* would be completed.

The Afro-American wearing the white mask left the stage. The white man wearing the black mask placed a white mask over it, and started playing an imaginary scene; the white man playing the black had become a black playing a white man, addressing an imaginary black. "Who do you think you are, nigger? Do you think you're a big shot, nigger?" The laughter snapped off like a light switch. Then the white mask *and* the black mask came off, and the face was immediately not a masked but a human one. "Who am I? *Who am I?*" Into a moment of desperate questioning the audience poured the epithets and inhumanly murderous names used by racists: "Boy! Boy! Where are you boy? Boy! Come here boy! Boy! Boy! Boy!" The cries rose and filled the theater, then ceased as abruptly as they had started. The man on the stage slowly stood up. He was human and white, white and human, and he had been playing a black man. "I am not boy. I . . . am . . . not . . . boy." The applause, in that old Mississippi theater which was segregated for "niggers," rose, in a giant roar, and sounded like London or Broadway. The theater owner was clapping his hands in a staccato movement against the peoples' applause and he was shouting in counterpoint to the roar: the performance is over, you must leave immediately, quickly, *get out*.

But still it could not be stopped. The crowd and the

performers clasped hands. "We Shall Overcome." The words were shouted, the music was starkly simple. Jaded Northern liberals may misuse this song by singing it too frequently at respectably uninvolved church or social meetings; and Black Nationalists may wish the song could be banned for five years so that it would not be substituted for serious economic and political community planning; yet, inside that Mississippi theater, it was a hymn, a creed, a shared public statement of intention and solidarity.

So went one night of our tour. Filing out, the people shook hands with us. Shortly afterward, we joined them at the restaurant which was the black gathering place in that town, and talked for several hours about the readings, the plays, the movement, the young Black Nationalists, riots, LBJ, Adam Clayton Powell, and whether freedom would really ever come.

Every night of the tour was different. But always it was hot . . . sometimes 110 degrees . . . and in the crowded, airless centers where we played, we would sweat, and be wringing wet by the end of a performance.

One night, when the white man in *Boy* hurled a coin at the Afro-American shoeshine man and ordered him to "pick it up," a small black youngster . . . seated quite close to the small wooden stage in the packed community hall . . . ran in front of the actors, picked up the coin and handed it to the black man wearing a white mask, telling him, "You dropped this." The audience laughed and applauded, but immersed itself almost immediately back in the flow of the drama.

In Palmer's Crossing, Mississippi, I read the "Jerry and the Dog" sequence from Edward Albee's play *The Zoo Story*. ("We neither love nor hurt because we do not try to reach each other. And, *was* trying to feed the dog an act of love? And, perhaps, was the dog's attempt to bite me *not* an act of love?") The individuals in the audience identified either Jerry or the Dog with black or white, and also related themselves, in various ways, to each one.

(When I had read this speech, a year before, at the Ecumenical Institute of the World Council of Churches, in Switzerland, white man from South Africa had come up to me during tea the next afternoon and said, "The dog was the colored man.")

After I read the Harlem funeral scene from *Invisible Man*, at several of our stops, people would often ask me questions about Malcolm X, although he is not mentioned in any line of the reading, and again I found how deeply imbedded is his legend in the consciousness of Southern blacks. ("Here are the facts. He was standing and he fell. He fell and he kneeled. He kneeled and he bled. He bled and he died. . . . He was shot for a simple mistake of judgment and he bled and his blood dried and shortly the crowd trampled out the stains. It was a normal mistake of which many are guilty. He thought he was a man and that men were not meant to be pushed around. But it was hot downtown and he forgot his history, he forgot the time and the place. He lost his hold on reality. . . . Forget him. When he was alive he was our hope, but why worry over a hope that's dead? So there's only one thing left to tell and I've already told it. His name was Tod Clifton, he believed in brotherhood, he aroused our hopes and he died.")

One of the Freedom Singers often read the fantasy TV commercial from my play *The Job*. ("Now you can be as stark white or jet black, as rosy-cream or golden-brown, as you have secretly always wished to be.") In the north, on college campuses and at civil rights meetings, I was warmly received when I read this; but not in Mississippi or Alabama, where only a black actor could be accepted reading these lines. A Freedom Singer and I portrayed, several times during the tour, the two roles in my play *Study in Color*.

Within each audience that saw a performance, we were really playing to four different audiences: local black adult residents, black and white volunteers from different parts of the country, local Afro-American youth,

and staff members of the Student Nonviolent Coordinating Committee and the Freedom Democratic Party. Most
people seeing our performance were looking at a play for
the first time in their lives and had never before been
inside a theater. A man in southern Mississippi, after the
reading from *Invisible Man,* told me that he had once
read it but now understood its meaning for the first time.
And I remember the elderly lady, who, after *Study in
Color,* said simply, "That's it. That's the way it is."

Our tour was entertaining; but the audiences did not
appreciate it so much as entertainment as an "identifying-
with"—an expression of what had been individually
known but not shared, corporately. In getting across a
human message—directly and disturbingly—at best our
art had all the impact of a freedom ride.

During the summer of 1963, Robert Sherwood, the
producer-director at WMSB, the educational television
station at Michigan State University, expressed an interest in presenting the trilogy—*The Job, Study in Color*
and *Boy*—on the station. Little did I suspect that it
would be the start of yet another controversy.

In January, 1964, Woodie King, Jr., and Cliff Frazier
—actors who had appeared in the initial performances
of my plays—taped *Boy* and *The Job* at the WMSB studios in East Lansing. Mr. King and I taped *Study in
Color.*

As Mr. Sherwood had expressed considerable satisfaction with the taped plays, I was jolted to receive a letter
from him in March which stated: "I am very sorry and
embarrassed to have to inform you that we cannot
broadcast *Study in Color, Boy* and *The Job.* The Director
of Broadcasting Services made the final decision on the
point that the plays do not reflect the proper function of
the University in either approach or method of dealing
with the social questions involved." He added: "Please

accept my apology for the problems and inconveniences I have caused and for any embarrassment I may have inadvertently caused you. In spite of the negative outcome, I still do not regret making the tapes. In fact, given opportunity, I would probably try the whole thing again and for the same reason—I still believe they ought to be broadcast."

Upon receipt of this letter, I asked Mr. Sherwood if he would come to Detroit to meet with me because I found the cancellation unacceptable, and wanted an explanation. He said there was a great furor within the station management concerning the plays, with one executive claiming they were "anti-white." (I found this in sharp contrast with *Variety*'s comment about *Boy*, on March 14, 1962: "[It] becomes a lesson in race relations . . . It brings the whole issue down to person-to-person relations and how a few kind words, so easy to say and mean, could help bring peace and friendship rather than war and hatred.")

Evidently there was further discussion at the station, with the result that two of my plays, *The Job* and *Study in Color*, would be scheduled for viewing on WMSB; however, *Boy* was censored. Thanks to Mr. Sherwood's negotiations, the Anti-Defamation League of B'nai B'rith agreed to make films of all three plays available for national distribution, both for television and private showings. B'nai B'rith paid the costs of making film negatives from the three video tapes and some twenty prints of each of the plays.

The telecast of *The Job* and *Study in Color* was scheduled for July 12, 1964, on WMSB. I telephoned Mr. Sherwood four days before that date to ask again if *Boy* would definitely not be shown. He said it would not because it was considered "too strong" by some executives at the station. One day before the telecast I announced to the press that *Boy* was being censored by the station.

On the day of the program the Sunday edition of the Detroit *News* front-paged the headline:

MSU BANS CHAPLAIN'S PLAY ON TV

"He certainly has been censored," Armand Hunter, director of the division of broadcasting at M.S.U., was quoted as saying. The reason given was that "officials at the East Lansing school say it 'contains too many curse words.'" The so-called curse words were two: "damn" and "nigger," the latter being used, of course, as an exhibit in the anatomy of racial prejudice.

> Nigger! Shine my shoes, nigger. No, dammit, spit on the shoe, black boy. Spit. How much is your spit worth anyway, boy? Who do you think you are, nigger? You think you're a big shot, nigger?
>
> (From *Boy*)

The next day the Detroit *Free Press* asked: "Are the words 'damn' and 'nigger' too strong for Michigan television viewers? The director of the Michigan State University educational television outlet thinks so, and refused to broadcast a social-protest play written by a Detroit minister."

Mr. Hunter clarified his position in his remarks to the *Free Press:* "We would have screened the play if the words had been left out," he said. He explained that "the two words have never been used over the station in his eight years as director, and he also said they were not vital to Boyd's play."

Actually, the words "damn" and "nigger" *had* been used on WMSB. Both were contained in my play *Study in Color* which was telecast on July 12, pointing up the fact that the words themselves could not have been the reason for banning *Boy*. (In addition, a taped program featuring James Baldwin had been shown on the station several weeks before, and he had used both words liberally in the course of his remarks.)

Mr. Sherwood, whose support I deeply appreciated, stated that *Boy* was the best of my three plays and that the station "probably objected to the dramatic intensity of the play. It's a very strong piece. A frightening piece." (It is worth mentioning that in the station's original explanation to me nothing was said about an objection to the language in the plays.)

My use of "nigger" is a dissection in public of a fantasy "nigger" world of whispers, ignorance, and stereotypes. Educational television, as well as community theater, must offer an opportunity for experimentation with forms of communication and breakthrough of new ideas. Whites must begin to experience racial pain at profounder levels if they are going to be able to comprehend how an Afro-American suffers in white America.

JOHN (*Slowly, wonderingly*) I am not boy. (*With a growing realization, not so much of who he is, as of who he is not; the words are to be read as if they were followed by a comma, and the audience must complete the final, uncompleted phrase*) I am not boy . . .

(From Boy)

The American Civil Liberties Union of Michigan protested to M.S.U. that the reason given for not showing the play reflected ". . . a shocking lack of sensitivity in dealing with controversial issues." It continued: "The Lansing community is indebted to Boyd for publicizing this action of censorship rather than remaining silent because two of his three plays were produced. The American Civil Liberties Union feels that Michigan State University should judge the merits of this play by the same standards used generally for the fine arts. The works of Shakespeare as well as the Bible use language at least as objectionable but the overall context in which they are used make them an important part of these works. An author or playwright has the right to see his works presented in the form he feels best expresses his ideas. A great university should be particularly sensitive to this problem and respect this right even though it may upset the sensitivities of some individuals. Therefore, we urge Michigan State University to reconsider its hasty action and offer the play as soon as practical."

Writing in the *Saturday Review,* Robert Lewis Shayon called *Study in Color* "a provocative exploration of racial attitudes" and commended it and *The Job* as "fresh, vital explorations with social bite and contemporary relevance." Then he commented on *Boy,* calling it "honest, uncompromising, and poignant." Mr. Shayon went on to say that the reasons offered for the censorship by WMSB spokesmen, "on and off the record, simply don't wash, and one is justified in suspecting that the buck is being passed . . . Such an affair disappoints educational television's friends, and it sets back the creative people in the field who want desperately to have their branch of the medium step out with courage and style and become meaningful in American life." He made this observation, too: "Somebody was apparently afraid of someone, and the shock of having the timidity and dissimulation come from the academic community—where freedom of expression is presumably prized—undercuts the station's presentation of the two plays that were aired."

The incident seemed to be closed. But shortly thereafter, when I was in Switzerland giving lectures at an international conference there under the sponsorship of the World Council of Churches, the Associated Press telephoned me. Did I know I had been attacked by my bishop? No, I said, I did not.

In a diocesan column, the Rt. Rev. Richard S. Emrich, Bishop of Michigan, had written: "A newspaper article informed us that a play on racial justice, written by a clergyman, was banned because of its profanity by the radio [sic] station of a great university. Since the clergyman preaches and practices high and sensitive standards in race relations, it astounds me that his standards in language are so low. Rejecting the sin that divides man from man, it is astonishing that he is willing to offend men by accepting the vulgarity and profanity of the modern avant-garde stage." The wire services had immediately distributed his statement. So the *Boy* controversy had not ended. The *New York Times* headline of the story, "PRIEST IS REBUKED ON WORDS IN PLAY . . . EPISCOPAL BISHOP DEPLORES HIS PROFANITY IN DRAMA," reflected the general misunderstanding.

But the bishop had not seen the play. It was only upon reading a newspaper report of the incident involving the TV station that he wrote his criticism of my use of "profanity." The bishop's mistake was certainly human, but his public, and sensationally treated accusation that I had used profanity in the play unfortunately created images of considerable durability.

I replied publicly to the bishop's published statement:

I am a Christian priest trying to do the work I was ordained to do. My work is not always exemplary, not even very good, but surely criticism of it could be made by a bishop in a private conversation with me, or by telephone, or letter, rather than in the sensational, scathing denunciation issued publicly.

If I have no priestly rights in such a matter, I must be granted human rights. I stand on my right as a human being to live and work without the kind of harassment to which I have been subjected . . . A number of racial bigots, fundamentally despairing over my views on racial freedom and equality, have criticized public readings I have presented before university, church, and civil rights groups taken from the writings of James Baldwin, Ralph Ellison, Richard Wright and Edward Albee. My attackers, labeling as immoral the profoundly moral work I have read from these Negro and white contemporary writers, seem never to have questioned the immorality of their own residence in soundly segregated housing areas.

I seek a reconciliation with the bishop but must know that I am loved even when I am not understood. The bishop had apparently neither seen nor read my play 'Boy,' which he attacks. The play has nothing to do with sex. Its language is neither vulgar nor profane. It is simply a strong statement against racial prejudice and bigotry . . . If the church is to be open to the life of God's world for loving and blessing it, it must not pillory, harass or attack those of us who work in experimental ways to achieve contact with men and women who have rejected Christianity or are indifferent to it. The church cannot ever become a private club with such membership qualifications as puritanism concerning the arts, race, economic status or social respectability. To become such a privileged club would represent blasphemy.

My resignation from the chaplaincy in Detroit was announced at this time. Most people therefore assumed that this controversy was the direct cause. It was not. In point of fact my resignation had been requested by the diocese several months before, when the Rt. Rev. Robert L. DeWitt, a warm and loyal friend who was then Suffragan Bishop of Michigan, was elected Bishop of Pennsylvania. When I was serving under him, he had stood effectively between me and many determined critics within the diocese, explaining my motives and actions with great understanding. I acceded to the request of the diocese, submitting my resignation confidentially, dating it to take effect about one year later so as to give myself adequate time to seek a new position. Some critics had threatened financial recriminations if I was not silenced. Others had insulted me, on purely racist grounds, at public meetings. My hunger fast against nuclear testing had aroused angry resentment. Then, one night on an interview program for the Canadian Broadcasting Corporation, which was taped in Toronto, I discussed Jesus' humanity and said he had "a head, shoulders, a stomach, a penis, legs and feet." In Canada there was no reaction; but the program was also seen in Detroit. The people there who had had violent reactions to my statements before were again up in arms. It seemed to me that many of them were saying, in effect, "Don't let Jesus be real because, if he were, we could not go on being anti-black and living in neighborhoods where Jews are barred. So don't refer explicitly to Jesus' humanity. Keep him locked inside a stained-glass window or nailed to a cross over an altar. We won't let Jesus be real!"

So now my resignation would soon take effect—and would have even without the furor about the plays. It seemed to me that I was unemployable within my church, inasmuch as an episcopal rebuke which had been so sensationally publicized would not be treated as a minor matter. While they seemingly accomplished their purpose of opening up discussion about racism, and stinging Christian consciences, my plays had caused me personal anguish and difficulty. During this time of banishment, when I was ostracized by former "friends" and my telephone was as silent as a cold stone, I was mercifully able to function in my writing. Out of this period came my book of prayers, *Are You Running with Me, Jesus?*

I lived in the heart of the inner-city. When I walked down Third Street, passing its slum dwellings, I could look up and see an old man seated by a third-story window, a box of cold cereal placed on the table before him, a breeze gently moving a soiled kitchen curtain by his side. He entered into one of my prayers: "Look up at that window, Lord, where the old guy is sitting."

When I looked out the window of my own apartment, I saw workmen tearing down, floor by floor, an old house directly across the street; and I wondered about the people who had lived there, who might wish to return for a look at their old home. As I gazed, feeling sadness for its fate as well as my own uncertainties, another prayer evolved: "The old house is nearly all torn down, Lord."

As the book of prayers assumed form and shape, so did faith and hope stir once again inside my cold, frightened soul. I could reach out to life and not be simply afraid. The hurt inside me, and the impelling desire to isolate myself from other human beings, would gradually be healed.

Unmailed Letter 4

Dear D.,

You seem to be caught in some ridiculous middle-age vise, some acute attack of accidie, some relentless feeling that you can't struggle anymore. You're dying, every part of you but your body, which is thriving. You'll undoubtedly live to be ninety.

You say that nothing is so dead as a dead cause. Yet,

in quite a true sense, there is no dead cause. As some people die for a cause it achieves resurrection and new life. Certain life may take new form. Yes, all this can be baffling and disconcerting to a person looking for "signs" of neat historical continuity or genealogical structure. But the cause (civil rights) which seemed to fill you with life—and then, as abruptly, with death—is not dead. It has emerged in new forms of black revolution and peace-liberation. You have mistakenly mourned its passing in, to say the least, a very protracted way. You have fantasied it as Albert while you, my friend, are an unlikely and absurd Victoria, puttering about in widow's weeds.

Come off it. Creep outside it. Life is going on, even if it does not now contribute so munificently to your compelling need to feel indispensable. You must let your mighty Excalibur sink below the cold waves of a gray sea; remove your helmet, hang up the war banners on the dining-room wall (next to the museum posters from Prague, do you think?). You can't *lead*. You can't hold those exciting midnight councils of war. You can't even "help" anyone else now, precisely because of your own desperate need of help.

Good. If you survive, it will be as a maturer man. You won't play missionary *or* war king any more. There is a place and purpose for you. You detest Black Power, while enjoying the manipulation of White Power which you previously could bring to bear upon the treatment of black misery and need. So you have become patriarchal even in middle age! You want to stalk the native villages of black jungles, bearing salvation (alleluia! amen!). Yet inside you there is a void. *You* need salvation. You need a *black* missionary or war king to come walking up your path with a cross or banners, holy bread or bronze sword. You could kneel down, kiss a black hand (perhaps while receiving holy bread or absolution), and say thank you. This might heal the messianic fever inside your body, that fever which rages in your mighty acts of giving. Your recovery depends on your learning how to receive.

Life is not so ordered as you would have it. You did not *want* Vietnam to happen now; first, one hundred years of progress and peace under the aegis of civil rights legislation, aided by Negro patience and slow integration. You did not *want* ghetto blacks to appear as unruly demons out of a bad movie, making unruly demands for radical structural changes now. No! Let them rather bless and thank sincere and hard-working white liberals, learn Jesus in order to forgive white bigots, *and march on* (oh glory! Mine eyes have seen the coming . . . Onward, Christian Soldiers! O 'twas a joyful sound to hear! Brightly gleams our banner! Alleluia! Alleluia! Hearts and voices heavenward raise! Forward! be our watchword.)

Demythologize yourself.

V

Father Boyd prefers to think of himself as a latter-day Luther or a more worldly Wesley trying to move organized religion out of "ghettoized" churches into the streets, the business offices, the union halls, the CORE chapters, the theatres and even the night clubs where the people are. His efforts are considered by sympathetic churchmen to be part of the secularization of the church that began at the end of World War II and has included such activities as the worker-priest movement and the involvement of clergymen in civil-rights protests and on the side of union members in labor disputes.

The *New York Times Magazine*, November 13, 1966

MISSION

I remember when a minister some-
where in the Midwest asked me if I had experienced the
act of conversion. I told him that I sometimes have three
in a good day and can go five weeks without one.

I meant that "conversion," like "loving" or "education,"
is a continuing process; it cannot be shut off in
isolated moments, or given a cut-and-dried definition. Always, it involves relationships with others—confrontation, forgiveness, and healing. One's relationship to God
is totally wrapped up in life experiences with fellow
human beings. I have come to understand evangelism
and mission as two-way streets: they do not mean only
my influence upon others, but the effects which other
lives have upon my own.

My ideas concerning the meaning of Christian mission—outreach to people in the spirit of God's concern
and love, and relating the gospel to significant life issues
—had been molded during my year of graduate theological study in England and Europe, then at Union Seminary, the Taizé Community in France, my first parish in
Indianapolis, college chaplaincies in Colorado and
Detroit, in the course of involvement with the black
freedom movement, and while being invited to share the
views and feelings of American college students. Many

years of experiences with people helped to form my convictions and beliefs. My style of ministry developed alongside my very style of consciousness.

I remember trudging up a muddy path at the Trappist Abbey of Gethsemani in Kentucky and suddenly coming face to face with Thomas Merton, whom I was seeking. Moving inside his hermitage nearby, we spent the afternoon talking and sipping bourbon. He astonished me; he lived as a hermit, yet had the new Bob Dylan album and all the most recent books. He was deeply involved in the life of the world, while not physically active in it. We discussed subject after subject in a torrent of conversation—war, race, spirituality, literature—knowing that our time together was limited. We gossiped. The one flaw in his experience was that he could not see films, because he lived an isolated rural life and was not allowed to spend his time outside the abbey. Yet we still included Jean-Luc Godard in our conversation. Humor, easy grace, and gentle openness marked his warm adventure of involvement in all of life.

While serving as a university chaplain, my concept of the parish developed until I saw it as the whole university—every corner of it, every nook and cranny in it, every activity taking place within it—instead of merely as my denominational center.

Once, addressing a student gathering, I said that everybody has faith in something, for example, that a toilet will flush. The meeting erupted in gales of laughter. I was informed that the plumbing in the student union, where I was speaking, had broken down that same afternoon.

During my first year as a chaplain in Colorado I remained inside the Episcopal center, seated *behind* a large desk, confronting students on the *other* side of it who came in to discuss "religious" questions ("What is the Trinity?," "What is the correct definition of salvation?"), and sexual problems ("My roommate masturbates," "I left the dorm to meet Tom but didn't sign out . . ."). After a year of this, I decided that I must put into practice my definition of the parish. It was difficult for me on the first morning when I walked, alone, into the snack bar of the student union. It was packed with students, seated at tables drinking coffee, reading or talking. I was new and marked by my clerical collar. I have never approved of glad-handing and what I call "personal imperialism"; hence I did not wish to inflict myself upon a group of students who did not want me to join them. I like to be available to other people (by being present in a public place) but wait for the others to make initial personal contact. So, on that first morning in the student union, I purchased a newspaper and sat down at an empty table. I was very tense, seemingly absorbed in my paper, wondering if anybody wanted to talk to me. After about ten minutes there were nearly a dozen students seated around the table. In no time the snack bar had become my morning headquarters. I have always found that students draw back from slick, contrived "answers" to questions they have not asked, and from religious pep talks (or any other kind). Students are trying to articulate their own questions about their identity and life.

The drive to achieve is a strong part of me.
I'd be phony to deny it in myself.
I can't stand completely apart from the system which produced me.

There's good and bad in this.
I hope I can hold onto the good while letting the bad
  go.
The Protestant Ethic is in my bones.
My ancestors helped build empires including the
  American one.
My ancestors contributed to sending missionaries
  to convert heathen natives.
This is in my bloodstream.
Can I keep the impulse to help, yet not be tied up by
  paternalism?
Is there a chance that I might find out what servant-
  hood means without the do-gooder corruption?
Can I find a way to achieve without feeling guilty,
  and also stand in the world as an honest servant?

Surveying a campus scene, one frequently sees the
chaplain's office and doll-house denominational centers
scattered about its fringes, looking like cute ecclesiastical additions to a monopoly set: Canterbury Club—to
replace the Boardwalk or Kentucky Avenue—Westmin-
ster Fellowship, Newman Center, Wesley Center, et al.
Students who have rejected the traditional forms of
Christianity often have not rejected Jesus or a style of
life rooted in his life. Rather they believe that such a
style of life is alien to institutional church life in America. If not (they argue) why do churches maintain segregation and inequality? Why do churches (they ask)
explicitly proclaim Christ's lordship and implicitly deny
it by perpetuating a gulf between the "sacred" and the
"secular"? Why (they ask) do churches accept cultural
norms about sex, refusing the freedom in responsibility
which the gospel affirms? Why do churches (they ask)
resolutely strive to keep Christ out of politics, econom-
ics, sociology—out of contemporary life?

Is it too late now?

Perhaps my deepest responsibility is not to be found in preserving anything which exists. Could it be that the dying of present existence represents honest faith and creative discipleship? Could it be that ours is uniquely an age for the planting of seeds for a new life to emerge?

I do not want to impose any pattern upon the future. The worst paternalism and colonialism seems to issue from exploitation in the name of love. I have told students that I could completely accept their devoting their lives to tearing down what I had spent my life building up, if such action on both of our parts represented honesty.

I feel strongly that my own basic commitment must now be found in as unselfish as possible a concern about who and what can follow here after we are gone.

I discovered that evangelism must concern these students (and faculty) who assumed they had been exposed to Christianity and rejected it, when they had instead—and as an act of conscience—merely repudiated cultural, provincial and sectarian perversions of Christianity. On the basis of their original assumption about the nature of Christianity, they were clearly not interested in the usual species of "inquirers' classes."

Evangelism means "proclamation" of the Word of God, "witnessing" to the presence and redemptive lordship of Jesus Christ, and "servanthood" in the corporate ministry of individual and social responsibility toward other people. Evangelism means outreach. Dialogue, as outreach, cannot ever be manipulation of others for the purpose of turning them into statistics or prospects for conversion, but rather must be a standing together in mutual trust and servanthood.

I tried to apply this definition when, as a chaplain at Wayne State University, I wrote a paper on the theme "Christianity and the Arts" which was choreographed by the university's dance workshop. I was to read the paper while a dance interpretation was given. However, I did not stand passively outside the action; the dancers integrated me into the choreography itself. In preparation for the event, I joined the dance workshop for several months. Changing into my leotards at a gym locker, I worked out with the students, marveling at their poise and dexterity in contrast with my own inability to communicate freely with my body. The choreographed presentation of the paper was an attempt to communicate the meaning of the gospel to people who were largely alienated from corruptions of it.

The students developed a remarkable dance in which the participants all carried masks. The tribal or ritual dance commenced with five persons taking part, each holding a grotesque mask in front of his face. Suddenly, one of the dancers was forced out of the movement. He withdrew with a mixture of sadness and anger. The dance continued and a second person was forced out by the others. Then a third was ruthlessly removed. This left two dancers. They performed a duet, each holding a mask. Suddenly, one of the two dancers seized the mask of the other. The dancer whose mask had been taken away fled in terror from the stage. The remaining and sole dancer, now gloating and triumphant, held both masks in front of her face. She looked at one and then the other. Gradually, unmistakably, she was overcome by panic. One sensed that she did not know which mask she should relate to—soon she went to pieces. I was making the statement, that many have tragically settled for a mask, a role, a rigid interpretation of life, a dogmatic definition. They allow no leeway, no fluidity or flexibility, no openness or possibility of change.

Near the end of the dance concert, there was a movement in which the five dancers were on stage together and I was with them, seated on a high stool. Four of the dancers remained in lifeless positions. My back was turned to the audience, my position representing an absence of life or feeling. One of the dancers moved to each of the others, trying to lift a hand, or inject life into a form. Each time this proved to be an abortive attempt. Finally, the first dancer grasped the limp hand of one dancer and placed it upon the limp hand of another. After this, the two stirred and came to life. As the dance progressed, it was by relating one dancer to another that life was restored on the stage. Then all five dancers reached out to me. When I came back to life, we all turned, facing the audience and holding out our hands. As we had been restored to a relationship in life, now we sought to become engaged in relationship with the audience.

Early in 1965 I was invited to the Diocese of Washington by the Rt. Rev. Paul Moore, Jr., the Suffragan Bishop. I moved to Washington, D.C., from Detroit. Bishop Moore had been dean of the cathedral in Indianapolis when I was rector of St. George's parish; the two churches had worked closely together in trying to confront urban problems. Paul and Jenny, his wife, had remained close friends of mine through the succeeding years. Now I felt as close to their children as to them, and our relationship was very much a family one. It was possible, then, for one's bishop to be one's friend, and a "brother in Christ" as well as a "father in God."

As assistant priest at the Church of the Atonement, I served under two black priests, both of them old friends. I met the Rev. Quinland R. Gordon on the 1961 freedom ride and we were later together in McComb, Mississippi, in 1964; and I had served under the Rev. Henri Stines at Grace Church in Detroit. When Father Gordon left Washington to accept a position with the Executive Council of the Episcopal Church in New York, Father Stines succeeded him as rector of the Church of the Atonement.

Bishop Moore assured me that I was meant to travel, write and express myself freely. I began to spend more and more of my time with college students in virtually every part of the country, traveling at their invitation to various campuses. They confronted me with their uncompromising questions, hunger for truth, and startling honesty.

At first, I used to read some of the favorite works from the civil rights days (the funeral oration in Ralph Ellison's *Invisible Man*, the sequence about Jerry and the Dog from Edward Albee's *The Zoo Story*, Kim's Letter from *Dying We Live*) as a part of my presentation. Later I read my own prayers and meditations, and quoted from my plays on racial themes. But finally I did not read anything at all. Instead, my talks became dialogical—interlaced with questions from beginning to end. Often these sessions with students lasted more than four hours; in the final two hours I sensed that masks were coming off, real questions being asked, and communication developing in a shared mood of silences, relaxation and easy probing.

My work with students has been criticized on the grounds that I tell them "what they want to hear." In other words, I have been accused of courting popularity with students by telling them how great they are and by withholding needed hard criticism of their ideas and movements. This is seemingly second-hand descriptive data. The fact is that I make it a point to offer students extremely hard prophetic views of their activities, divesting these of romanticism and that absurd self-righteousness which obscures an awareness of moral ambiguities. I have tried to cut against what is fashionable, placing honesty ahead of "effectiveness." Some people have even taken me aside and tried to counsel me: "Don't you understand?" I have been told on such an occasion. "You have created a communications barrier by saying that. Why don't you delete it now and write it in the future? It's not *that* important. Without it, you'll make no enemies. People will be able to accept the rest of what you're saying." But, for me, it could not be deleted. My friendly critics could not seem to understand that I did not wish to be effective at such a high cost. The hard truth simply had to be a part of communication. Student reactions to my talks are always considerably mixed. Once a student told me publicly: "My roommate didn't want to come and hear you because he said you're full of shit." After a talk which I gave at a college in the midwest, a student wrote me: "The first half hour of your lecture made me want to belt you right in the mouth. Your thoughts (as you speak them) seem to pounce on your audience." A Vassar freshman told me, "I don't think you're sincere" and a Sarah Lawrence sophomore announced, during coed week at Yale in 1968, "Malcolm Boyd is passé." Nothing, in years, had so encouraged me. So I was not avant-garde, after all. Having been in and out of "vogue" a half-dozen times, I had finally managed to die as a "Now" person, and was now resurrected. I was out of mere fashion. Holy Jesus, I was free! I am not in a popularity contest, cautiously picking safe words. I am running neither for bishop nor guru.

Following my formal sessions with students, when I usually sit on a tall stool which has a back (because a continuing bout with a slipped disc prevents me from standing for a long period behind a podium), we often adjourn to a coffeehouse, beer joint or dormitory for a more intimate discussion. Some of these meetings have lasted most of the night. I remember one in the back room of a West Virginia saloon, others in an old house in south Georgia, and in a student's apartment in California.

People unfamiliar with my work, except from a distance, have tended to consider one of its principal weaknesses to be a "hit-and-run" aspect because I am frequently at a campus for just one day or night. I used to agree with this judgment, preferring week-long visits with students in a given setting. But now I think otherwise. The letter I received after one campus visit may explain why:

> I hope you got more sleep than I did last night, as I got to bed at 1:30 this morning. By way of introduction, I am the young priest, a Roman by the way, who sat on the sidelines last night, met you after your talk, and invited you to the Newman House for coffee. I'm writing to you now, because I just want to react. It's as simple as that.
>
> At first we were disappointed that you could not come to dialogue later in the evening. But may I say, without fear of offending you, thank God you had to go on to catch a plane! If you would have been at the Newman House, I'm sure you would have been the center of attraction. But as it was, we all had to turn to ourselves and to each other. Four guys from the Afro-American-Union were there, and a mob of us whites—Catholics, Protestants, Nothing in Particulars, Clergy, Kids—but all human persons—few with any answers, all with many questions.
>
> You told us to learn to ask questions, to search, to probe. We began again last night. As you would have

wanted it, the three-hour bull session centered around social morality—blacks, whites, Power, Love, Hope, etc., etc. Not too much time was spent on private morality, or even on Malcolm Boyd. May I say we do love you, but we're trying hard to love you enough to listen to what you said, rather than sit around and congratulate you on how you said it.

I finally could understand the meaning of a particular ministry which moves into a given situation upon invitation, speaks prophetically, opens up people by confrontation with the gospel, and departs—leaving the people themselves to react and relate together, bind up individual wounds, and decide what to become and to do.

During my stay in Washington, D.C., Charlie Byrd, the guitarist, and I became acquainted at the Showboat Lounge. One night early in 1965, I stood up in the club and read two pieces which I had written, which later appeared as secular meditations in my book *Free to Live, Free to Die*. As I read them in the Showboat Lounge, Charlie and his jazz trio improvisationally accompanied me. One piece was about inner freedom, the other an expression on the theme of "cool" and its relation to passion. Charlie was intrigued by the prayers in *Are You Running with Me, Jesus?*, so we had some work sessions together in a Washington studio which we rented; I would read my prayers aloud while he improvised on his guitar. As a result of this we presented a concert in the National Cathedral.

Charlie and I appeared together in a New York City church on Good Friday for a three-hour service in 1966. It was divided into seven twenty-minute portions (paralleling the traditional seven-section Christian observance of Good Friday). Again I read prayers from *Are You*

Running with Me, Jesus? while Charlie improvised on his guitar. The *New York Times* said that, "the liturgical gave way to the colloquial," describing the service as "a gentle blend of Bach, the blues and prayer in the contemporary vein." Next came an appearance at the 1966 Newport Jazz Festival when we presented a forty-minute concert. (At Bailey's Beach in Newport one day Hugh D. Auchincloss, Jacqueline Kennedy Onassis' stepfather, asked me why I had not written any prayers for stockbrokers. It is one of the things I intend to do.)

It was odd being called a performer. I felt that reading my prayers was not a performance—any more than the Mass is a drama, and the priest an actor playing a role. I was, in the jargon of our day, doing my own thing—being myself, and becoming absorbed in my dialogue with Charlie Byrd. For he was not "accompanying" me, really; we were communicating verbally and nonverbally with one another.

One day I was reading a few of my prayers over a radio program. An irate woman phoned in and said, "Your prayers are dirty." She meant prayers about a pregnant unmarried girl, a bleak slum, loneliness, an extramarital love affair, hypocritical Northern middle-class whites refusing to rent an apartment to a black schoolteacher. The woman on the phone was living a kind of pseudo-Christianity, locked inside church instead of life. It's not a question of secular or sacred—for me, everything is sacred. Puritanism is the division of what is supposedly sacred and holy from what is considered secular and evil.

In the fall of 1966 I performed at the hungry i, a nightclub in San Francisco. I was there as a priest, not an entertainer—because I am not an entertainer. The four thousand dollars I earned in my four-week engagement I gave to the black liberation movement. I read a few prayers from *Are You Running with Me, Jesus?*, a few meditations from *Free to Live, Free to Die,* and then replied informally to people's questions. Nothing in recent years intrigued me more than the uproar which greeted my performance. Even quite recently, a critic disparagingly referred to it in print as my "Prayer Act."

What was a priest *doing* in the hungry i? Wasn't it heretical for him to be in a nightclub? This priest was taking a knife and slashing through the utterly false, dreary, pretentious, theologically unsound, personally burdensome dichotomy between "church" and "world." It was simply another Expresso Night. Being at the hungry i meant the same to me as reading my prayers to jazz accompaniment at the Newport Jazz Festival, or appearing in one of my plays in a coffeehouse theater.

There is another reason I played the hungry i. It is akin to why I went on the freedom ride in 1961. In each case I was invited to put my body where my words were. When I was asked to take part in the freedom ride, I sat up one night, trying to weigh all the factors which seemed to be involved and make a decision. I decided that if I didn't go I should shut up on the subject of racial justice. When I was asked to appear for a month at the hungry i, I felt that if I didn't accept I should have the decency to shut up forever concerning the church's involvement in the world. I decided to complement rhetoric with action.

Critical reaction to my performance was extremely varied: The San Francisco *Chronicle* deplored it; the *New York Times* strongly recommended it; the *Christian Century* attacked it, the *National Catholic Reporter* praised it; *Life* said it "bombed"; the Huntley-Brinkley TV program said it succeeded.

Audiences at the hungry i seemed understanding, friendly, and basically open to what I was doing. Certainly, there were dissenters—sharp and loud. One lady exited in the middle of my prayer readings, shouting out, "Goodnight, ex-priest!" Another night, two people got up and walked out. A man in the audience asked me, "Why do you think those people walked out on you? Did they disapprove of what you are doing?" Frankly, I didn't know. But a note handed to me cleared up the matter. It had been left with a waiter, and read: "My apologies for leaving, but we are students and my date must return to the dorm before midnight. Thanks."

One morning in San Francisco I took part in a simple and moving event. Peter Yarrow and Barry Feinstein called me at five in the morning. Would I come right out to the beach before sunrise? They were filming a sequence for their motion picture *You Are What You Eat*. I got into clothes and drove out. Fifty or sixty students were already on the beach, huddled under blankets and coats. I joined them. We talked, losing some of our words in the strong morning wind which lashed against our faces. Then some kids started making love, others sand castles, and a few ran into the ocean water. We held a *Seventh Seal* kind of march along the seashore, splendidly and freely being ourselves, yet within the context of a consciously corporate action. We broke loose and ran and danced spontaneously—in small clusters, then in giant circles. We related to one another enthusiastically; ours was a celebration of the dawn and life, the vast stretch of ocean which lay before us, and being together in that place.

Dick Gregory headlined the show at the hungry i. (We had become friends after once being jailed together in Chicago during a civil rights demonstration.) We appeared twice on Monday through Thursday nights, three times on Fridays and Saturdays. (The club was closed Sundays.) Never have I worked harder. Peter Yarrow (of Peter, Paul, and Mary) flew out from New York to accompany me on the guitar and stage my readings. I tended always to stay on stage too long, trying to answer too many questions. On weekends, when we had three performances, I had to cut my readings due to the pressure of time. Sometimes during intermission I would take friends who were catching the show out into an alley behind the hungry i and read for them the prayers and meditations which had been deleted, as a young student accompanied me on guitar. Generally, between shows, I was in the club's bar talking with people who had either seen one performance or were waiting to catch another. People were intensely anxious to ask questions; often a virtual mob scene built up inside the bar, with men and women shouting comments and questions.

What did I feel? I was scared. There were flashing, agonizing, confusing images between people in the audience and myself—could they see me at all or only my clerical collar and "Father" sitting up on the high stool in the hard light? Would it be possible for us to annihilate isolated roles and rigid separation, and to construct bridges of feeling and encounter between ourselves? I knew that silence could speak louder than articulated responses or applause. Yet, in my weakness, I welcomed the audience reactions I could *hear*. They were comforting and reassuring. Though I kept an inner silence and cool, I drove myself to the edge of physical and emotional exhaustion during that month.

The hungry i experience has deeply affected the way I look at a number of things. For example, I used to enjoy the challenge of speaking to large groups of people (I once gave an address before ten thousand). Now I dislike the element of show business which seems inevitably to be a part of keeping a large number of people responsive to a speaker. Technique has a way of taking over when it is needed; this includes the injection of humor, dramatic emphasis on key points, shifting of mood, projection of "sincerity," and the necessity to have an irresistibly strong opening (which may determine the course of the whole presentation) and ending. My objection to most traditional sermons is their grounding in technique. I have never practiced in front of mirrors or taken speaking lessons; but to claim that one does not develop a technique, as a matter of course, while delivering a large number of public speeches, is altogether naive. Now I prefer speaking to a very small group of people; the give-and-take is simpler, less mannered, and genuine conversation seems to result. A university student, a good friend of mine, walked out of a meeting of around sixty people which I was addressing. "I never intend to listen to you speak again to a group of more than five or six people," he told me afterward; I knew exactly how he felt.

What I disliked most about the hungry i was that technique had to take over when I was too fatigued or concerned about audience reactions to be human. One night NBC-TV's crew photographed my presentation in front of an audience at the hungry i; on the next two nights CBS-TV and ABC-TV sent crews to do the same thing. It was almost impossible to relate to persons in the audience amid the physical distraction of cameras and technicians operating, as well as the psychological distraction of knowing they were there merely as observers and not participants. This virtually precluded the possibility of everybody in the room becoming a community.

If you don't like the fire, the saying goes, stay out of

the kitchen. My experience at the hungry i taught me that if one cuts against the grain of accepted preconceptions and the public relations which accompanies them one has walked straight into the kitchen. What I did was to make myself well-nigh totally vulnerable by moving into an altogether new and untested experience and, in that context, smashing traditional images—in my opinion evangelism required this. By evangelism, I do not mean generating media publicity about an event; I mean trying to build a bridge between alienated people by moving vulnerably onto somebody else's ground where *his* ground rules will be the law. Trying to learn how to hear a new language—because people express themselves with it. Trying to enter into the experience—the world view, the thought forms, the ethics, the social mores—of people who stand outside one's own experience. If one refuses to do this he remains in a ghetto, and surely cannot engage in communication of the gospel outside it.

Yes, I had once worked in Hollywood. But now I had been an ordained priest for eleven years. These years had been spent in theological seminaries, monasteries, a parish, church chaplaincies on campuses—a world of religious publications, religious books, religious people and religious rules. For me, as a priest, to walk out on the stage of the hungry i was to break out of one culture into another. I felt it had to be done—for the sake of the Christian gospel in a highly secular society; for the sake of the church, largely alienated from the lives of millions; for my own sake as I struggled to find radical meanings of priesthood in the world in which I lived.

Before appearing at the hungry i, I had already become aware of the ambivalent nature of publicity. Once I had been able to approach it casually, believing nothing was deader than yesterday's newspaper, and anyhow, surely this was not *serious* business—it only molded images, which could be (I thought) shaped and reshaped at will. I found out now that publicity, in a world of mass media, is deadly serious; that persons can be trapped in public images far more securely than in iron masks; and that, in fact, a number of political, social and religious figures desire such entrapment in images of their own devising, and can successfully perpetuate the imagery because the public is trapped, too. I realized that I do not wish to be so trapped. At the hungry i the event was so highly unusual that it meant, in news parlance, "man bit dog" instead of "dog bit man." I was buried beneath an avalanche of news print, which I thought would be useful in helping to make my point that the church needs to become radically engaged with the world. My expectations backfired when the sheer notoriety of the happening obliterated, in the news media, an explanation of the motivations underlying the happening. Too, I was given a new iron mask when "nightclub priest" replaced "espresso priest," "freedom rider" and "hip-prayer priest" as a headline category. Yet I was in a nightclub for only one month out of my life! I never repeated, at the hungry i or any other club, the presentation which I gave there for four weeks. Would I do it again? Yes, I believe so. For while it cost me personal misunderstanding and pain, the event did accomplish, in part, what I had intended. It contributed, simply as one part of a movement of related events, to freeing many priests, ministers and nuns to work in new forms of expression. It made a statement about both the gospel and the church in relation to the world.

Another lesson was contained in the wholly disproportionate news value which was accorded my appearance. So the church moving outside its isolation into the fast, hip life of a great city's night world was *news*. I had preached for years about the existence of a mighty gulf between the church and the world, but I had not actually *experienced* it. The effect upon me was devastating, especially when some critics representing both "sacred" and "secular" announced clearly, "Run back to your ghetto, man—or Father—and stay there!" Was I, at the hungry i, a success or a failure? That is perhaps the best part of it—the widely disparate judgments which prevented a final judgment either by myself or anyone else. Beneath the superficial carping there lay a deep controversy which defied any consensus.

The most difficult times at the hungry i came for me at the main shows on Friday and Saturday nights. People stood in line outside, the room was jammed, and many men and women, out for a good time on the weekend, had been drinking for hours. A festive, curious mood made it harder for me when I talked about war, poverty and racism. Conversely, my best time at the hungry i was at the third, and last, "show" on the same weekend nights—or early mornings. It was past midnight when I was introduced and walked onto the stage. The thinned-out crowd was quiet. People in the front row put their feet and drinks on the edge of the stage. It reminded me of the best times I have known in church; indeed, this was church. Soberly, cautiously, and with deep mutual feeling, we talked and prayed. We took the skin off of man, and man's myths about gods off of God.

God,
I do not want to be calm or serene.
God,
I fear that the worst death is false peace.
God,
I will fight against permanent dreaming or total sleep.
God,

I am not afraid to be wounded.
God,
I am afraid . . .

I always used to wear the clerical collar. Increasingly, students asked me why. I explained that I considered it a symbol of paradox, mystery, and the Absurd, in the midst of a life and a world which I would characterize as paradoxical, mysterious, and Absurd. I explained (only half-jokingly) how, if I could change the seating pattern of an airplane by wearing the clerical collar, why should I give it up too easily? I referred to the fact that, on a crowded airplane, late-boarders would trek to the rear of the machine, making their way down a crowded aisle, jostling other people and carrying heavy luggage—rather than sit down in a convenient front seat beside a man wearing a clerical collar. So the collar obviously said *something*—something that might be used as a point of departure for serious thought. I told Dick Gregory how sometimes I would sit down next to an infrequent black on an airplane and say "Do you mind if I join you? We could free *two* seats." (Now I tend to dress casually, exchanging archaic clerical symbolism for contemporary clothing.)

Acting out of my dislike of the false church-world dichotomy, since my Colorado chaplaincy days, I have been a reviewer of films for various church publications. For five years, I met a regular monthly deadline as a film critic. In February, 1961, I explained my views as a reviewer to the *New York Times:* "Obviously, self-labeled religious subject matter does not mean that a movie is a religious one. Such films as 'Room at the Top' and 'A Streetcar Named Desire' must be understood as possessing more religious significance than the Hollywood biblical extravaganzas . . . Good religious films are those that deal realistically, poetically, probingly and unerringly with the human condition and pose the right, hard questions about the meaning of life and suffering and joy." When Vincent Canby of *Variety* (who now reviews films for the *New York Times*) asked me to define "a family film," I replied: "It would be a film which brings the family together for a discussion of topics ranging anywhere from sex and love to political or social problems. Principal effect of most of today's so-called family films is to send a family off to Howard Johnson's for chocolate sundaes. Most church people have no conception of what makes 'a good film'—they are looking for photographed Sunday School tracts. How many of these people, supposedly so concerned with the world around them, would go to see a film like 'Breathless,' a legitimate reflection of a time and place and attitude?"

For two years, as an extension of my duties as a reviewer, I served on the film awards committee of the Broadcasting and Film Commission of the National Council of Churches. In 1966 we honored *The Pawnbroker* and bypassed *The Greatest Story Ever Told*, and, in 1967, selected *Who's Afraid of Virginia Woolf?* for honors over *The Bible*. I have never had any illusions about the importance of my work as a film critic. My main concern has been to try to mold new attitudes toward films and redefine "morality" in motion pictures. I have tried not to use a bad film as a whipping boy, and have sought films which aroused my enthusiasm. To review *The Ten Commandments, The Greatest Story Ever Told,* and *The Bible* was a painful task; I knew that I was cutting against the grain of firmly held beliefs about miracles, myths, the nature of God, and the very definition of religion. On the other hand, it was a great delight to review *La Dolce Vita, La Strada, Hiroshima, Mon Amour,* and other innovative foreign films, as well as such American pictures as *Dr. Strangelove, The Pawnbroker, Bonnie and Clyde* and *The Graduate.*

I had always written out of a sense of Christian mission; I considered my books to be "preaching" in the sense of contemporary evangelism. I certainly never expected them to interest a vast public. However, commencing with *Are You Running with Me, Jesus?,* they did. In that book, I tried to write prayers in a style that would be honest and meaningful for me, if not for anyone else. I feel it is anti-orthodox to lock up content inside stale, outmoded forms of expression. So, in *Free to Live, Free to Die,* I tried to do the same thing with meditations. In my *Book of Days,* I endeavored to work with the very traditional concept of "a thought for a day" and revolutionize it (thereby preserving the core of its traditional integrity) for use today. In *The Fantasy Worlds of Peter Stone,* I worked with fables simply as an extension of this same overall impulse. As Langston Hughes used to call my prayers "poems," so various people may call my meditations, thoughts, and fables by other names.

The germ idea of a book can sometimes be traced in one's consciousness, other times not. Harvey Cox, Stephen Rose and I were together in Chicago one evening in 1966. When Cox expressed a concern that there existed a serious need for a spirituality to reflect the concerns and realities of the secular, I was influenced to develop the "secular meditations" which later appeared in *Free to Live, Free to Die.* Of course, there are books that take shape in one's consciousness, yet never get written. William Stringfellow and I made plans in 1964 to write a book together. I remember the day when we went out in a rowboat on a lake near Atlanta in order to outline the book in detail. Bill rowed as I made notes on a scrap of paper. We became so engrossed in the subject of our book that we stayed out on the lake for two full hours. It was a hot Georgia summer day. My resulting sunburn was a broiling disaster, matched only by the sad dénouement that we never wrote our book.

As my books became popular, I learned that a writer is expected to *meet* his public. He cannot sit quietly by his fireplace in a country retreat (if, indeed, he has one), a teapot whistling on the stove and a fat cat purring on a cushion in the window seat, as he quietly writes, far, far removed from the madding crowd. Very prominent authors have blazed the trail to major cities to do newspaper, radio and television interviews, and a new writer is asked to follow it.

Would St. Paul undertake such a tour, if he were living today and had written a book of prayers or meditations? I believe so. Abbé Michonneau speculated that if St. Paul were to come back to our world in the flesh, he would become a newspaperman. It seems to me that he would use all possible God-given methods and tools to communicate the gospel to people, as author, public relations specialist, or newsman. My own apostolate on my first author's tour was, it seemed to me, a remarkable opportunity to meet and talk with many different people; I would be moving in secular, not religious, circles. I would be living out a number of problems in Christian communication which I had written about, safely and academically, in my seminary thesis and first book. My tour was, in effect, a laboratory; my theories would be tested. I had earlier written the book *Christ and Celebrity Gods* and, during seminary days, glibly moralized from a detached point of view and a safe distance about realities with which I should now have to be existentially concerned.

The tour also represented my first time out on the

road as a worker-priest. I had recently terminated church income. Henceforth I would support myself by means of writing and occasional lectures. This income would also permit me to assist financially in the peace and black freedom movements.

Shortly before the tour began, I found myself in a strangely traumatic moment. I felt dwarfed, gobbled up, miniscule, surrounded—*a product*. I blew up. I knew I could not permit myself to be turned into a commodity, that I must fight hard to remain vulnerably human.

One morning, as I was walking through a hotel lobby after having appeared on an early TV interview show, a man passed me and swore under his breath. "Weren't you on television this morning?" he asked. I said yes. "Goddam you," he retorted, and walked on. Fun and games. On that program I had expressed my opposition to war, as well as my commitment to racial justice. Another interview, in yet another city, brought me a letter addressed to "Malcolm X Boyd." It commenced: "You damned nigger-lover. No wonder black men burnt Watts. They don't know God."

Once I tried to keep a journal during a publisher's tour, but gave up almost immediately because there was little or no time to write during the day, and at night I was too tired. Such a journal would have been monotonous in its recording of fairly similar happenings, day after day, city after city, hotel room after hotel room. (The people I encountered were different and highly individual, however—they would have made the difference.)

My journal-keeping effort did last one day. It expressed my feelings as I was leaving Boston. I was finding that for a modern Christian writer to relate to a mass public responsive to his "preaching," was very, very hard work.

Saturday

Today I guess I could (Roman collar notwithstanding) kill everybody connected with this tour. Why am I on it, anyway? Why can't writers just write: Why is America so loused up that everybody is supposed to get out on the road—statesmen, politicians, artists, stove salesmen, priests, foreign dignitaries, insurance men *and* authors?

It's been a tough week in Boston. I've tried to pace myself, do all the things on my schedule—nicely, without temperament or blowing up or replying to a blast with anything but a decent smile and a logical, rational, human statement—and *now,* here I am standing in the airport and there's no plane. I mean, the plane on my ticket doesn't run on Saturday, the day for which the ticket was written. So, loaded down with a suitcase, newspapers, a book I am to review for the *Times,* and my rubber overshoes (it isn't snowing today), I've got to sit for two hours while airplane employees keep shouting over the P.A. information about flight arrivals and departures, lost wives and waiting limousines.

A lady seated in the same waiting area just leaned over and quietly said to me: "I've met *two* celebrities this week. You, Father Boyd, and a man in Boston who went on TV to tell about how he finds all kinds of valuable things in old antique and junk shops. I see you on TV, too, Father, and you're wonderful. So the Lord's been good to me this week. *Two* celebrities. Would you please sign this piece of paper for me, Father?"

My departure from Boston was further confused last night. I had stayed over for a TV program which had to be taped late yesterday. At around 4 P.M. I noticed a Western Union message had been left, an hour earlier, in my hotel room box. "Call Western Union, Operator 1." When I did so, I found that the star of the program had, at the last minute, "reshuffled the format" and that I had regretfully, been "preempted." So an entire day had been shot, or lost, or swept under a rug, or whatever one might call it. I mean, I had been badly needed in New York and had

had a dozen pressing commitments in Washington. But such human concerns can get lost in the jungle of authors' tours—or, admittedly, a number of other things. I realize I'm quite tired, and need to get outside airports, big downtown hotel lobbies, and restaurants, hotel rooms, airport limousines, and also off airplanes. A walk in the country for an hour would be very, very healing.

Actually, my last working assignment in Boston was a healthy, lively, honest one. I was on the radio last night from 10 until 1 A.M. (It's a program I could have done earlier in the week, if we'd known I was not to tape that last TV interview.) The radio show comprised an interview with a vigorous, hard-hitting young man who seemed really concerned about issues of peace, race and poverty. He pulled no punches at all, so far as I could tell, in stating his views, which are clearly not out of a John Birch Society handbook. Then the phones were opened up for calls from listeners. These calls weren't nervous, bitchy, non-dialogical, hysterical ones (as encountered on some programs, in some cities. Dallas is bad, so are Atlanta and Los Angeles). These callers seemed either to want specific information or to engage in some good dialogue; if they disagreed, they were able to say so without becoming loud or insulting. What fun!

Why will it seem so good to get back to my own home, bed, typewriter, coffee pot and easy chair, even for only a few hours, after a trip like this one? Because hotel living, day in and day out, is one vast impersonal hell. Going up and down in elevators all day: there is no relating of persons at all. One's hotel room is the most transient single factor in modern living: there is no *connection* between the persons using it, day after day, night after night. The stone shafts upon which one looks from the same dreary hotel windows. The thermostat-controlled air, not quite human, not hot, not cold. The Kleenex dispenser in the bathroom, the cellophane cover over the drinking glass (this is provided *every* day, so that one can't even get used to drinking out of the same glass for three or four days), the Gideon Bible in a drawer with a

folded hotel laundry bag and a local telephone book. To
add a pragmatic note, I don't eat properly on a trip like
this. I always miss breakfast, often miss lunch, and end
up in some TV studio at 3 P.M., starving. Then they bring
me yet another cup of coffee.

They're calling my plane. I won't believe it until I've
boarded and we're in the air. So the first stop, Boston, is
completed. I had some clam chowder, a great look at the
Charles River at night when lights were shining on the
ice, called some friends, managed to leave messages with
some other people's friends, and had a few surprises. One
was the visit, for a half day, of a publisher's representative from New York. He made me realize how little the
public relations specialists who plan these trips know
about what it's like to *do* them. Such P.R. experts, map-
ping campaigns from New York, have no idea what it's
like to *ride* the planes, *check* into the hotels, *eat* the road
food, *run* to the appointments—always fresh, alert, and
"a good guest," manage to *fall asleep* on cue at night in
order to *get up* at dawn for that very, very early interview,
and, in dozens of ways, be a damned nice, attractive,
expendable commodity. So I shout or cry or jump up and
down, whenever I can, to remind my publisher that I'm
human and therefore not a commodity. Of course, I have
to remind myself too.

My own life soon took a very different turn, placing
me in a situation where I would once again build and
mend fences, dig for roots, nurture seeds, and enter into
close relationships and deep involvements within community. In 1968–1969, I was asked by R. W. B. Lewis,
the Master of Calhoun College at Yale, to live and work
there as a Fellow. The Rev. William Sloane Coffin, Jr.,
the chaplain of Yale, graciously asked me to act also as
"visiting chaplain."

It was strange and wonderful, at forty-five, to be living in the midst of students. I ate my meals with them. I
was able to do a lot of listening to them. They came to

my room, or I to theirs, and we would talk together way
past midnight about the things that mattered to us. I
conducted a few seminars. I led a Free School course in
Creativity. A black director of a ghetto theater, a black
priest, and I conducted a seminar on "Black Consciousness—White Consciousness." The *Yale Daily News,*
which proudly calls itself "the oldest college daily,"
asked me to write a weekly column; I gratefully accepted
and thereafter spent up to ten hours a week preparing
my Wednesday morning journalistic offering.

In my first column (September 24, 1968) I explained
my reasons for coming to Yale. I wrote: "My preoccupa-
tion now, as I commence my stay at Yale, is to stay alert
for signs of new forms and new content. In the theater.
In the church. In politics. In the University. I hope for
dialogue instead of debate. I want to listen to what students are saying, especially underneath or despite
words. And, as I feel strongly that we have come to a
period of necessary and painful silences, I hope to share
these in creative community instead of bearing them
simply in isolation." My best remembered column was
an interview with Hugh Hefner of *Playboy* magazine,
which the editors of the *Yale Daily News* illustrated with
a four-column horizontal photograph of a sexily reclin-
ing nude. I was invited to senior societies, the Yale Political Union, college groups, a commune of nine students
living out in the country, and SDS. The Yale Drama
School asked me to participate in a discussion following
the opening of a new Jules Feiffer play. A student helped
me pick out a guitar and gave me lessons. I bought some
gym equipment, signed up for a locker, and worked out
three days a week with students at the Payne Whitney
Gymnasium.

When William Sloane Coffin, Jr., asked me to be the
first guest preacher of the year in Battell Chapel, I re-

sponded with mixed feelings. I admired him and wanted to be a part of the worshiping community at Yale. However, I had not "preached" in a church for approximately one year; I had come to feel that preaching must be an expression of life-style, not a verbal exercise within a prescribed ritual. On the morning that I was to give my sermon at 11 A.M., I had been present at a performance of the Living Theater's *Paradise Now* until 2:30 A.M. I was moved by its openness and vulnerability, its juxta-position of new content and new form. I knew that I should have to discard my prepared manuscript and also any kind of outline in my mind. I did, sharing these feelings with the congregation. At the conclusion, I said that a sermon cannot "end," and simply walked out of the pulpit. I was grateful that many people chose to discuss the sermon with me, sympathetically entering into the spirit in which it was given.

In one of my *Yale Daily News* columns, I quoted from a letter I had received, postmarked Detroit: "Malcolm, I'm 24 and black. Why won't they wake up before it's too late, and I'm dead? Just once in my life I want to be free. Is that asking too much?"

A couple of days after the column appeared, I received this note from a Yale student:

malcolm
i am rich and therefore an outcast from life
they don't trust us
we aren't in close
my mind bleeds to communicate—but
the gardol shield keeps
me from touching anything real
malcolm
i am 19 and white
why can't i wake up before it's too late?
just once in my life i want

to be free
is that asking too much?

Many changes were coming to Yale. One of these was
women, following a successful coeducation week which
led to a decision to change the old all-male way of life in
1969–1970. During coeducation week, in fact, it had
been my interesting lot to conduct a discussion, for both
men and visiting women students, on the theme "Man
and Sex at Yale."

My Yale experience has been, on the whole, exceedingly happy. I recognized it as a bridge-time in my own
life. I was breaking with some past things and preparing
myself—for what? I did not know. Often I have sat up
past midnight sharing ideas with Bill Coffin; he has been
like a brother to me. "I don't find rough edges on you," I
told him once. "It is healing, and doesn't cut and hurt, to
communicate with you."

When Norman Mailer, a nonresident Fellow at Calhoun, visited the college in December, 1968, I experienced a head-on collision with celebrity and, I think it
must be granted, genius. Mailer fascinated and dis-
turbed me. For days after his visit, I was grappling furiously with myself and could not organize my thoughts
or write a coherent page.

Some thirty people joined him for two hours of informal discussion in the afternoon. He responded to questions on politics. He was kind, in communion with most
of us in the room, and seemingly without edge. But later
that night, when he addressed three hundred people in
the college dining hall, it was another matter. His late
entrance was stagey. He was on a high. At first, he
played with the crowd, putting us on, placing himself in
obvious roles and then deftly leaping out of them. It was
an enormously enjoyable and very warm performance.

Mailer seemed to be obliterating distances. One felt
highly welcome inside the joke.

Without warning, the mood shifted. His jokes were no
longer amusing. Mailer seemed to start out in one direction in his thoughts, fumble, lose track altogether, ca-
reen into stream-of-consciousness, change the subject,
pose in solitude, and peter out in a jibe or a *non sequitur*.
He said he was going to read us the text of an article
about race which he had written for *Look*. Incredibly, he
removed the long galleys from a coat pocket and read
them, line by line, aloud in an uncertain and flat voice.
When he finished, he consented to answer questions.
Several of these bothered him; he wanted to change the
subject, requesting some fast, direct questions covering
a wide variety of themes. Yet Mailer and his questioners
immediately got mired down in a repartee marked by
bang-bang-bang delivery on his part, and embarrass-
ingly personal references along with stumblings into
verboten subjects, on theirs.

The reactions to Mailer were legion. "He's a phony,"
announced a student who, I remembered, had said the
same thing earlier about William F. Buckley, Jr. "He's a
genius because he plays all these roles in order to get
interaction," a young faculty member told me over lunch
two days afterward. The latter seemed a working hy-
pothesis which I could accept. However, I had to admit
that I never found Mailer underneath the roles and images. He remained an absolute mystery to me, an
enigma which smiled, strutted, scowled, aroused hard
tensions inside other people, exploited the status of
American super-star, and wrote the best prose of anybody around.

Norman Mailer carried a lot of personal meaning for
me because, in 1965, Ralph J. Gleason of the San Francisco *Chronicle* wrote a column entitled "Two Moments

in a Revolution," in which he drew a comparison between the two of us. I was in San Francisco to preach at
Grace Cathedral in a service which presented a new
modern setting of the Choral Eucharist, while Mailer
had come to Berkeley to address a Vietnam Day protest.
Mr. Gleason apparently attended both events.

"Would it shock you to compare Rev. Boyd with Norman Mailer?" he wrote. "The comparisons are obvious if
you pause a moment to accept the idea.

"The Rev. Boyd spoke of the reality of God in our
society, of how Christianity must return from formality
to actuality. Norman Mailer spoke of the reality of death
and life and how the society's very existence depends
upon a moral revolution, a return from formality to
reality, from symbol to the thing itself.

"Both were concerned with truth, both with salvation
and both with the link between the here and now and
posterity.

"Agnostic that I am, Rev. Boyd's sermon was the most
impressive I have heard in years, and a veteran journalist remarked, as Mailer stood on the platform, the applause thundering in the air, that his was the most impressive political speech in a generation."

Mr. Gleason's remarks later intrigued me because,
while he liked me in Grace Cathedral, he intensely disliked me in the hungry i sixteen months later. This is
one reason why I so searchingly studied Norman Mailer
at Yale, trying to get ahold of him as a man and find the
clue to his mystery. I failed.

While I was at Yale, Janet Lacey came to visit me.
(She was the British Council of Churches executive
who, when I was a graduate student at Oxford, had put
me in touch with church experiments in England and
sent me off to the Ecumenical Institute in Switzerland.)
By now she had retired, and was on a speaking tour of

the States sponsored by the Church Women United. When Janet's schedule included New Haven, she had time for a long afternoon's chat with me. She had great dignity and presence, and was quite beautiful, having lost none of her gaiety, verve, and downright zest for life. She told me how she had been to Buckingham Palace for lunch with the Queen and Prince Philip; she spoke knowledgeably about politics in every part of the world, singling out for special reference her fear of a renascent Germany in Europe; then we talked about the theater in London, a favorite mutual topic. Janet laughed. "I've always been a night person, and had to be a day person *too* because I had a job," she said. "Now, retirement means I can be simply a night person."

Janet's life and mine had remained in touch—I had stopped in London on my way home from the Taizé Community in 1957; I had met her at an international church gathering in Strasbourg, France, in 1960. Over the years we met in Los Angeles, or Geneva, or New York. Janet had even come to Indianapolis—on a national speaking tour of some kind—and had spoken in St. George's Church. Being a woman, she had not been asked to mount the pulpit itself; she spoke at the top of the chancel steps and wore an appropriate head covering of black veil. Janet introduced my isolated, poor, determinedly all-white congregation to the facts of world ecumenism, racism, and refugees, linking all these to the Christian gospel.

Our meetings were brief but we made them happen— we worked at staying friends. And I never ceased to be amazed at the sheer time she gave to others, with what it represented of essential life energy. As she spoke, seated across from me at Yale in the fall of 1968, I gloried in the durability of our friendship which had survived awful distances, unshared experiences, and the ruthless passage of time. I felt totally relaxed with her. Our conversation did not attempt to fill cavities of experience; it was not heavy or pretentious about "events"; we did not at all try to catch up with each other's lives. Instead we permitted ourselves the luxury of random talk, dipping briefly into this, dabbling unhurriedly in that—topics we knew were happily inconsequential. Although we might never see one another again, we did not frame formal remarks or compose epitaphs. By mutual consent, we spoke without a beginning or an end, allowing ourselves unalloyed fun and play in a middle current. As I basked in Janet's comfortable presence, I was aware how friendship comes as close as anything else to realizing the mystery of life.

I was speaking to a group of women about peace when word came to us that President Kennedy had been shot. Before we even got outside that room, where the only news we had received was the stark assassination notice itself, I heard a woman saying "A Negro did it." When Malcolm X was shot, I was in a social situation with a group of middle-class Negroes who were patently uninterested in the news announcement; then, getting into a taxi, I told the white driver that I wanted to find a newspaper, no matter how far out of the way it was necessary to go, because I wanted to read about Malcolm. "That nigger son-of-a-bitch," he said.

I was in Honolulu, in the spring of 1968, as the guest of students at the University of Hawaii. A Chinese student had driven me back to a hotel where the students had housed me. Suddenly he ran into the lobby, following me. Martin Luther King, Jr., had been shot, he said. He had just heard the news over his car radio. We sat together in his car for an hour, hearing repetitions of the stark announcement, and talking. I said that I would feel different an hour later, after I had had time to link memory with the present. An hour later I felt crushed, wanting to burrow deep inside myself; instead I had to address the students of the University of Hawaii in what would be my final talk there, trying to interpret for all of us what had happened.

A few weeks later, in the spring of 1968, I was in a hotel room in New York City when I turned on a TV set early in the morning to find out how Senator Robert F. Kennedy had fared the night before in the California primary election. The news of the shooting of Robert Kennedy had been repeated many, many times during the preceding hours, so that by now it was no longer presented as news; the news was each subsequent development in the context of what had become a death watch. Thus my first knowledge of the event came when the commentator referred to the shooting somewhat in passing. I did what millions of other people did: raged, wept, prayed, and shouted in futile desperation. As many others did, I made long-distance telephone calls to the people who were close to me. This was a time of tragedy to be shared with family and close friends. But there had been no time for healing after Dr. King's murder, and one wondered now if there would ever be. How could these events be placed in a proportion with which one could come to terms?

In this moment I find myself asking deep and painful questions about life. I can't help crying out in the midst of a world in which complexity and feeling lost seem to be more and more of a reality.

Many of us are crying out from an underground

church—you may call it a new church, an open church,
an innovative church, the confessing church, or an experimental church. So much attention has been given to
the name. Sometimes I feel like calling the new Christian movement "underground—schmunderground." In
Dallas, on February 14, 1967, I first used the phrase
"underground church." Yet I spoke of a revolutionary
movement within the church which I described as essentially "nameless." The fact that an enormous number of
people in various parts of the world identified strongly
and immediately with a casual and secondary allusion I
made to the underground church—and continue to do so
—is not without significance. I made my remarks when
I was a speaker at the 1967 annual meeting of the Division of Christian Education of the National Council of
Churches. In the course of my remarks, I reported that a
new Christian movement cutting across denominational
lines was "rapidly spreading across the nation" and that
"bypassing official structures and leadership, a real but
nameless revolution" was taking place in American
church life. I explained how I had first become aware,
about six months before, of an underground church. It
simply means that, for many thousands—maybe millions—of us, the game of church-as-usual isn't sufficient
now. A revolution is taking place at virtually every level
of American life—in sex, politics, race, the arts, education, mass communications—while the church, largely
unaware because it is out of touch, stands archaically as
the chaplain of the status quo. If, God forbid, America
should veer sharply toward becoming a police state, the
underground church might take on a reality which now
is only whispered about.

Our cry comes out of real need. The meaninglessness
of churchianity is acutely painful to us: An unchanged
Sunday morning charade with the *same* prayers, *same*

form of sermon, *same* hymns, *same* separation between clergy and laymen, *same* unrelatedness to life, *same* liturgy (be it in old English, new English, rock-and-roll jargon, or Latin), and the *same* feeling of not-touching-base.

We feel a need of prayer and worship in our own idiom and style, reflecting our individual and social experiences and joys, dilemmas and visions. As a result, in underground worship situations, which are often intimate circles of people within private homes, indigenous liturgies and prayers are spontaneously cropping up in every section of the United States.

For Catholics, Protestants and Jews alike, time seems to be running out. This is a time of open crisis, personally and collectively. Increasingly, people feel there is a neon-lit, Muzak-filled vacuum at the pit of their lives where there used to be at least a clear memory of faith. These people will tell you they are experiencing a desperate need for raw, unvarnished honesty if faith is ever going to be possible for them again. But they don't want just honesty. In an age of supposed unbelief, people are yearning for something to believe in. The institutions of organized religion have, they feel, frustrated and betrayed this yearning again and again.

This need for honesty and belief has caused men and women to dig into the underground church. It isn't only that Catholics and Protestants and Jews and agnostic humanists are often not *supposed* to worship together, according to various religious rules. Even if rules were relaxed people don't *want* to gather as isolated individuals in huge congregations within impersonal "houses of worship." People don't *want* to engage in a cold and mechanical ritualistic exercise, terribly unrelated to their actual problems, under the direction of a religious leader who hides behind his role like the Wizard of Oz.

More and more people are finding reality of experience in new forms and settings which bring a feeling of authentic community.

The cry from the underground church is the cry for courage to face the future instead of the past; an ethic rooted in human need instead of ecclesiastical legalism; a concern for people instead of statistics and things; and a passion for life rooted in Biblical faith instead of a passive living death masked by pasted-on smiles, incestuous concern for self-perpetuation of an organization, and yet more slick public-relations and fund-raising drives to create bigger and better real-estate interests.

The cry from the underground church comes out of a curious common sense of loneliness. It is always more acute at times of celebration, and amid crowds and even family circles. Somehow, at such moments, we clearly catch a vision of death and our own participation in it. So, at the very moment of warm lights, traditional music, shared food and close-knit relationship, we stand more starkly alone than at any other time. We seem to be standing outside ourselves, looking on. . . .

In such a moment, we ruthlessly examine ourselves. "Who am I? Am I white or black—or human? Am I American or German, Vietnamese or Brazilian—or human? What, precisely, am I doing in this sad and beautiful world? My life is draining out of me with each heartbeat; what is its meaning? I don't want to waste it. Have I faced myself? Where am I going?"

We don't want to go on crying out such questions in the midst of cold, vast echo chambers. We need to hear one another. We want to stand together. Tennessee Williams expressed this poignantly in his play *Camino Real:* "In a place where so many are lonely, it would be inexcusably selfish to be lonely alone."

We want to learn not only more of our own cultural or

psychological experience, but that of another man with a different experience. We want to listen not only to endlessly repetitive utterances of our own convictions, spoken within the confines of our own ghetto—but to hear new sounds, new words, new concepts and new ideas spoken in another ghetto. Any ghetto represents alienation from other people; we want to communicate across ghettos.

Looking back over the years of the U.S. freedom struggle, I wish that we had tried harder, while attempting to register black people for voting, to communicate with white people whom we often merely—arrogantly—judged. I wish that we had not allowed ourselves to be caught in a process of polarization: We vs. They, the Good Guys vs. the Bad Guys, Us vs. the Enemy. We tried to change laws instead of hearts; we generated publicity instead of engaging other people's minds. We even sank into the pitfall of self-righteousness.

Activism *without* involvement can be a most insidiously effective way of cutting off communication. One's wheels are spinning, silences are filled by noise, ego needs associated with the Protestant Ethic are met by ceaseless work, guilt is assuaged by the satisfaction of a slight achievement, everything can be organized on a big basis—and, sadly, there can be no true feeling at all. Whatever one's iron-masked category, one is tightly locked inside it, and operating on a computerized basis from that vantage point to "help" others. A freedom fighter might assist blacks as statistics yet never actually enter psychologically into the black experience; a middle-class welfare bureaucrat might work from nine to five surrounded by "poor people" as card cases—yet not know what it is to *think* poor; a youth from an affluent background—yet deeply alienated from it—might receive financial benefits from his middle-class parents, yet lose the capacity to *feel* middle-class (indispensable for his task of changing its attitudes from within, after he has been changed himself).

There is always a danger of isolation. For example, blacks need to understand the subtle changes taking place in that spectrum called white opinion, as whites need to realize that they confront not a monolith, but individual black people representing a myriad of views.

Openness to communication came threateningly close to me once when I lived for a period of weeks in suburbia, near New York City. A man across the street from where I stayed had worked hard for everything he earned. His home was indeed his castle; he was leery of Jews and antagonistic to blacks moving into the neighborhood because he believed they might endanger his real-estate investment.

Each morning I saw him depart at 7 o'clock, carrying a lunch pail, when his car pool picked him up for work. Suddenly I realized that if communication could not take place between us, because of our different and very deep beliefs, we would be responsible, in microcosm, for despair and pessimism elsewhere. Building bridges between people must begin with *us*.

Real communication meant that I should not smilingly play a missionary role to change his views so that they would match mine; I had to be as open to his way of thinking as I wanted him to be open to mine. I sought him out; we talked; we related as human beings; we shared our views. Hopefully, both of us had undergone some changes in the dynamics of open communication.

The cry from the underground church is this cry for communication. We seek, and are sought out by, new people in spontaneous or planned encounters. We *do* connect, and often by means of words. While the nonverbal meaning is fundamental, the word is still the

vehicle. We write, and receive, letters. Mine come almost equally from students and older people. They talk
to me directly and here are some of the things they are
saying.

"What a straight jacket I was in for so many years,"
someone wrote me recently. "There has been so much
junk getting in the way for so long. Guess what, here I
am after seven years again ready to acknowledge the
reality of God and my Lord. You and others have shown
me that Jesus is the kind of person who will run with
me. Who understands when I can't take being human
any longer. Hang with it, Luv."

The need is acute, the pain unsupportable by oneself.

Someone else wrote me: "When I first heard about
you, I really didn't care much about civil rights, unwed
mothers or poverty. I was attending a church girls'
school and was perfectly content to live a life naive of
the reality of pain, suffering and frustration. Then I
found that there are people who are living in a modern-
day type of slavery. I found that completing high school,
something I had taken for granted, was a terrific accom-
plishment if you have to bring up yourself and eight
brothers and sisters. But most important of all, I found
that the color of your skin, your religion, and where you
live have nothing to do with your basic right as a human
being. I learned to respect others and at the same time to
truly respect myself. It took me almost nineteen years to
learn these things."

The need is to learn to comprehend one's brother as
well as oneself.

"I look around and see nothing I can do. (I am fifteen.) What can be done?" asked another letter-writer
who entered my life not long ago. "If I ask nuns or
teachers, they say to pray. But, when people are starving, they need food, not prayers. Isn't it better to do what

is right, even if everybody says it's wrong, than to go along? Malcolm, I know you are busy, thanks for listening."

The need is to feel truly useful.

"When I first read about you, I said, oh well, another damn priest trying to prove he's one of the boys; more power to him, but who cares?" someone else wrote me not long ago. "I apologize. I heard you on TV. I went out and got your books and for the first time thought maybe it is possible to be a Christian/christian. I do not want a remote, theologically-ridden Son of God, whose incomprehensibility excuses me from imitation. I do not need a church of ritual and beauty whose dogma and promises encompass humanity, yet cannot hear a human cry. I loved it and long for it, but reject it. I can relate to you because you wear your psychic wounds showing, maybe bleeding a little. I hate the good taste that cures its sores under sterile bandages and antiseptic powders of platitudes and denial."

The underground church, having started from a strong dissident Catholic base—an indication of a rising tide of resistance to traditional centralized authority— will rapidly embrace more and more Protestants. For people are reacting against repressive ethical and social mores in local church structures. Many protest what they believe is a betrayal of Christ in normative American church life.

"Unless a grain of wheat falls into the earth and dies, it remains alone; but if it dies, it bears much fruit." The underground feels that the institutional church, which speaks the words of Jesus to others, must itself will this same dying to self in order to be renewed by God and thus live for others.

When "my" God becomes "our" God, then something

wonderful can happen. "My" world becomes "our" world. "My" life becomes "our" life. Suddenly we are alive together. The alternative is to be dead together.

On a visit to Rome several years ago, I had a lengthy private conversation with the sensitive, renowned and extremely down-to-earth Cardinal Bea. He had acted as confessor to Pope John XXIII and was one of the fathers of the ecumenical movement. His death, in 1968, saddened Christians throughout the world. He told me, during our talk, that he considered himself neither an optimist nor a pessimist, but a realist. What he said has deeply affected me.

I, too, am trying to be a realist. I consider this one of the most challenging periods in human history and, consequently, in the church's history. It is harder and harder to play lukewarm Christian. We are faced by the alternatives of annihilation or enormous betterment of human life. There is incredible hope in the very presence of sharp alternatives.

We humans are summoned to our mission of becoming human.

How?

First, by discovering what our words mean. We ought not to say "I love you" unless we mean "I love you." We ought not to say, alone or in a group, "I believe in . . ." unless we believe in it. Very specific definitions are in order. Who *is* God? Do you feel God is a man, a woman, white, black, American, a busy heavenly switchboard operator, love, Charlton Heston-in-the-sky, a hating creature who runs torture chambers, a kind elderly bishop with a beard . . . ? In my own experience, God is the spirit of loving instead of murder, of relationship rather than fragmentation. To me, the meaning of Jesus is God's sensitivity, involvement, nearness, and intense loving. Prayer, for me, is not asking God for either small favors or great miracles, but wanting to place my life with God in loving and relationship.

Second, by closely relating our words to our attitudes and actions. Communication isn't just words; it is life-style. If we make pledges about democracy, then we must practice it in our cities, schools and neighborhoods. If we profess Christianity, then we must reject churchianity. If we say that we are against war, then we must give ourselves totally to working for peace. Our words in themselves are no longer taken seriously by most people, and even our actions may be looked upon rather cynically. But our way of life—the expression of our whole being—is regarded with a startling seriousness.

Third, by understanding that we are a part of everybody and everything. One cannot point to the church over there; it is right here. I am the church, you are the church, we are the church. [In the reality of the Judeo-Christian tradition acting as the nerve of our social conscience, this touches almost everybody.] Vietnam is not far away—it is where people like you and I are suffering. It is where a man whom we know—a nephew, a son, a friend, a husband—is fighting. Remember: a human face is a human face. Look into it and see. ("I see white and black, Lord. I see white teeth in a black face. I see black eyes in a white face," I wrote in *Are You Running with Me, Jesus?*) A human heart is a human heart; transplant it and see.

Fourth, by listening carefully to what people really mean—underneath mere words. For example, if someone speaks of "revolution," he may not be speaking of anything new. He may have in mind original meanings, turning over the soil, and getting back to essentials that have undergone corruption or been forgotten in the midst of convenient idolatries. If someone says, "I'm dreaming of a white Christmas," he may really be declaring "I'm lonely." A black student saying "Black Power" may be talking about social equality, whites' recognition of the beauty of blackness, and the absence of separation in genuine opportunity. We must listen, not only with the head, but with the heart. Sometimes it is painful; but listening is, I think, a beautiful thing. It has so much to do with people.

Fifth, by jumping into life. This is not merely identification with others—it is active participation in their lives. Love means openness, spontaneity, a radical transformation of individual and social life. Let's knock down ghetto walls. And quit acting like a brother's keeper—who wants one? Does a brother even want a brother? Maybe he's been burned too many times and feels he cannot trust a brother. So we must understand now that, in terrible and great truth, we are more than brothers—we are one another. So we must live together. Shall we do this joyfully and creatively? Anything else would be less than real life.

Hope, like love, is considered by many people to be very, very corny. This year, as I write these lines, I am forty-five. I have learned a few essential things during the short and long years of my life. One of them is that I cannot live without hope. If hope has substance it is closely related to need. For me, the meaning of Jesus is God's radical, total involvement in all of human need, including my own.

Will the church, claiming to be the body of Christ, develop the reality of authentic community as well as a style of life which resembles the prophetic passion and selfless love of Jesus?

This is the cry from the underground church. Despite its name, the time has come for the underground church to surface and witness clearly to the questions it asks and the life-style it seeks to develop. The underground church must participate in the meaning of sacrifice and the radical restructuring of organized religion.

Unmailed Letter 5

Dear E.,

I liked being able to visit you at your college and see you in your world there. You're becoming much more real to me as a person in your own right (remember, I knew you first only as the son of your father and mother). Now I feel we are friends, you and I, independent of any relationship with your family.

What you said when we had lunch the other day has stuck in my craw. You feel as if you were being shot out of a cannon. Your pace is ridiculously fast and gaining momentum. The demands of success are tightening their hold on you. In the midst of all this, you would like to be able to stop and get your breath. (As I said to you, this is only the beginning. The pressures will become far worse with the passing of time.)

Aside from the question of the draft, you don't know yet what to do with your life. You're caught between a strong idealistic drive to give of yourself to others and a strong pragmatic drive to achieve results and success, as traditionally defined by our society. To figure things out, you would like to take a year or two for travel or some other subterfuge for deep thought. In any case, what to do about the draft looms up straight ahead. After that, graduate school seems to be on your map.

Yes, you seem to have a map. That's what is actually bothering you most, isn't it? The damned map, with its cross-sections of expectations and clover-leaf patterns of almost rigidly iron probabilities. You feel that you are not free to strike out, yet this is the only life you've got, and you would like to be kind to it, or, at least, treat it as if it were your life.

Unlike many students whom I know, you are not being pressured by your parents. They're absorbed in their own lives instead of reliving them in yours and, to an astonishing degree, trust you to make your own decisions as a maturing human being.

Your decision not to go after the class presidency is terribly significant in reaching any understanding of you at this point in your life. The class presidency was waiting for you; you passed it up. You told me that you are questioning the meaning of achievement. This office at a prestige school like yours would have meant a lot, after college, in hard currency of lining up what you want in an overly competitive situation. (Okay, you probably wouldn't need this bonus, but who can say?) Anyway, you made a decision. It cuts you off from a whole traditional way of looking at achievement and success; yet you haven't completely stopped valuing these things—you still want some of them.

What, specifically, do you want? It might help to put it this way. What, specifically, don't you want?

Visiting your college, and seeing you there, I realized suddenly that I probably couldn't survive as a student today living under the kinds of pressure you live under. And I sensed, underneath all that we talked about, your uncertainty about what in this society is worth preserving and what should be destroyed so that something else can take its place. You realize an even bigger question is *how* to preserve, or to destroy and rebuild—but *how*? And you don't yet know what you'll be able to live with in this society which your parents and I are graciously handing to you on a plastic platter.

VI

He explains the Christian church may be seen
as embodying an objective ideal. It doesn't
stand for what people think of each other.
It stands for what God thinks of man. It
constitutes a point of reference, therefore,
that remains untouched by dogma and by
outward trappings. It offers society a true
"open end." That is why, in Malcolm Boyd's
view, a man may challenge the formalism,
the institutionalism of the church and still be
its true lover. . . . Speaking of organization
as an end in itself, Malcolm Boyd says,
"It has broken down for me. It has broken
down for a great many other people and I
think particularly for students. There's a
certain sadness in this—you don't have the
padding, the comfortable security. It's sharp.
You bleed. You hurt. But you don't hurt
alone, and there's a great deal of beauty, a
great deal of joy, in that."

The Christian Science Monitor,
November 5, 1968

STRUGGLE

Sometimes I wonder how I have been able to survive during the past dozen years of my existence. I remain, as always, a private person. I need great stretches of silence. I have found that, as Marianne Moore pointed out, the cure for loneliness is solitude. Friendship means a great deal to me, and I am nourished by the gentle love of people, but not in roving packs—with clichés unthinkingly manufactured and mere activism roaringly rampant. Sometimes I get out of bed in the middle of the night, put on a robe, turn on a desk lamp, and just sit thinking for two or three hours; maybe I do some writing if I feel like it, or I may choose to clean out a desk drawer (this can be an art form!) or answer letters by scrawling notes on five-cent postcards.

Yet, as a private person, I have found myself caught between my beliefs and the kind of world I happened to be born in. So I *had* to act. This, despite an innately acute shyness, a natural and strong laziness, and a great desire to *be* instead of to *do*. To be a rock beside a sloping road in springtime. To be a rocking chair on a shaded porch in summer. To be a watermelon, ripening on the vine. To be the sea, roaring and churning on a windy day under a warm sun. To be a voluminously crammed Sunday newspaper, resting on an ice-cold newsstand on a blizzardlike day in February, then to be retrieved by an anxious buyer and carried into a warm study, there to be jealously guarded, studied, and appreciated prior to being burned in a great fireplace. To be a good book *and be read.* To be a poem. To be music. To be myself—but, oh God, if I am to find who that is I must have deep silences, then a knowing rhythm in my relationships with other people, and an uncluttered vision to comprehend distances and time, both inside and outside myself.

I became more strongly myself, conscious of my own strengths and weaknesses as an individual, as various writers sought to characterize me in a paragraph, a colorful caption, a brief newsworthy phrase. "What is Malcolm Boyd really like?" a young woman reporter for *Newsweek* asked some forty startled college students to whom the question had never occurred. *Playboy* described me as "a balding, battling Episcopal priest" whose prayers "take the form of a slang-packed monolog to the Almighty" and represent a "gutsy new approach to religion." Within a period of six weeks, two writers assembled my various fragments and functions under startlingly different headings. A writer in *Look* said: "Father Boyd is part Old Testament prophet and part stool-straddling entertainer. He calls himself a worker-priest, and speaks in what he calls 'poetry.'" And a reviewer for the *New York Times Book Review* called me "a sort of balding Holden Caulfield become Episcopal priest." These circumscribed phrases freed rather than imprisoned me. They helped me to hang loose, know myself as a suffering and laughing human being, and maintain the capacity to act spontaneously and radically. As my public images proliferated, they became increasingly alien to my self. I even learned to find them highly amus-

ing. It would require an army of different people—albeit
all balding—to fit all the conflicting descriptions.

What am I *really* like? I don't know. Surely there is no
uniformity. I am *really* like this at 2 P.M. and then *really*
like that at 8 P.M.—at least, I hope so: I welcome vast
and beautiful changes within the hours. I hope, however, that I am never a locomotive. I have a friend who is
a locomotive and, whenever we meet, I must brace myself against the charge of sound and fury.

Sometimes I am criticized for my refusal to enter into
the workings of bureaucratic machinery, where I should
be content to "do my share." But it is not a refusal at all;
it is an inability; I cannot play an institutional role and
preserve my sanity. However, I have enormous admiration for certain friends of mine who can succeed in
playing such a role gracefully while maintaining compassion as well as high humor.

I have come to shun socially important gatherings
with huge crowds, and formal ground rules. I will not
make an appointment to see someone on two weeks
from Friday, but will be delighted if he calls one morning to arrange to see me that same day. I *have* to keep
things somewhat plain and simple, and at least function
in terms of my tested capacities to survive and relate to
other people. But, damn it, I want to be able to relate,
not coexist with; and to live with other *people,* not ma-
chines.

One afternoon I was out walking. It was a fall day
and leaves had turned to bright yellows, reds and
browns. It was windy and the sun was shining. A man
stopped me on the street. He was a Jesuit and had
heard me speak somewhere. We talked for a few minutes. He explained that he, along with some other

Jesuits, was living in a house near a university where all of them were pursuing secular studies. "We're trying to find out what it means to be human," he said. I told him that is what I am trying to find out too.

Do I know where I am? No. Only that I am still on the pilgrimage which is the context of life's meaning for me.

Do I know where I am going? No. A career or a mapped destination is a kind of ultimate absurdity now amid nuclear weapons, deodorants, racial conflagration, gin and pot, affluence, poverty, politics-as-usual, the Pill, the Moon, nationalism, tourism, orgasm, television, communism and The Star-Spangled Banner.

Where have I been? In my skin . . . wasting and celebrating life . . . doing a lot of different things with many different people. The clock has not stopped, even when electricity has temporarily been cut off. Bloody time has marched on. I run to keep up with it—even while I know, in a curious sense, that I am freed from its sovereign power. It's 7 A.M.—I must hurry out of bed for there are appointments to be kept, people to see, deadlines to be met, work to be completed, life outside the window beckons me. It's noon—I must hurry to catch a cab. It's 1 A.M.—I must hurry to sleep. Bloody time is pushing and stomping me, seducing and raping me, sucking my life juices.

How do I feel now? My mind is in a dozen places, leaping and soaring to connect with fragmented thoughts; my face appears calm if you do not perceive a twitch in the left eye or my lips which are ready to part in a shout. Yet I am conscious of interior silence. There is calm within the hurricane's eye. I am meditating in the midst of activity and noise. Mysticism and pragmatism have come together; there are no longer any dichotomies. My body is *here*, yes, but what does that say? for

STRUGGLE 271

we live in a mobile age. My personality is already mixed with the ages and the personalities of dozens or hundreds of other people; and it is color-splashed—now crucified, now free of the nails and furiously engaged.

"Where were you on December 7, 1941?" Someone will smile and say, "I wasn't born yet."

The madness of passing years.

How can I cope with them? My life is careening absurdly out of all control and its passage has become illogical. Where did Wednesday go? Shall I send Christmas cards? August is half spent. It is 3 P.M.: I remember nothing after 9 A.M.

My God, someone else has died. (He was young, only forty-three.) I saw a youthful face from my childhood yesterday (we used to sit on a porch and play monopoly); it was wrinkled.

A symposium is being planned on the subject of life fifty years from now. Top speakers will be assembled; a great hall will be rented; the event will be televised; the press will cover it.

I will no longer be here fifty years from now. (Where will I be? I will miss this life which I love and hate, intensely fear and fiercely laugh about.) I want to be here. It isn't fair to hold the symposium if I am implicitly excluded from the topic.

I will no longer be here twenty-five years from now. I'm sure of it. I feel the truth of this.

Therefore I no longer have the option to waste time. But I want to waste it. This is a part of my freedom.

In this very moment, I am heavily depressed and light as a feather, filled with sad cries and belly laughs, ready to climb the walls and sit here quietly.

My pilgrimage has antecedents with Abraham's. He didn't know where he was going either. Faith. (My God,

that sounds religious.) My pilgrimage has the same destination as Jesus'—a cross, and then Easter and Em-
maus.

I am Christian and secular, denominational and post-
ecumenical, Jew and Greek, white and black, American
and Asian, a priest and a prophet, false and true, a child
and a man, a prince of the church and a pauper in
Christ. I am simply myself. Yes, I have a vision—don't
you? Yes, when things are at their worst I die, and wake
up either laughing or crying, and go on—don't you? Yes,
I am lonely and fulfilled, sure of myself and unsure,
loving and self-loving, faithful and apostate—aren't
you? I look for home, longing for it, yet know I will not
completely find it here or now; this is why I am thankful
for the part of it which I can find. I don't break my heart
for love; my heart is already broken, and, besides, love
does not require this. Love requires nothing.

I was a child, visiting distant relatives for a few
days at a mountain cabin. I was away from my governess and with children of my own age. There was a
stream outside the cabin where we played. The water
rolled easily over the bed of the stream and smooth
stones in it. I had never been so happy, I felt. I was in
a family.

I looked up from the empty street—I was in my
twenties—and saw a lighted window. It was in San
Diego, California. The window beckoned me. It
seemed to offer security, warmth, and even love.
Happy people, I thought, were inside. For them, things
were so simple.

It was late afternoon in Detroit. I had just celebrated Mass in the student center. Garbed in the vestments of a priest, I had left the altar (a dozen students
were still kneeling in pews before it) and had started

walking toward the sacristy with the Eucharistic vessels in my hands. I saw the sun-warm church in the late afternoon, its gentleness and dignity; I thought, This is my home, this is my refuge.

The plane was leaving West Virginia. It was a spring day in 1969. I had been with students at a college. An elderly woman faculty member had joined us. I had seen her home—it was over a hundred years old, situated against solemn hills and green trees. She had a garden, four dogs and one cat. Her eyes were mysteriously peaceful. The students were open and friendly. One of them said, Why don't you come here and stay with us? As the plane sped away, it flew low over a tiny West Virginia village—to me it was a mythical Glocca Morra.

In certain moments, I simply give up trying to make sense out of life and my own portion of it. Then I find I am not only still here, but that I care intensely, passionately, and even with a curious lack of selfishness about the human enterprise.

Relationship, I have learned, has a nerve of commitment to it. "For better for worse, for richer for poorer, in sickness and in health, to love and to cherish": these are words not alone for the marriage of a man and a woman. These words are a vow for all people in relationship—between friends, in a job, between neighbors, on a campus, in the city, everywhere.

Relationship with anyone is a specific symbol of one's basic, pervasive responsibility for the universe outside oneself. Any relationship therefore signifies one's membership in the human race.

The waiter asked me which salad dressing I would have.

I asked him to list the dressings from which I might choose.

"French, chef's, oil and vinegar, or Green Goddess."

I thought about it.

"Make a decision, you son of a bitch," he said.

Living and dying, dying and living: the common pattern of our life together. The personality is, I know, not destroyed by "dying"—that funny and terrible moment of severing which, yes, I fear. But I don't fear the moment after it. Malcolm, who lives, will no longer live? I certainly do not feel I shall be any more with Jesus before the moment of "dying" than in it or after it. Anyhow, I anticipate no geographical hells or heavens to visit. This means, for me, that my personality will live after my body has been utilized for medical research and cremated. My body, too, after it is consumed by flames, will still mysteriously live as a part of the totality of my being. This fierce thing, the personality—the essence or the soul, embracing the totality of body and mind— touches life violently and tenderly. This *is* I. After "dying," I must live.

It is easy for me to forget this, especially when I am sad or lonely. Public as well as private events can force me into new and tight compartments of depression and hurt. Withdrawal can seem a physical and psychical necessity to breathe and dream. Then, once again, comes a call to community with other people. This means involvement in their lives (and so, in life).

Involvement and activism. Always I juggle the two. They are different, but possess strong similarities. It is nice sometimes to rationalize that one is involved because activistic; but this just doesn't hold true. (What about motives? What about depth of relationships?) Yet it is not fair to make a blanket assertion that activism is only a cheap and shoddy substitute for involvement. (What, then, are the alternatives? Should one indulge only in rhetoric, and with special emphasis on criticism of activists?)

The fear of failure and the desire to succeed. I juggle these, too. (Did we win our objectives? Can we issue a press release announcing victory?) I have learned that triumphs can be empty and flat, especially if they are on paper. What of triumph in the heart? Too, I have learned that failures can be exciting and freeing experiences; sometimes, having failed, one comes upon a brother whom one can meet without pretense. There is simplicity and sharing within such a breathlessly lovely moment of integrity. I should reiterate that, for me, the greatest symbol of success is Jesus' wooden, bloody, criminal's Cross. There is mystery in "success" and "failure," as there is paradox in "honesty" and "phoniness." Always we are confronted by other people's motives as well as our own: never completely dirty or clean, never totally wrong or correct.

When my heart broke. The organic destruction.

There was the long moment of severing (I remember it: the day, the weather, the faces, the time, the sun, the voices, the rain, the decision, the moon) and suddenly fragments.

It is these fragments I have struggled to find.

Didn't love mean community, acceptance, healing and belonging? Love me! Love me! I called—in sounds of hurt and fury—to strangers. I discovered then the curiosity of love. Love is not taken or given. I found it can be shared.

I am Malcolm.

Underneath a number of titles, roles, functions and images—this is who I am.

I can't help wondering: who are *you*? I wonder what are your dreams, the things that make you laugh, the people you love, the deep loyalties which stir you to act, the basic dictates of your conscience, and the vision of truth which cuts through your life?

As Malcolm, I have lived through events which I cannot begin to comprehend. Six million Jews were killed by Nazis. This, even as I ate ice cream, drank beer, saw movies, read books and went swimming. I have lived through a World War (actually, it was the *second* one). Hiroshima was set afire by an H-Bomb. Hungary and Czechoslovakia, struggling to become free, were tortured. Mass killing occurred in Indonesia, India, and Pakistan. And Biafran children starved to death. America has nearly succeeded in blowing up a small nation in Asia while failing to obliterate poverty at home. Racism took off its smiling mask and we saw a monster when we looked into our mirrors.

When I stop to think, I am not sure that I can. Have I not somehow deluded myself, somewhere numbed my senses, in order to be able to survive?

Yet here I stand, still alive, still aware.

I am struggling.